NORTH-EAST PASSAGE TO MUSCOVY

STEPHEN BOROUGH
AND THE FIRST
TUDOR EXPLORATIONS

KIT MAYERS

SUTTON PUBLISHING

First published in the United Kingdom in 2005 by
Sutton Publishing Limited · Phoenix Mill
Thrupp · Stroud · Gloucestershire · GL5 2BU

British Library Cataloguing in Publication Data
A catalogue record for this book is available from the British Library.

ISBN 0-7509-4069-7

Typeset in 10.5/14pt Photina MT.
Typesetting and origination by
Sutton Publishing Limited.
Printed and bound in England by
J.H. Haynes & Co. Ltd, Sparkford.

Contents

Appendices

List of Illustrations in the Text

Illustration and Text Credits

The author and publisher gratefully acknowledge permission to reproduce illustrations from the following: The *Serchthrift* in 1556, and The three ships of the 1553 expedition, drawings (2004) by Mark Myers, artist, Woolley, Cornwall; Borough, the manor house, *Transactions. Dev. Assoc.* lviii (1926) p. 193, The Devonshire Association; The village square at Northam, Marion Northcott, Northam; Stephen Borough's signature, Centre for Kentish Studies, County Hall, Maidstone; The Thames and the Tower of London, Placentia Palace at Greenwich and Dr John Dee, Ashmolean Museum, Oxford; Sebastian Cabot, Bristol Industrial Museum; Small merchant ship by Hans Holbein, Städelsches Kunstinstitut, Frankfurt am Main; The *Dragon* (ADD. 22047), English ships off Dover (Cotton Aug. I.i.22.23), The 'Haven of Death' entry (Cotton Otho E VIII 6: f 16), William Borough's chart (Royal 18.D.iii. f 123: f 124) and Hugh Smyth's sketch map (Cotton Otho E VIII: f 38) British Library; Ships at Antwerp, 1468 [Cartes et Plans manuscrits No. 351] Archives Générales du Royaume, Bruxelles; The *Teager* (detail from MPF 1/75) The National Archives; portrait of Sir Hugh Willoughby, The Lord Middleton, Birdsall House, N. Yorks; The great whirlpool (Olaus Magnus, *Description of the Northern Peoples*, Hakluyt Society Series II/182) David Higham Associates; The Old English Court in Moscow, John Powers, Instow. The maps are by the author.

Note: It is regretted that despite various attempts, it has not yet been possible to find the copyright holders of Zeigler's map of northern Europe or Olaus Magnus's *Carta Marina*.

The author and publisher also gratefully acknowledge permission to reproduce a quotation from Alistair MacLean, *HMS Ulysses* (HarperCollins, 1994), pp. 106–7.

Preface

When my father died, I found among his books a version of Richard Hakluyt's *Principal Navigations*, originally written in 1589. The first story in the book that I came across was that of Stephen Borough. He was a shipmaster, born in Devon, who in 1553, and again in 1556, was given the job of sailing in search of a north-east passage to China. Such a voyage would be remarkable even today; in those days, it must have been astounding.

The bare facts of the voyages were there in Hakluyt, but I conceived an irresistible desire to know much more. I wanted to know about the reasons for the voyages, how Stephen came to be selected for the job and how he did it, what sort of ships he had, and about the effects and consequences of the voyages.

This present book is an attempt to find some of the answers. It has three main subjects: *the exploits*, the first brave voyages to search for a north-east passage from Europe to the Orient; *the effects* of the voyages, one of which was the setting-up of the Muscovy Company, the first English company to trade outside western Europe; and *the man* who did it, Stephen Borough, his origins and connections. (This book is not a biography, as we know virtually nothing of a personal nature about him. He lives on only through his exploits, but these are more than enough to put him into the pantheon of great Tudor sea captains from Devon.) The other topics in this book include the sizes and shapes of the ships of the time, the state of geographical knowledge, the state of the art of navigation and a brief history of subsequent attempts to find a north-east passage.

Before 1553 the English had done almost nothing by way of overseas exploration.[1] Stephen Borough's voyages were the first that had been organised by the English. They were the first English voyages to set off in a previously unknown direction, and they were also the first voyages of which we have any detailed account written in English.

A principal source of information throughout has been Richard Hakluyt's book, *The Principal Navigations, Voyages, Traffiques and Discoveries of the English Nation* (1589).[2] Hakluyt (*c.* 1552–1616) made it his life's work to gather the stories of English seamen and explorers. His perseverance in accumulating so much material on the early days of exploration and trade with Russia has come in for particular appreciation.[3] It was entirely due to his diligence that the original accounts of the voyages were collected together in his 'troublesome and painful' work. On one occasion, as he himself said, 'I rode 200 miles onely to learn the whole trueth of this voyage.'[4] On other occasions, he was supplied with material by his friends and acquaintances, such as William Borough and Anthonie Jenkinson.[5]

Hakluyt himself had staunchly Protestant views, but he kept them separate from the narratives that he collected.[6] He made a point of copying the original accounts' *ipsissima verba*. Hakluyt himself wrote, 'Whatsoever testimonie I have found in any authour . . . I have recorded the same word for word',[7] and G.B. Parkes, the Hakluyt scholar, has commented that 'Hakluyt emphasised the value of the original sources' and 'the majority of the narratives give no sign of his part in their making'.[8] A few of the original documents that Hakluyt copied still exist, such as the 'Haven of Death' account of Sir Hugh Willoughby's voyage.[9] Comparing this original with Hakluyt's version shows that he copied it word for word. I make no apology for quoting from him on numerous occasions.

As to the other important sources, it is extremely fortunate that some of them ever survived. The Lisle Letters, for instance, were seized and impounded when Lord Lisle was incarcerated in the Tower of London, and they have survived in the national archives ever since. The wills of the members of the Borough family are another important source of information. The original wills, or most of them, were destroyed when the Exeter Register Office was bombed in the Second World War, but fortunately a Mr Oswyn Murray had previously made abstracts of them, and those abstracts have survived.

It is not obvious why Stephen Borough's epic voyages have received so little attention hitherto. A few later authors have retold the tale of his exploits, but they have done little more than paraphrase Hakluyt's original account.[10] By contrast, Martin Frobisher's voyages in search of a north-west passage, some twenty years later than Stephen Borough's, have had a good press, even though his expeditions produced relatively little result and were a financial disaster. Perhaps Stephen suffered because his great exploits were peaceful: he never fired a shot in anger. The other great Tudor sea captains such as the Hawkinses, Drake, Raleigh, John Davis, Oxenham, Cavendish, Fenner, Howard, Towerson, Grenville and Frobisher, as well as all the pirates and privateers, all relied on their cannon, their swords and their swashbuckling for their fame and fortune. Incidentally, all these sea captains came later than Stephen Borough, with the single exception of William Hawkins. This book is an attempt to remedy the neglect and to throw some new light on a Tudor hero from Devon.

Acknowledgements

A large number of people have helped me in finding out about Stephen Borough and I am very happy to thank as many of them as I can. I acknowledge my debt to my deceased parents. I thank my wife, Heather, and my son, John Henry, for their great patience and encouragement.

This book started life as a dissertation in the Maritime History Department at Exeter University. Since then it has been considerably enlarged, extensively changed and completely rewritten. I am grateful to have had Dr Stephen Fisher as my first supervisor at Exeter University. He was a wise and erudite adviser who became my friend, and his death in the spring of 2002 was a great loss. Fortunately for me, Dr Michael Duffy was able to take over the supervision of my dissertation in a very able manner. I also appreciate the stimulating tuition of Dr Roger Morriss and Mr Ian Mortimer and the comments of my fellow students in Maritime History.

I am very happy to have this opportunity to thank a number of individuals, including Mr Robert Baldwin, National Maritime Museum; Dr David Barraclough, British Geological Survey, Edinburgh, for correspondence about changes in magnetic variation over the years; Mr Peter Christie, Bideford, for some research suggestions; P.L. Dickinson, Richmond Herald, College of Arms, for information about Walter Borough; Mr S.M. Dixon, Borough Archivist, Rochester, for information about Stephen Borough's house there; Mr Alastair Dodds, National Museums of Scotland, for information about ship models; Mr R. Foster, Chatham, for information about the Medway Heritage Centre; Mr Ian Friel, Littlehampton Museum, for advice on medieval shipbuilding; Dr Alastair Grassie, Isle of Arran, for his comments on Viking navigation; Captain J. Johnson for comments on the chapter on ships and ship design; Mr Danny Koolen for his comments on the whole of the text; Mr David Loughborough, owner of the house at Northam where Stephen Borough spent his childhood, who kindly showed me round; Mr Jim Moulton for an engraving of the old house at Borough; Mrs Marion Northcott for information on Northam; Mrs Carole Pavitt, Chelmsford, for information about John Vassall and the *Mayflower* connection; Mr John Power, Instow, for photographs of the Muscovy Company house in Moscow; Dr Owain Roberts, University of Bangor, for helpful correspondence about the sizes and shapes of ships; Mr Philip Rose, Bideford, for discussion on the chapter on navigation; Mr Jim Row, Bridgend, for his experience with the Arctic convoys; Mr James Saumarez, Bideford, for useful comments on the text; Mrs Pat Slade, Bideford Archives at Northam, for advice about the Borough family; Mr Peter Towey, Teddington, for a helpful summary of the Star Chamber cases involving the Borough family; and Victor Winstone and his wife, Joan Cory, for their most helpful and constructive criticism.

I am grateful too for courteous help on my visits to, or in response to my letters to, various record offices, libraries and other archives, including Archivo General de Indies, Sevilla; Barnstaple Library; Bideford Library; Bodleian Library, Oxford; Bristol Record Office; British Library; Centre for Kentish Studies, Maidstone; The Church of Latter Day Saints (Mormons), Exeter; College of Arms, London; Devon and Exeter Institute; Devon Record Office, Exeter; Exeter Central Library; Exeter University Library; Family Records Centre, Myddleton Street, London; Guildhall Library, London; Hampshire Record Office; Lambeth Palace Library; London Metropolitan Archives; Medway Heritage Centre, Chatham; National Archives (formerly the Public Record Office), Kew; Naval History and Local Studies Library, Plymouth; Newberry Library, Chicago; North Devon Local Studies Library; Rochester upon Medway Studies Centre, Strood; Royal Commission on Historical Manuscripts; the Society of Genealogists; UK Hydrographic Office, Taunton; and the West Country Studies Library, Exeter.

I am also grateful to the representatives of several societies for their help, particularly the Hakluyt Society; the Royal Geographical Society; the Society for Nautical Research (publishers of the *Mariner's Mirror*); and the South West Maritime History Society.

Several museums and their staff have also been helpful with advice and information, including Guernsey Museum and Art Gallery; Mary Rose Museum, Portsmouth; Merchant Adventurer's House, York; Merchant's House Museum, Plymouth; National Maritime Museum, Greenwich; North Devon Maritime Museum, Appledore; and Tucker's Hall, Exeter.

The errors and omissions in this book are all mine.

Introduction

Besides the foresaid uncertaintie, into what dangers and difficulties they plunged themselves . . . I tremble to recount.
Hakluyt, introducing the story of the Northeasterne discoveries.[1]

On Friday 7 August 1556 Stephen Borough and the ten men of the crew of the *Serchthrift* were very far from home. They were in the Arctic, more than 500 miles further east than any west European had ever been before, searching for a north-east passage to the Orient. They had tried to find shelter from 'a cruell storme' by anchoring in the lee of a small, featureless island near the southern end of Novaya Zemlya, but this time it looked very much as though the end had come and the ship would founder from the buffets of ice floes.

They had seen sea ice before, but never anything like this. This was much more menacing. It was a wall of pack ice driven by the wind, and it advanced on them, coming round both sides of the island behind which they were anchored. From the deck they could only watch in horror as the two arms of the ice field swept on around them and closed some way behind. The ship floated in a black pool of the sea, hemmed in by gleaming masses of white and pale-blue ice. The wind increased from the north-north-east and the swell grew, though the ice itself acted as a damper and kept the waves from building up. The dark surface of the open pool of sea was buffeted all the time by heavy cats-paws of wind. The mast and rigging roared and whistled with the wind, though all the sails were tightly furled. The small ship strained at her anchor cable and veered violently from side to side as the storm increased. Then the mist came, rushing past them and bringing snow, so that they could hardly see even so far as the low, black island which gave them some protection from the ice.

All that night the storm raged. With the sun only just below the horizon, there was enough visibility in the twilight for the crew to keep a constant watch on the ice as best they could through the driving murk. From time to time, large pieces of ice came free from the pack towards them. Most of the crew were on deck, using poles and oars to try to fend off the ice. A few lay below, awake and huddled in their blankets, listening to the thumping and crunching along the waterline as stray floes, some of them as big as houses, drifted along the side of the hull. They all knew that at any moment a floe could crack the hull with a blow or carry away the anchor cable.

By the following morning the storm had abated slightly, but the mist had turned into fog and they could see no more than a cable's length from the ship. They could do nothing but stay put where they were, and hope and pray that the anchor cable would continue to hold.

The next day, Sunday, the mist lifted for a while, and they saw that the ice had mysteriously departed. They sailed out from their anchorage at four a.m., but then the mist came down again and they were forced to reduce speed by taking down all the sails and drifting slowly before the wind.[2]

They had survived 'by the Grace of God'. They would have had no chance if the wind had changed direction while they were surrounded by the ice or had blown even more violently, or if a larger floe had borne down upon them, or if the anchor cable had parted or the anchor itself had lost its hold. This was just one of the many times on the voyage when they had faced death and yet escaped. Stephen Borough was undoubtedly a very competent sea captain, but on this occasion, as on a number of others, he was lucky. Perhaps, at his birth, the fairy ladies had indeed danced upon his hearth.[3]

The 1556 voyage was itself an epic. It involved travelling some 500 miles beyond the entrance to the White Sea, through the Arctic Seas, which we now call the Barents Sea, trying to find a route to China. They were in a dreary and desolate region of the world, entirely uncharted, facing unknown hazards of many kinds, including rocks and shoals, currents and tides, storms, frequent fog and pack ice, not to mention the monsters of the deep, and possible encounters with the Samoyeds, who were said to be cannibals.

Stephen went on to survive this and many other voyages in Arctic waters; he became a national hero and deserved to be so. His voyages were the first of the great Tudor explorations. They set the example. They ignited the flame of exploration for the English and were followed by other feats and voyages, including Frobisher's attempts to find a north-west passage in 1576–8, Drake's circumnavigation of the world in 1577–81, the defeat of the Armada in 1588 and the founding of the English Colonies on the east coast of the New World.

Another result of the voyages was the birth of the Muscovy Company, the first of the English joint stock overseas trading companies. It was the Muscovy Company that established the very first English trading stations outside western Europe and that set the pattern for all the other overseas companies, including the great East India Company. These London-based businesses were the principal mechanism of England's commercial expansion overseas.

The British political empire, at its peak, covered a quarter of the land surface of the globe and embraced, under the diminutive figure of Queen Victoria, 400 million people. It was enormous. But the British commercial empire, the 'informal empire', was an even greater phenomenon. In the years around 1870 there were few areas of the world into which British trade and commerce had not penetrated.[4] In most cases, it was not 'trade following the flag', rather the opposite.[5]

The merchants of London took a big step in the growth of this commercial empire when they set up the first trading company and the first trading stations outside western Europe – in Muscovy. Stephen Borough and his crew were the men who made it possible.

CHAPTER 1

The Times

Stephen Borough made his first voyage of exploration in 1553. That was about four and a half centuries ago; it may seem so, but it is not really very long ago at all. For instance, most people can remember their grandparents and can remember talking to them. Mine were born in the 1870s. If we suppose that there are about fifty years between batches of grandparents, it would only need eight or possibly nine lots of grandparents to take us back to the 1550s.

The time may seem short when measured in cohorts of grandparents, but what a lot has changed! Things were very different then: for instance, we do not now set fire to our archbishops, as they did then ('Bloody Mary' had Archbishop Cranmer burnt at the stake in 1556). Our attitudes and thought patterns, and a great deal else besides, have changed enormously since then.

How can we possibly get into the mindset of Stephen's time, a time when a belief in God pervaded everyday life, when the sun and the planets circled the earth[1] and the order of everything in the cosmos was taken for granted?[2] The Tudors' concept of the four elements (fire, air, earth and water) may seem bizarre to us, but to them it was a system by which they could apprehend and explain many of nature's mysteries. We may think them odd, but I wonder what they would make of our concepts of the spin of gravitons or the charm of quarks by which we seek to explain the behaviour of the elementary particles.

The physical world that they knew was also very different. In Stephen's time, the population of London was about 50,000,[3] which is about the same as the population of Keighley or Macclesfield today, and slightly less than that of Stourbridge or Weymouth.[4] London was small, which meant that anybody who was anybody knew everybody else who mattered. (At that time, the total population of England was only about 3 million.)[5]

Looking back at England then, we can see that she was little more than an underdeveloped off-shore island. There was a good deal of internal trade, but as far as exports were concerned, wool and cloth were almost the only commodities that the English could offer, and together they accounted for over 85 per cent of the export trade.[6] The quantity of wool and cloth that was produced increased slowly and steadily. For instance, the flock of sheep owned by Norwich Cathedral Priory increased from 2,500 in 1470 to 8,000 in 1520, and the output of traditional woollen broadcloth trebled in the first half of the sixteenth century.[7] Bowden has calculated that there were about 11 million sheep and lambs in England and Wales in 1540–7.[8] The wool and the cloth were traded overseas for wine and manufactured goods from the Continent. The woolsack that the Lord Chancellor sits on today is a surviving symbol of the erstwhile dominance of the wool trade. Many people all over the country found employment in the production of wool, from shepherds and shearers to those involved in the processes of spinning, weaving, fulling[9] and dyeing. The term 'spinster', which applied to all unmarried women, reflects the very widespread involvement of the English people in the textile trade. The finished cloth was mostly sold through Calais, which, apart from Ireland, was England's only overseas territory at that time. It was through the wool market at Calais, the 'Staple', that the customs dues were levied on wool and textiles, and these provided a large part of the Crown's income. The Crown levied 40s on every sack of wool exported by Englishmen and 53s 3d on every sack exported by 'aliens' (foreigners).[10]

In Stephen's day, the supply of food in England depended entirely on the harvest, as very little food could be imported from abroad, and the harvest in turn depended very much on the weather, and it was cold in the 1550s. It was the beginning of the period which later came to be known as 'the Little Ice Age' and which lasted from about 1550 to 1700.[11] There were bad harvests in 1549, 1550 and 1551,[12] and people starved. To add to the problems, there was an outbreak of 'the sweating sickness', or *sudor anglicus*, in London in 1551.[13] It seems to have been a form of influenza, and it could kill young adults within twenty-four hours.[14]

The king at the time was Edward VI. He had been 9 when he was crowned in 1547, and he was heavily guided by his 'Protectors': first his uncle, Edward Seymour, Duke of Somerset, and then, from 1549 onwards, by John Dudley, Duke of Northumberland.

His father, King Henry VIII, had spent all the money derived from the dissolution of the monasteries, and more, on vainglorious wars, his navy and a chain of forts and castles along the east and south coasts to defend England against the very real threat of attack by France or Spain, or both of them together.[15] Fortunately for England, these two countries were much occupied at the time in fighting each other, and when peace was, for a short time, declared between them, neither had the strength left or the inclination to mount an attack on England. But King Henry had left the nation bankrupt.[16]

The whole economy of England was upset: landlords raised rents[17] and tried to enclose land, local manufacturers went down, prices rose in what has been called 'the sixteenth-century price revolution', especially the price of grain, and real wages declined.[18] There were popular rebellions in 1549 in Norfolk and the West Country, and serious riots in the Midlands and southern England, triggered largely by the sharp rise in the price of corn and also in part by opposition to Edward VI's religious reforms.[19]

Then, in 1551, Northumberland was forced to honour some of the nation's debts to the Continental bankers. This meant a dramatic rise in the prices of England's textiles, which caused a sharp drop in sales on the Continent. The number of shortcloths exported from London fell from 133,000 in 1550 to 85,000 in 1552.[20] This dramatic drop in the sales of England's chief export commodity affected the whole nation. The situation is described by the Duke of Norfolk in Shakespeare's *Henry VIII*:

> The clothiers all, not able to maintain
> The many to them 'longing, have put off
> The spinsters, carders, fullers, weavers, who
> Unfit for other life, compell'd by hunger
> And lack of other means, in desperate manner
> Daring the event to the teeth, are all in uproar,
> And danger serves among them.[21]

It was the sudden fall in cloth exports that impelled the English merchants to seek other overseas sales outlets and that prompted Stephen Borough's voyages of exploration.

At this time, the English had done very little in the way of exploration, though there is no doubting the fact that they were excellent sailors. They had been making regular voyages to Danzig for many years,[22] to Iceland,[23] to all the ports on the Atlantic coasts of Europe, and into the Mediterranean.[24] English ships had also reached Morocco[25] and Guinea (the Ivory Coast),[26] and had crossed the Atlantic to Newfoundland in the wake of Basque fishermen.[27] At least one English ship, the *Barbara of London* under Captain John Phellyppes, had reached the Caribbean in 1540, with 'one Robert Nycoll of Depe' (Dieppe) as pilot (a Frenchman, despite his Scottish name). There they seized a Spanish ship and some valuable charts of the Americas.[28]

The most adventurous of the English seamen had sailed to Brazil, led by William Hawkins, who made three voyages there in 1530, 1531 and 1532.[29] He almost certainly used foreign (probably French) pilots to get there,[30] as did Robert Reniger and Thomas Borey, who sailed there in about 1540, and 'one

Pudsey' (as Hakluyt calls him), who also sailed there and built a fort at the Baya de Todos Santos in 1542.[31]

But none of this was pioneering. The Portuguese had been sailing to Brazil regularly for thirty years or more before Hawkins arrived, and a Frenchman, de Gonneville, had sailed there from Harfleur in the *Espoir* as early as 1504.[32] The English could certainly sail the high seas, but apart from the voyages to Brazil they had until the 1550s confined themselves to the North Atlantic and the Mediterranean, and all the sailing routes that they used had been anticipated by others.

By contrast, the Iberians had already circled the globe, and by the middle of the sixteenth century ships of Portugal sailed regularly to East Africa to trade for gold, which they then took on to Goa and Malacca (on the Malay Peninsula), where the gold was traded for spices to be taken back to Europe. At the same time, Spanish ships were sailing regularly from Seville to ports in the Caribbean Sea to collect silver and gold from their mines in Mexico and Peru.

When the English did at last set out to explore, it was many years later than the Iberians. Like them, the English also hoped to reach the Spice Islands and the fabulous Orient, which were 'the most richest londes and ilondes in the worlde, for all the gold, spices aromatikes and pretiose stone', according to Roger Barlow, who had found out a great deal about the Portuguese and Spanish explorations. He went on to propose a route that was not already dominated by the Portuguese or the Spanish, 'out of spayne thei saile all the indies and sees occidentales, and from portingale thei saylle all the indies and sees orientalles, so that betwene the waie of the orient and the waie of the occydent they have compassed all the world . . . so ther resteth this waie of the northe onelie to discover'.[33]

Thus it was that Stephen Borough of Devon and his colleagues became the pioneers of English exploration when they set out in search of a northerly route to the Orient in two expeditions, one in 1553 and another in 1556. Twenty-odd years later, the English tried again, this time to the north-west, sending out three expeditions under Martin Frobisher in 1576, 1577 and 1578.

This book is about Stephen Borough and the part he took in these English expeditions, the ones in search of a north-east passage to the Orient.

CHAPTER 2

Stephen Borough at Home

In this chapter Stephen Borough's family and home life, as far as we know them, are discussed. His nautical career occupies most of the later chapters of this book.

Stephen Borough, the future sea captain, navigator and explorer, was born on 25 September 1525, at a small manor farm called Borough, in the parish of Northam, North Devon.[1] (The family name of Borough – spelled in several different ways – and the name of the farm where he was born were the same.)[2] His infant world consisted almost entirely of his mother (née Mary Dough) and his nurse. A little later, he would get to recognise the faces of his father, Walter Borough,[3] and his uncle Thomas,[4] who between them ran the farm, and the faces of the servants, one or two servant girls in the house and three or four men and boys who worked in the fields.[5]

The infant Stephen was the centre of attention. He was for a long time the only child in the family, as it was not until eleven years later that his younger brother, William, was born, in 1536.[6] For the first year of his life, Stephen would have been wrapped in strips of cloth (the traditional swaddling clothes) and then, when he started to toddle, he would have been put into a small jerkin and breeches.[7]

His first explorations were of the fields and woods of the farm which slope steeply down from Borough to the nearby River Torridge. Borough is about a quarter of a mile from Northam, an ancient village set on a hill. The whole parish of Northam is almost surrounded by water, with the Bristol Channel to the west and the estuary of the Taw and the Torridge rivers to the north and the east.

From Borough, Stephen could see ships coming in across Bideford Bay from the Atlantic. He could also have seen ships anchored in the bay, waiting for the tide to rise before they could come in across the formidable bar, and later he could watch them working their way in on the tide, up the zigzag channel towards Appledore, until they disappeared from sight behind Lookout Hill.[8] He could also see Northam Church, standing up as a silhouette against the evening sun. The church tower was used by sailors as a seamark, and it was whitewashed regularly until 1846 to make it stand out better.[9]

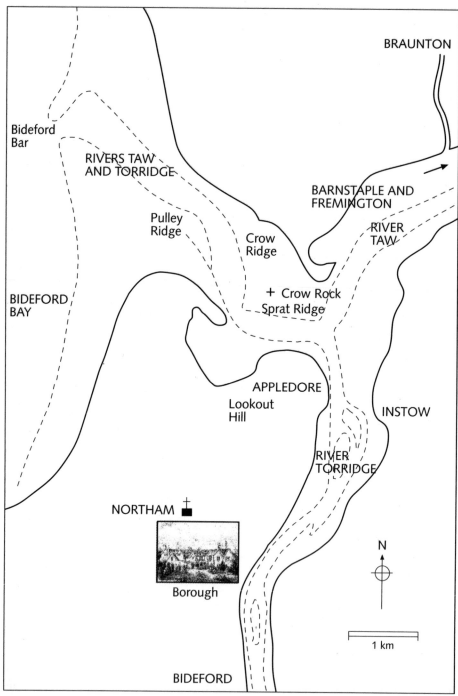

BRAUNTON

Bideford
Bar

RIVERS TAW
AND TORRIDGE

BARNSTAPLE AND
FREMINGTON

Pulley
Ridge

Crow
Ridge

RIVER
TAW

BIDEFORD
BAY

+ Crow Rock
Sprat Ridge

APPLEDORE

Lookout
Hill

INSTOW

RIVER
TORRIDGE

NORTHAM ✝

Borough

BIDEFORD

N

1 km

The estuary of the Rivers Taw and Torridge in North Devon, showing Northam and Borough surrounded by water on three sides.

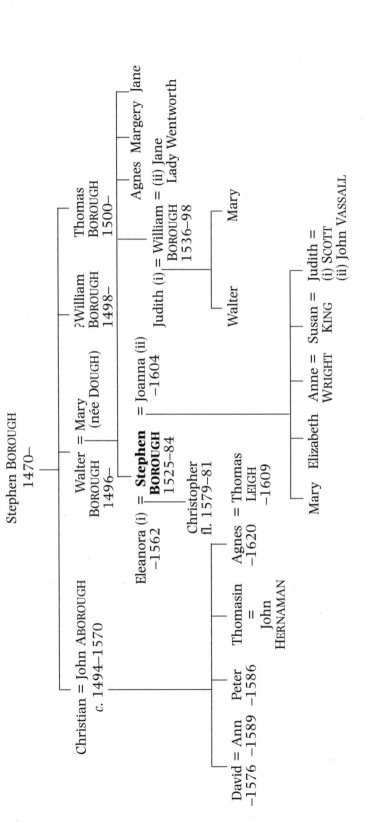

The Borough family tree constructed from many sources.

The Borough family consisted of three brothers, John (Aborough), Walter and Thomas.[10] John was born in about 1494 and appears to have been the oldest of the three brothers and head of the household, to judge from the Subsidy Rolls,[11] although he must have been away at sea a lot of the time. The Borough family worked in farming and in shipping, a common combination all round the coasts of England in those days.

Information from the so-called 'Mormon Index' confirms the general structure of the Borough family tree,[12] though it does show one or two additional members of the family, such as William (born 1498), another brother for the three brothers, John Aborough, Walter and Thomas. It also shows a certain Stephen (born in 1470) as the father of the three (or four) brothers and a certain Walter (born 1444) as their grandfather.[13]

The connection between John Aborough and Stephen may have been crucial to Stephen's later career, and for this reason I have investigated it as far as possible. In 1926 Chanter had suggested (correctly as it turned out) that John Aborough was Stephen's uncle.[14] Others have (incorrectly) stated that he was Stephen's father, and others again have indicated that there was some connection but that they did not know what it was.[15] John Aborough was married to Christian,[16] and they had two sons, David and Peter, and two daughters, Agnes and Thomazin, a son-in-law John Hernaman and a grandson, also called John Hernaman. John Aborough had two brothers, Walter (the father of Stephen) and Thomas. These names are all in his will[17] and they all tie in with the details in the wills of the other members of the family, including those of Stephen and William (John's nephews through his brother Walter), David and Peter (his sons) and Ann (David's widow). The numerous cross-references between the names in the various wills, especially the fact that John had two brothers called Walter and Thomas, confirm that John was definitely Stephen's uncle.

Stephen's first lessons in reading and writing may have been with his uncle, John Aborough, on one of his occasional visits. We know that John could read and write, but his own father and mother almost certainly could not.[18]

When he was 5, Stephen would have started school. He would have walked along the muddy track from the farm to the village of Northam, and then between the low houses of what is now Castle Street to Church House in the small square at the centre of the village. (Some of his young friends were not allowed to go to school: they had work to do, such as clearing stones from the fields or herding cows or cutting furse for the cloam ovens.)[19]

Church House was, and still is, a stone building on the west side of Fore Street, backing onto the churchyard, on the south side of the church gate and separated from it by one other property.[20] Stephen's first lessons were held in the long room that ran the whole length of the house, at first-floor level, reached by means of a flight of external stairs that no longer exist.[21]

Nobody knows how old Church House is, but it was certainly used as a schoolroom for many, many generations, up until 1839. The ground floor beneath the long schoolroom was used as a prison, later as a barber's shop, then an off-licence, and recently it has been converted into a spacious sitting-room.

Stephen's first teacher was probably not John Smyth, the parish priest of Northam from 1524 to 1554, but Richard Walter. He was the stipendiary or auxiliary priest, employed by the religious guild of Northam, principally for the purpose of saying masses for the departed souls of members of the guild.[22] He was also expected to teach some lessons. For these duties he received a rather niggardly stipend of £3 16s 6d, but he probably had a small house and garden included.[23]

He taught Stephen to read and write, and he seems to have done a good job for, in later life, Stephen's handwriting was good, regular and legible, as is shown in his will and in one or two other documents that he wrote himself. Stephen could certainly express himself very clearly in English, as he did, for instance, in the account of his voyage in the *Serchthrift* in 1556 and 1557.

By the age of 6 or 7 Stephen may well have discovered the excitement and the bustle at Appledore. Appledore was about a mile and a half away from Borough, though still in the parish of Northam,[24] and it had been a port since time before memory. Boys of his age probably enjoyed working on or playing about in boats then just as they did in Victorian times when, as we know from local photographs, boys worked on boats there. One photograph of Appledore, taken in the 1890s, shows three boys tarring the bottom of a ship's boat.[25] One of those three boys went on to become Captain W.J. Slade, who started his seagoing career in 1904, at the age of 12.[26]

It would be surprising if Captain Stephen Borough, some 350 years earlier, had not done much the same as Captain Slade, and spent many of his boyhood days down at the waterside in Appledore, learning to handle small boats belonging to, or part-owned by, some of his relations, and learning about the skills and the hazards of the seafaring life.

Appledore was an excellent place in which to learn. It sits beside the estuary of the two rivers, the Taw and the Torridge, where they join together before flowing out over the Bideford Bar and into the Bristol Channel. Appledore was busy with trade in those days, when transport by water was much cheaper than overland by packhorse or wagon.[27] The inland trade from the hinterland of North Devon came in carts or by packhorse to the navigable parts of the Taw and Torridge rivers, and then downstream in barges to

Appledore, or to one of the other 'bar' ports (ports inside the bar, i.e. Bideford, Barnstaple, Braunton and Fremington).[28] There the goods were transhipped into larger vessels capable of going out to sea into the Bristol Channel, a rough stretch of water, exposed to Atlantic storms and with very few places of shelter. The Bristol Channel trade in Tudor times extended to South Wales, Southern Ireland, Bordeaux and the Spanish wine ports.[29]

The principal hazard to local shipping was then, and still is, the Bideford Bar, at the seaward entrance to the estuary. It has a fearsome reputation as a wrecker of ships. It can only be crossed at or near high water, and even today must be approached with considerable caution. As the Bristol and Severn pilot says, 'Bideford Bar can be dangerous in heavy weather. . . . Do not try to enter the Torridge Estuary in poor visibility or in fresh onshore winds.'[30] The other problems of the estuary include the zigzag channel and the tidal stream, which flows at 3 knots, on to Pulley Ridge, Crow Ridge, Crow Rock and Sprat Ridge (see p. 6). The entrance to the Taw–Torridge Estuary is hazardous to any vessel, but especially to one relying entirely on the wind and sails for its propulsion.

We do not know where or how Stephen got any further training. This is not surprising, because we know very little about where most people in Tudor England got their education. It has been said that 'Apart from isolated and fanciful tales, we begin to know most important sixteenth-century people only when they are already public figures.'[31] Stephen could have been a pupil at a grammar school or at a local private school, or he could have served as a page in the household of a noble family, or perhaps gone to sea to learn the mariner's trade with a relative.

The nearest grammar school was at Barnstaple, about 12 miles away.[32] It is possible that Stephen's family could have afforded to send him away, to stay in lodgings in Barnstaple and to attend the grammar school there. We do know of one North Devon boy, John Jewell, who did just that. Jewell was born in 1522, only three years earlier than Stephen; he was sent successively to three local schoolmasters, at Heanton Punchardon, Braunton and South Molton, before he went to Barnstaple Grammar School. John Jewell later became Bishop of Salisbury.[33]

Stephen could have attended a private school instead. There were a number of private schools at the time, run by persons licensed by the church to do so, where children could learn such subjects as book-keeping and the elements of mathematics needed for land-surveying or navigation.[34] There is, however, no surviving evidence that there was such a school locally in Stephen's time.

After some formal education, many boys were sent, usually at about the age of 12, to live in another household, preferably one of a superior social status to their own, to serve as pages and to perform such menial tasks as serving at table while they learned about etiquette, riding, hawking, hunting, shooting and military skills. Most noble or superior households had a number of such pages, or 'henchmen', as their protégés, and the household of the local gentry, the Grenvilles, was well known for this a few years after Stephen's time. There is, however, no evidence that Stephen was ever one of the Grenvilles' henchmen.

It is more likely that Stephen spent his apprenticeship years under a master mariner. As Scammell points out, 'families already in shipping sent off their boys to learn the trade, either in their own vessels or in those of friends and relatives'.[35] Stephen's uncle, John Aborough, was the most skilled and successful mariner in the Borough family, and he owned ships, as did other members of Stephen's family, such as his cousin David. Although there is no evidence for it, it would be surprising if Stephen had not spent at least some of his formative years as a page or 'gromet'[36] learning all the practicalities of ship-handling under the tutelage of John Aborough, and it would not have been at all unusual if he had started his seagoing career, as Drake did, when he was 10 or 12 years old.[37]

JOHN ABOROUGH, STEPHEN'S UNCLE

Stephen got his start in life entirely through his uncle, John Aborough, who was the crucial, and the only, connection between the remote farm in North Devon where Stephen was born and the Court in London. His story is summarised here because his position was to prove so important to Stephen.

John Aborough was born in about 1494[38] and died in 1570.[39] In 1531, he was employed as a master mariner by Lord Lisle in a ship called the *Mary Plantagenet*, sailing between the West Country, France and Ireland. By October 1532 he had left the *Marie Plantagenet*. He then made a number of voyages to the Mediterranean: for instance, he turned up in Sicily in 1533 and made a voyage to Venice in 1534.[40]

It is interesting, in view of Stephen's later navigational exploits, to see what a comprehensive set of navigation instruments John Aborough had in 1533. In that year he put in a claim before the High Court of Admiralty for the loss of two sea chests, the contents of which included: a 'Balestow' (a cross staff), a quadrant, a lodestone, a running glass, Portuguese ephemerides, a rutter (route card) in 'Castiellan', an English rutter compiled by himself, two Spanish compasses, two other compasses and two charts, one of the Levant.[41] It is apparent that he was well ahead of most English sea captains of the time in his knowledge of navigation.

His employer, Lord Lisle, was appointed Lord Deputy of Calais from 1533 to 1540. As previously mentioned, Calais was England's only overseas possession then apart from Ireland, and it was only (with some exceptions) through its wool market, the 'Staple', that wool could legitimately be exported to the Continent. John Aborough was put in charge of the service boats, delivering packets to and fro across the Channel between Calais and Dover, from 1535 to 1539. Lord and Lady Lisle were effectively trapped in the English enclave at Calais by their duties there: they had to conduct all their business to England by letter and had to rely entirely on John Aborough and his service boats for the safe delivery of all their correspondence and packages. In 1540 John Aborough was listed by the Calais Commissioners as having three ships regularly repairing to the town: a ship of 50 tons, a ketch of 25 tons and another ketch of 18 tons.

In March 1539 he was sent on a spying mission to Flanders. Henry VIII was greatly concerned that the Holy Roman Emperor, Charles V, might be preparing to attack England. Aborough had to ride on horseback from Calais along the coast about 70 miles to Sluis in Flanders, and report on the state of readiness of the ships that he found there.[42]

Later in 1539 John Aborough and Robert Couchye, another experienced shipmaster, were sent to the Netherlands, in great secrecy, to discover a route and make a chart so that Henry VIII could send his fleet over to Harderwijk in Holland to pick up his next bride, Anne of Cleves, and bring her back to England. In 1540 he was employed on the design of the king's 'Water works at Dover', to draw up plans to improve the sea defences there. By 1544 he was in command of a navy ship, the *Great Pinas*, of 80 tons, at the time when Henry was involved in attacking south-east Scotland and also Boulogne, though it is not known what part Aborough took in these campaigns. In 1548 and 1549 he was employed carrying supplies for the fortification of the island of Alderney against the French. His name also appears in connection with various properties in Calais, London and Hampshire, and particularly with several properties in North Devon.

This was the man who almost certainly was Borough's mentor during his early years, and who was the critical link between Stephen and the authorities in London, without whom Stephen would never have been appointed as master of the *Edward Bonaventura*.

STEPHEN BOROUGH'S ADULT LIFE

Stephen was 27 when he was appointed. By that time he was a skilful sea captain, experienced enough to be selected as the master of the largest of the three ships of the 1553 expedition sent to search for a new sea route to the East and wise enough to survive numerous long voyages to Russia and back. His training for all of this could not have been better if he had grown up learning to master the various hazards of the Bristol Channel trade and the 'Western Navigation'.

Stephen's first wife was Eleanora, the daughter of John Smithe of the parish of Clive in Shropshire. It is not known where or when they married. They lived at Ratcliffe on the north bank of the Thames, downstream from the Tower of London, and they had one child, Christopher. Eleanora died in February 1562; Stephen was the administrator of her will, in which he is specified as 'Stephen Aborough, Mariner, of Ratcliffe'.[43]

A year after Eleanora died, Stephen married again, on 26 March 1563.[44] His second wife was Joanna Overye of the parish of Stepney, and by her he had five daughters.[45] Joanna outlived Stephen; she eventually died at Chatham in 1604.

Stephen occurs again in another Deed of Administration in 1572.[46] This time the deceased was a man called John Rabelo, and Stephen was the executor of his will. The relationship between him and Rabelo is not known, though Rabelo was a mariner and he left the lease of a house in Barking to Stephen. Stephen was recorded as still living at Ratcliffe at this time.

Stephen and his brother William both apppear in a register of ships in 1572.[47] Alongside theirs is the name of a certain Robert Burrow. Each of the three is listed as the master of a ship in the Port of London: Stephen of the *Black Greyhound*, of 200 tons; William of the *Margaret*, of 120 tons; and Robert Burrow of the *Black Burre*, of 100 tons. It would be very interesting to know if Robert was any relative of Stephen and William.

Stephen Borough's signature, from his will, which he wrote himself shortly before his death in 1584.

Stephen Borough wrote his own will and signed it 'S. Borowgh' on 1 July 1584. This was just eleven days before he died.[48] In it he refers to his wife Joanna; his 'first' son Christopher (presumably referring to him as his first child, as he only had one son that we know of); his five daughters Judith, Susan, Mary, Anne and Elizabeth, some of whom must still have been young at the time, as he refers to them as 'my young children'; and he also mentions

Here lieth buried the bodie of Steven Borough who departed this life the 12th of July in the yier of our lord 1584 and was borne at Northam in Devonshire the 25th of September 1525. He in his lifetime discovered Muscovia by the northerne sea passage to St. Nicholas in the yere 1553. At his settinge foorth of England he was accompany with two other shippes, Sir Hugh Willobie beinge Admirall of the fleet, who with all the company of the said two shippes were frozen to death in Lappia the same winter. After his discoverie of Koolia and the coastes there to adioyning, to wit Lapyia, Novazemia and the Cuntreie of Samoyeda et: hee frequented the trade to St. Nicholas yearlie as chiefe pilot for the voyage until he was chosen for one of the fowre pricipall masters in ordenarie of the Queens majestie's royall Navy where in he continewed beinge imployed as occasion required in charge of sondrie sea services till time of his death.

The text of the memorial plaque to Stephen Borough, which is on the wall of St Mary's Church, Chatham.

his brother William. He refers to his three houses, one of which was called 'the Signe of the Mayden Hedd' and which stood somewhere in East Street, Gravesend. From its name it sounds as though this house was an inn, and in fact it was documented as a public house from 1584 (the year of his death) until 1712.[49] Another of his properties was 'my house over against Barking Church, which I hold in the right of John Rabelo deceased'. His third house was 'my house in Chatham called Goodsight'. This was the house that he was living in when he wrote his will and where he died not long afterwards.[50]

His was a remarkable family – a dynasty almost. Four other members of the family achieved national fame. John Aborough, his uncle, worked directly for Henry VIII on several important projects, and it was he who was the vital connection for Stephen between North Devon, where Stephen was born, and the Court in London. The other relatives who became famous were Stephen's brother William, who eventually became Controller of the Navy; his son Christopher, the traveller and explorer of parts of Asia; and his son-in-law John Vassall, who was one of the founders of the colony of Virginia, the first permanent English colony in America, and possibly the owner of, or even the builder of, the *Mayflower*. (Their stories are summarised in Appendix 2.)

It is fortunate that enough evidence still exists to construct a family tree for Stephen Borough and, at least to some extent, to enable us to construct a context for his life in different localities. The evidence shows that the focus of Stephen's life, like that of John Aborough and William Borough, moved from the remote manor farm in North Devon to London, though they did retain connections with Northam. They were not alone in this migration to the capital: the records of the High Court of Admiralty clearly show a movement of seafarers from Devon and Cornwall to Thames-side, as trade and shipping became increasingly concentrated in London.[51]

Stephen had obviously done well financially. He had started life on a small and remote country manor farm but died in possession of three houses, at Gravesend, Barking and Chatham. The records also show that Stephen, his uncle and his brother all achieved what would now be called upward social, as well as financial, mobility.

CHAPTER 3

The Aims and Organisation of the 1553 Expedition

'Many things seemed necessary to bee regarded in this so hard and difficult a matter.'[1]

The organisers of the first English overseas expedition were well aware of how difficult a matter it was. They were preparing for a leap into the unknown, as they knew almost nothing about the proposed route or the difficulties that would have to be faced. They were, however, buoyed up by tales of the riches of the spice trade (Vasco da Gama's first voyage is said to have repaid his investors 100,000 times over in gold, spices, pepper and ivory). The English had inside information about the great Spanish and Portuguese expansion from several well-placed sources, one of whom was Sebastian Cabot. He had been in charge of all the Spanish voyages when he was the Pilot Major of Spain, and he was now living and working in England. There was also information from the English merchants who lived and worked in Seville, such as Robert Thorne and Philip Barnes.

The control centre for all of Spain's overseas trade was the 'Casa de la Contratación' in the *ataranza* (arsenal) at Seville,[2] and it is perhaps not surprising that the original proposal for the English expedition came from Seville, specifically from Robert Thorne, a merchant of Bristol, who had been living there for a long time and was thus well placed to know all about the overseas activities of the Spaniards.[3] In a letter to Henry VIII in 1527 he urged that:

> With a small number of ships there may bee discovered divers New lands and kingdomes, in the which without doubt your Grace shall winne perpetuall glory, and your subjectes infinite profite. To which places there is left one way to discover, which is into the North.

He went on to enunciate the benefits of a northern route to the Orient, whereby the English could profit from 'golde, precious stones, balmes, spices and other things that we here esteeme most'.

He pointed out that a northern route would be some 2,000 leagues (6,000 nautical miles) shorter than the route used by the Portuguese, that there would be perpetual daylight along the way and that, once they were past the North Pole, they would find, as he supposed, a temperate climate.[4] Thorne advocated the northern route because it would allow the English access to the riches of the Orient without conflict with the routes already established by the Iberians. However, for a number of reasons, Henry VIII was not able to act on the proposal at that time.

THE AIMS OF THE EXPEDITION

What exactly were the aims of the expedition? What was it that galvanised the English into action? Richard Chancellor's original account of the expedition partly answers these questions. He became the second-in-command of the expedition and later wrote an account of it, in which he described the aims as follows:

> At what time our Marchants perceived the commodities and wares of England to bee in small request with the countreys and people about us, and neere unto us, and that those Marchandizes which strangers in the time and memorie of our auncestors did earnestly seeke and desire, were nowe neglected, and the price thereof abated, although by us carried to their owne portes, and all foreigne Marchandises in great accompt, and their prises wonderfully raised: certaine grave Citizens of London and men of great wisedome, and carefull for the good of their Countrey, began to think with themselves, howe this mischiefe might bee remedied.[5]

Chancellor also talked of the wealth of the Spaniards and the Portuguese, which 'by the discoverie and search of newe trades and countreys was marveilously increased'.[6]

Another view of the aim of the expedition was put some years later by one Thomas Edge. He said that the merchants were 'incited with the fame of the great masse of riches which the Portugals and Spaniards brought home yeerely from both the Indies', and he also stated that at the time of the 1553 expedition, the trade of the kingdom was 'waxing cold and in decay'.[7]

The Muscovy Company itself, in a statement about its own origin made much later, in 1600, declared that 'the king and his councell, finding it inconvenient that the utterance of the comodities of England, especiallie clothe, should so much depend upon the Lowe Countries and Spaine, and that it should be beneficiall to have a vent some other waies'.[8]

These accounts show that the main aims of the English expedition were the lure of the riches of the Orient and the need to find other export outlets, because sales of cloth to the Continent had fallen.

Richard Hakluyt, who collected most of the documents relating to the early voyages to Russia, held strong Protestant views, and he produced Protestant arguments in support of English overseas expansion, which he hoped would counter the dominance of Catholic Spain.[9] He expected that Englishmen would take the (Protestant) Gospel to the heathens and 'reduce those gentile people to christianitie'. But none of the organisers mention religious or missionary motives for the voyages.

An examination of the crew lists of the ships of the expedition gives another indication of what the actual objectives were. There were three ships and a total of 117 men, of whom 11 were merchants and 7 others may have been merchants, although they were not specifically identified as such.[10] (Two of the seven later became members of the Muscovy Company.)[11] There was only one soldier, Sir Hugh Willoughby, the leader of the expedition, and there was only one minister of religion. The merchants on the three ships greatly outnumbered the priests and soldiers.

The economic pressure for the start of the English expansion can be seen by looking at the number of shortcloths that were exported from London each year. This number increased by 150 per cent between 1500 and 1550. The rise was fuelled, to begin with, by the general growth in trade at Antwerp, but later stimulated by exchange depreciation, largely due to several debasements of the English coinage under Henry VIII. The debasements caused the pound sterling to fall in value from 32 Flemish shillings to 13s 4d Flemish by 1551.[12] But then, in that year, the Crown was pressed to repay its debts to the Fuggers and the other financiers in Antwerp. It took various steps to restore the exchange rate, as a result of which English goods immediately became more expensive on the Continent. Consequently there was a sharp drop in the export of shortcloths from London, from a peak of 133,000 in 1550 to 113,000 in 1551 and 85,000 in 1552. This sharp drop in the export of the one commodity that constituted more than 85 per cent of England's total export trade was what triggered the search for new outlets. This is the view held by most, if not all, historians.[13] There were, of course, many other factors involved, not the least of which were wars on the Continent, epidemics and the rise of other trading centres.

However, in summary, it seems from a number of accounts, and from the crew lists of the ships, and from the economic indicators at the time, that the aim of the expedition was not conquest or religious zeal; nor was it prompted by the spirit of adventure or the pure pursuit of geographical knowledge. It was set up by merchants and for merchants, and between 10 and 15 per cent of the members of the expedition were themselves merchants. The aim appears to have been to find a new way to the Orient, to trade there, to sell more cloth and thereby to increase the wealth of the London merchants. Hakluyt himself summarised the position when he wrote 'Our chief desire is to find out ample vent of our woollen cloth, the naturall commoditie of this our Realme, the fittest places . . . are the manifold Islands of Japan and the Northern parts of china and the regions of the Tartars next adjoyning.'[14]

In short, it was a purely commercial venture.

The aims of the 1553 expedition were thus in contrast to those of the Spanish expeditions to the New World, and also very different from later Tudor expeditions. The Spaniards were intent upon conquest, gold and silver and the religious conversion of the people they encountered, while the main objective of the later Tudor seafarers, nicknamed the 'Sea Dogs', was privateering, piracy or pillage, whatever their ostensible purposes may have been.[15]

The English, when they did belatedly organise their first explorations, did it very differently from the Iberians. Both the Portuguese and the Spanish efforts were very much centrally planned and supervised and under royal control and patronage, whereas the English voyages were made by groups of private individuals, usually but not always with royal consent, and they were sporadic and haphazard.

SETTING UP THE 1553 EXPEDITION

According to Richard Chancellor:

> Certaine grave Citizens of London, and men of great wisedome and carefull for the good of their Countrey, began to thinke with themselve. . . . And whereas at the same time one Sebastian Cabota, a man in those dayes very renowned, happened to be in London, they began first of all to deale and consult diligently with him . . . it was at last concluded that three shippes should bee prepared and furnished out, for the search and discoverie of the Northerne part of the world. . . . Many things seemed necessary to bee regarded in this so hard and difficult a matter, they first made choyse of certaine grave and wise persons in maner of a Senate or companie.[16]

It was indeed a hard and difficult matter. It was the first time that the English had ever attempted any such expedition and the first time that they had attempted to sail in such a completely new direction. It was also, and this is perhaps even more astonishing, the first time that such a great consortium had been set up, involving so many highly placed members of the Court, as well as a large number of the merchants of London.

The instigators of the expedition, the two so-called 'principall doers', were Sir George Barne and Sir William Garrard, both of them wealthy and powerful London merchants.[17] Sir George Barne was a member of the Haberdashers' Company, an exporter of cloth, a grocer and vintner, and an importer of wine from Spain, where, as already mentioned, his son Philip was his factor. Sir George was also a promoter of voyages to Guinea in 1553 and 1554. He was Mayor of London in 1552–3, Sheriff of London, and knighted in 1553. He became a Charter Consul of the Muscovy Company.

Sir William Garrard was another of the great London merchants of his day. He was Assistant of the Merchant Adventurers' Company in 1564, Master of the Haberdashers' Company in 1557, Mayor of London in 1555–6 and knighted in 1557. He exported cloth and molasses, and imported sugar from Barbary (North Africa) and silk. He was a promoter of voyages to Guinea in 1553 and 1554 and of the slaving voyages of 1564 and 1567. He was a Charter Consul of the Muscovy Company and became Governor of the company in 1561. He was also Charter Governor of the Mineral and Battery Works.

Others who were active in setting up the new company were George Barne, Sir Rowland Heyward, Sir Lionel Duckett and Sir Thomas Smythe.

George Barne was the son of Sir George. He married Anne, the daughter of Sir William Garrard, thus joining together the families of the two 'principall doers'. He later became the joint Governor of the Muscovy Company in 1580. (Incidentally, George Barne's sister, Anna Carleil, formed another alliance, this time with the Court, when she married Sir Francis Walsingham, who became Queen Elizabeth's Principal Secretary, though she died only two years after the marriage.)

Sir Rowland Heyward was Master of the Clothmakers' Company in 1559, Mayor of London in 1570–1 and again in 1591, and an MP for London 1572–81. He was an exporter of cloth and importer of fustians, camlets, buckram and silk, and he became a great landowner. He was made a consul of the Muscovy Company in 1569 and its joint Governor, with George Barne, in 1580.

Sir Lionel Duckett was four times Master of the Mercers' Company and Mayor of London in 1572–3. He shipped cloth to Antwerp and imported wine.

Sir Thomas Smythe later became the Governor of the Muscovy Company and sometime ambassador to Moscow.[18]

SEBASTIAN CABOT

These were the men who called on Sebastian Cabot to organise the expedition. Cabot (*c.* 1474–1557) had had a complicated and controversial career. From 1512, he was in Spain, and from 1519 he was the Pilot Major to the Holy Roman Emperor Charles V. In 1526, he was put in charge of an expedition that was to sail to the Moluccas in the East Indies, via the Strait of Magellan. There is some doubt as to whether some of the expeditions he claimed to have undertaken ever took place. However, this one definitely did take place, and it ended in ignominy. He lost his flagship and spent four years in the area of the River Plate, near where Buenos Aires is today, building a fort and trying to lay the foundations for a Spanish conquest of South America. The expedition was such a failure that on his return Cabot was put in prison for a year, after which he was banished to Oran in North Africa for two years. However, there is no doubt that he was a brilliant cartographer, and he was eventually reinstated as Pilot Major of Spain. He seems to have been an excellent organiser but a poor executive. A comment was made by one of his contemporaries, that he was 'a good person and skilful in his office of cosmography . . . but it is not the same thing to command and govern people'.[19] This was the man who was to be the organising genius behind the 1553 expedition.

He returned to England in 1548, induced by Lord Lisle, the Lord High Admiral,[20] to return to Bristol by the offer of a pension of £166 a year. In 1552, at 79 years of age, he set about what was to be his finest achievement, the organisation of 'the Company for the exploration of unknown landes'. This new venture later became the Muscovy Company. It was set up as a joint stock company, the first in England.

THE FIRST JOINT STOCK COMPANY

Before this time the usual way in which a group of merchants had worked together had been in a 'regulated company'. Each member of a regulated company had to pay an entrance fee to the company to allow him to benefit from the company's assets, which might include the monopoly of a particular trade and an organisation to regulate the trade to prevent unfair competition between members and to maintain the prices of the commodities that they traded in. In a regulated company each member traded on his own account, i.e. he bought his own goods, and arranged for their transport and sale himself, often employing his own factor in some distant port for the purpose.

The Staplers and the Merchant Adventurers were both regulated companies. The Staplers had the monopoly on the export of raw wool and the Merchant Adventurers that on the export of English cloth. The Company of the Merchant Adventurers was described as having 'no banke, nor common stocke, nor common Factour to buye, or sell for the whole companie, but every man tradeth a-part and particularlie with his own stocke and with his own Factour or servant'.[21]

A 'joint stock' company was different in that the members did not trade as individuals. Instead they paid individual 'subscriptions' into the company, and the company used this money to pay its servants, to buy goods to trade with, to hire or purchase premises to store goods in and ships to transport the goods. It was the company, and not individual members, who employed the factors to buy and sell the goods. In a joint stock company, the amount of capital which accumulated from all the individual subscriptions could be much larger than that of a regulated company, which was a great advantage when buying expensive items such as ships, especially as the ships might make no financial return for a year or more.

The nobility and the landed gentry had little interest in the regulated companies, as they had neither the time nor the skill to trade on their own. However, they were attracted to the joint stock company, as it gave them the opportunity to invest any surplus money they might have without having to concern themselves with the day-to-day business of buying and selling the goods. They could invest and become 'sleeping partners'. There were at that time no banks, and no stocks and shares as we know them, and so the rich (and some of them were very rich) could do little with their wealth other than spend it on land, houses, clothes or conspicuous consumption, or else put it into trading ventures to foreign countries.[22] They welcomed the concept of the joint stock company as a new kind of investment opportunity. Another advantage of the joint stock company was that the share that an individual owned in such a venture could be inherited by his heirs and successors.

The scale and importance of all this was completely new. There had previously been a few small groups of London merchants who traded 'in joint stock', i.e. having common ownership of the goods traded. However, there had never before been in England a company run on a joint stock basis like this, nor for that matter had there ever been a commercial venture which brought together such a large number of merchants. Many of them knew each other, they lived in London in the same stratum of society, and many of them were members of the Merchant Adventurers, but they had never previously joined their resources together on such a scale. Nearly all the great merchant families of London joined in the venture, including the Heywards, the Lodges, the Barnes, the Ducketts and the Garrards.[23]

The notion of a joint stock company may have been introduced to England by Sebastian Cabot, who had had experience of the organisation and finances of overseas companies when he was Pilot Major at Seville. The original concept of joint stock trading seems to have come from Italy, which, with its several well-developed city states, was then in the forefront of the evolution of sophisticated financial organisations.[24]

The new company, which was originally called 'The Company for the exploration of unknown landes', was made up of the 215 subscribers, each of whom contributed £25.[25] In a short time a working capital of £6,000 had been collected, which suggests that there were 240 subscribers although the list shows only 215 names. Sebastian Cabot was made governor of the company for life, and there were four 'consuls' and twenty-four 'assistants', each appointed for a year at a time.[26] In the first year, the consuls were Sir George Barne, William Garret (or Garrard), Anthony Huse (or Hussey) and John Southecote.[27]

Some of the most powerful people in England invested in the venture. There were seven peers and twenty knights, many of whom were members of the Privy Council or of the Royal Household. The list included: William, Marquess of Winchester, Lord High Treasurer; Lord Howard of Effingham, Lord High Admiral; Sir Francis Walsingham, who later became Queen Elizabeth's Principal Secretary; the Attorney General; the Solicitor General; and many other notables, including five Privy Councillors, seven Aldermen and several past or future Lord Mayors of London. They were all from London, with the single exception of one merchant from Bristol, and there were two women.[28]

Not everyone believed in the new venture. There were some, 'sundry authors and writers', as Cabot calls them, who 'ministred matters of suspision in some heads, that this voyage could not succede . . . which have caused wavering minds and doubtful heads not onely to withdraw themselves from the adventure of this voyage, but also disswaded others from the same'.[29]

Stephen Borough was a charter member and also one of the twelve counsellors appointed by the company specifically for the first voyage,[30] but there is no record of what the counsellors did, or at what stage they were involved.[31]

CONCLUSION

It was the merchants of London who set up the first expedition to search for the North-East Passage, and their aim was entirely commercial. It was a huge undertaking for the English; nothing like it had ever been done before. Six of the merchants provided the impetus, and many of the other London merchants supported the venture by taking out a subscription of £25 each, as also did many of the highest officials at the Court of Edward VI. They managed to obtain the services of Sebastian Cabot, the most experienced organiser, to put the expedition together, and, as it turned out, it was their selection of Richard Chancellor and Stephen Borough as shipmasters that ensured the eventual success of this tremendous venture.

CHAPTER 4

The Ships of the 1553 Expedition and their Crews and Equipment

The only things we know for certain about the expedition ships is that there were three of them, their names and tonnages, and the names of all their crews. However, it is possible, using certain clues, to find out what the ships were like, and this is what will be discussed in this chapter.

Sir Hugh Willoughby's ship, the *Bona Esperanza*, was 'the Admirall of the fleete', even though, at 120 tons, she was not the largest of the three ships in the expedition. (It was the ship and not the man that was given the title 'Admirall'.) The *Esperanza* carried thirty-eight men, including Sir Hugh (the 'Captaine generall of the fleete'); the master was William Gefferson, and the crew included one gunner, several quartermasters, carpenters, pursers, two cooks, two surgeons and six merchants.[1]

The largest of the three ships was the *Edward Bonaventura*, of 160 tons, with Richard Chancellor as 'Pilot major of the fleete' and with Stephen Borough as master, and a total complement of forty-nine men, who included two merchants, seven unspecified, four gunners and one minister.

The smallest ship was the *Bona Confidentia*, of 90 tons, with a certain Cornelius Durfoorth as master and a total complement of twenty-eight men, of whom three were merchants and two were gunners.[2] Cornelius Durfoorth may have been of Dutch origin, to judge by his name.[3]

The three ships were for 'the most part . . . newly built and trimmed'.[4] They were built at Ratcliffe, now in the parish of Stepney. Ratcliffe was on the Thames below the City of London, as it had a low bank adjacent suitable for shipbuilding and launching into deep water. It was a site that had been used for ship-building long before any permanent docks were built there.[5]

THE REVOLUTION IN THE DESIGN OF SHIPS

The hundred years between 1450 and 1550 had seen a great leap forward in ship design, and the ships of the expedition, built in the early 1550s, incorporated all the latest developments in design and construction.

A Spanish carrack, *c.* 1500. The huge mainsail dwarfs the other sails.

The greatest single development was the change from the single-masted to the three-masted rig in the second half of the fifteenth century. This change started with the addition to the massive single central mast of a second mast, either a small fore mast or a small mizzen mast. Later, both a fore mast and a mizzen became standard. The ship seen above is a Spanish carrack of about 1500. She was at a halfway stage in this development. She carried an enormous great windbag of a mainsail on a massive tree-trunk of a main mast, and had very much smaller sails on the fore and mizzen masts. The huge mainsail must have driven the bulky hull along very nicely in favourable winds, but it is not difficult to imagine what a large crew would have been required to shorten sail in a hurry when a squall struck.

The fore and mizzen masts gradually increased in size in relation to the mainmast until, by 1540, the height of the fore mast was about eight-tenths the height of the main mast (above the deck), and the mizzen about seven-tenths. It also became usual to have a bowsprit, which was nearly as long as the fore mast; this projected at the bow at an angle of 30° to 40° to the horizontal and carried a spritsail (a square sail set below the bowsprit).[6] The fore and main masts carried fore and main courses and fore and main topsails, all of which were square sails, and the mizzen mast had a single lateen rigged sail. (Sometimes there were two mizzen masts, and in this case the after one was called a bonaventura mizzen, and it also carried a lateen sail.)[7]

By about 1540, the three-master was almost universal. A ship with three masts had several advantages over a single-masted ship. Not only were the sails smaller, which meant that they could be handled by a smaller crew, but also one or more of the sails could be furled at a time to reduce the sail area, a much more flexible system. However, the greatest single advantage was that the centre of effort of the smaller sails was not so high up as the centre of effort of a single big sail. In other words, there was less heeling moment, less tendency for the whole ship to blow over sideways.

Another important development was the introduction of heavy guns on board, placed low down, below decks, for reasons of stability. This was the beginning of the concept of the ship as a mobile long-range weapon platform, a concept still much in vogue today. Other major changes included the replacement of clinker with skeleton-built carvel-planked hulls and the replacement of rounded sterns with square transom sterns.

The outcome of the revolution was the three-masted ship, an invention that was so successful that it survived right through until the challenge of steam-power in the 1860s and '70s.[8] The ships of the expedition were nothing like so elegant or efficient as the magnificent tea-clippers of the nineteenth century, but they did have the same basic three-masted structure, and this is what gave them the ability to sail across oceans with a reasonable chance of coming back again.

WHAT THE SHIPS LOOKED LIKE

There are some magnificent pictures of the royal 'great ships' of the time, such as the 'Embarkation of Henry VIII' on the *Mary Rose*, and pictures of the *Ark Royal*, but these great ships are far too grand for our purposes. The ships of the expedition were much more modest craft. They were of a size that the great artists seldom bothered to portray, but there are nevertheless a few pictures that do show small merchantmen.

One is by Hans Holbein the Younger (1497–1543). His picture of a small Flemish or German merchantman of about 1532 shows a ship with a keel length of perhaps 30 feet, and therefore a tonnage of about 12 tons (see plate section). Her stern is of what might be called intermediate design, being modern and square above, but rounded and thus more old-fashioned below. She looks high above the water because of her upperworks at bow and stern. Her mast and sail plan are up to date, and her pronounced beak and figurehead are, if anything, ahead of her time.

Some other illustrations of contemporary ships are those in the *Anthony Roll*, a series of brightly coloured drawings made by Anthony Anthony, a clerk to the Ordnance, between 1545 and 1549.[9] They show every ship in Henry VIII's navy, all viewed from the starboard quarter.

The *Dragon* (see plate section), one of the ships from the *Anthony Roll* is a ship of similar size to those of the expedition, which were of 160, 120 and 90 tons. The draughtsmanship is amateurish but the pictures in the *Anthony Roll* show that all the ships in the navy had three (or four) masts, lateen rigged on the mizzen (and on the bonaventure mizzen if there was one). As ships of war, they were all equipped with high sterncastles and forecastles, and they all bristle with guns poking out through gunports set fairly low in the hulls. Other features visible in Anthony's pictures are prominent beak-heads at the bow, nets over the midships section to impede any enemy attempts at boarding, square transom sterns and marked tumblehome.[10]

Alongside each of his pictures Anthony listed the tonnage, the number of men, the number of gunners and an extensive list of the 'Ordenanunce, artillery, munitions, habillimentes for the warre, for the arming and in the deffence of the sayd shyppe to the see'.

Other pictures of small ships of the time can be found in the embellishments of maps and harbour plans. Such sketches show, among other things, how much the three-masted rig had replaced all others. There is, for instance, a sketch of Antwerp and its harbour, dated 1468, which shows that even by that early date two of the nine ships depicted were three-masted (see plate section).

By the mid-sixteenth century, nearly every ship was three-masted. There is an engraving of the entrance to the Baltic that shows a stream of about forty merchant ships sailing up or down the Sound in front of Elsinore Castle.[11] One of them is four-masted and flying a topgallant, but all the others, without exception, are three-masted, with square sterns, fairly high stern-castles and only modest forecastles. Merchantmen were similar to ships of war at that time, as they had to be capable of defending themselves against pirate attacks, though they did not bristle with quite so many guns, and their stern- and forecastles were not quite so enormous.

Another informative picture is that of Dover Harbour in 1538, which shows a merchant vessel[12] (see plate section). It is fairly high in the water, with a bluff rounded bow and slender beak, square overhanging stern, marked waist, three clearly shown wales running fore and aft along the hulls, and a low forecastle, with the stern upperworks much higher than the forecastles.[13] It has three masts and three top masts, and a bowsprit with a square spritsail below. The fore and main masts are square-rigged, and there is a lateen sail on the mizzen. Ratlines on all three masts are a prominent feature of the standing rigging.

All the illustrations mentioned so far have been of ships built a few years before those of the expedition. There are some other drawings that show ships built a little later than those of the expedition. These are in a document that dates to 1580, which is now referred to as the 'Smerwick Map'.[14] One of the ships shown in the plate section, very carefully drawn, is the *Teager*, a ship-of-war of 200 tons. She was rebuilt in 1570.[15] Rebuilding a whole ship was not uncommon at that time.

The *Teager* was three-masted, square-rigged on the fore and main masts, and with a lateen sail on the mizzen. She had a pronounced beak and relatively slight upperworks at the bow and a modestly raised sterncastle. She is listed as having twenty-four guns, though some of these may have been small, as only four (or possibly five) gun ports are shown on the starboard side. She has at least two guns in the stern, here seen firing furiously at a fort.[16]

Such illustrations show that the ships were only sparsely decorated, at least until 1560, and, perhaps surprisingly in such a flamboyant age, there do not appear to have been many figureheads until about 1580. They did, however, go in for numerous pennants and flags, some of which were enormous and must have been a hazard to ship-handling, if the artists have not exaggerated.

THE SHAPES OF THE EXPEDITION SHIPS

We know that Sir Hugh's three ships were of up-to-date design and were strongly built, and we can conclude from the pictures mentioned above that each of his ships would have had: a modest forecastle and a somewhat higher sterncastle; a low waist; marked tumblehome; a square stern raked aft; and probably only a modest beak and no figurehead. Each of them would have had three masts and a bowsprit; the bowsprit and the fore mast would each have been about eight-tenths as long above the deck as the main mast, and the mizzen would have been about seven-tenths as long. The mizzen mast would have carried a lateen sail, and there would have been two square sails on each of the main and fore masts, and a square spritsail on the bowsprit.

THE SIZES OF THE EXPEDITION SHIPS

It is also possible to make some reasonable deductions about the sizes of the ships of the expedition, as we do know their tonnages, and we do know something about the proportions of the ships of the time. There is a formula for calculating the tonnage of a ship from its length and breadth and depth, and from these three pieces of information it is possible to calculate the approximate dimensions of the ships.

William Borough's 'Proportions in building of Shyppinge'

The earliest contemporary comments that we have on the proportions of ships come from none other than William Borough (younger brother of Stephen), at the time when he was Comptroller of the Navy. He stated, in about 1590, that 'The proportions which suit several orders and kinds of ships are chiefly found by these 3 Dimensions, length, breadth and depth. That is to say length by the keel, breadth at the midship and depth from the boards [deck] to the keel.'[17] (This latter was presumably measured between the top of the keelson and the lower side of the main deck beams.)

The ratios he gave for the length, breadth and depth of different kinds of ships are summarised below:

For the Shortest, broadest and deepest ships – 2 (length) to 1 (breadth) to ½ (depth)

For the Merchant and general purpose ships – 2 or 2¼ (length) to 1 (breadth) to 11⁄24 (depth)

And for Gallions and nimble ships of war – 3 (length) to 1 (breadth) to ⅔ (depth).

These proportions, incidentally, had almost certainly been in use for many years before he noted them down.[18]

It would be reasonable to suppose that the expedition ships had proportions that were somewhere between those of William Borough's merchant ships and those of his 'nimble ships of war', i.e. a length of about 2½ times the breadth and a depth of about ⅔ of the breadth.

Mathew Baker's Old Rule

The usual Tudor formula for calculating the tonnage[19] of a ship was known as Mathew Baker's Old Rule, which he wrote down in 1582[20] and which may be summarised as:

Tonnage = length × breadth × depth below main deck (all in feet) ÷ 100.

Combining William Borough's 'Proportions' with Mathew Baker's Old Rule

If we take X as the breadth of the ship in feet, and use William Borough's proportions in Mathew Baker's formula, then we get this equation:

$$\text{Tonnage (cubic capacity)} = \frac{5/2X \times X \times 2/5X}{100}$$

As the tonnage of each of the ships of the expedition is known, it is possible to find the value of X, the breadth of the ship in feet, and from this to derive the length of the keel and the depth below the main deck. (The calculations are shown in Appendix 4.)

On this basis Stephen Borough's ship, the *Edward Bonaventura*, with a tonnage of 160 tons, would have had a breadth or beam of 25 feet, a keel 62½ feet in length, and the depth below the main deck to the top of the keelson would have been 10 feet. Further to this we could add that the rake of the bow and of the stern would have given her an overall length of about 113 feet.

For Sir Hugh's ship, the *Bona Esperanza* of 120 tons, the same formula gives a breadth of 23 feet; a keel length of 57½ feet; a depth below the main deck of 9¼ feet; and an overall length of 80½ feet. The smallest ship of the expedition, the *Bona Confidentia* of 90 tons, would have measured: keel 52½ feet; beam 21 feet; depth below main deck 8½ feet and overall length 73½ feet. (All of these dimensions are obviously very approximate.)

An anonymous treatise on ship-building

Another early source of information on ship proportions is an anonymous treatise on ship-building which dates to *c.* 1600.[21] In some ways this is less precise in its directions than William Borough's 'Proportions in building of Shyppinge' but, in general, the proportions it gives are similar and it can serve as a confirmation of the 'Proportions' that Borough proposed. For example it states that 'The breadth . . . must never be more than one half of ye (keel) length thereof nor less then ⅓. The depth . . . must not be more than ½ (of the breadth) nor less then ⅓.' The anonymous author goes on to describe many more dimensions, such as the amount of tumblehome in the ship's side, and he also prescribes the required rake at the stem and stern: 'the rake of the stem. . . must not be more than twice and a half (the depth) nor less than once and three quarters thereof' and 'the rake of the stern post aftward

. . . shall be any angle of degrees, and must not be more then 22½ degrees nor less than 18'.

He includes tables relating the length of the keel to the other dimensions. For example, for a ship with a 'length of ye keel of 99 feet, greatest breadth 33 feet, the depth from the breadth to ye keel in ye first bend of timber 12, the length of the higher sweep in ye greatest breadth 5½, the length of the futtick sweep 20, the length of the wrong head sweep 6½ and the length of ye higher sweep in ye fashion peece 16½'.

Similarly, there are detailed instructions on how to calculate the lengths of the spars. The length of the mainyard is calculated by taking half the length of the keel in feet and adding the breadth, and from this rules are given prescribing the lengths and dimensions of all the other spars.

It is probable that these rules and guidelines, or something very similar, had been well known for at least fifty years but had previously been kept secret as part of the 'mysteries' of the shipwright's trade. The builders of the ships of the 1553 expedition almost certainly used some similar guidelines.

ARCHAEOLOGICAL EVIDENCE FOR ENGLISH SHIP CONSTRUCTION IN THE SIXTEENTH CENTURY

Underwater archaeology is another way of finding out about shipbuilding at this time. The only two wrecks of ships that have been discovered so far and that were definitely English-built, and definitely of the sixteenth century, are the *Mary Rose* and the *Alderney*. There is a third, the *Cattewater* wreck, which may have been English-built, but she could alternatively have been built by the Basques. There are also several other known wrecks from the sixteenth century, but they were of Spanish or Dutch origin and were constructed somewhat differently and used different timbers.

The *Mary Rose* has been investigated in great detail. She was built in 1509/10 at Portsmouth, partly rebuilt in 1536, then sank ignominiously in 1545 and was raised again at Portsmouth (in part) in 1982.[22] The *Alderney* wreck is thought to have been a military supply ship, which went down in 1592.[23] Various artefacts have been recovered from her, including three guns of 3½ in bore (sakers) but, for various reasons, the only structural item that it has been possible to retrieve is the rudder.[24] The *Cattewater* wreck in Plymouth, dating from about 1530, has also been fairly extensively investigated. She was a three-masted skeleton-built merchantman, of some 200 to 300 tons, armed with at least three serpentines (guns with internal bores of 55mm, or just over 2 inches).[25]

The expedition ships could have had keels of elm like the *Mary Rose*,[26] or of oak like the *Cattewater* wreck. Elm was commonly used for keels and garboard strakes and often also for keelsons. Nearly all the other parts of the hulls of the ships of the expedition would have been made of oak, like those of the *Mary Rose* and the *Cattewater* wreck.[27]

Trenails and iron bolts were needed to fasten the various timbers together. The *Mary Rose* and the *Cattewater* wreck had their planks fastened to the frames by trenails, except for the butt ends of the planks, which were secured to the frames with iron fastenings.[28]

Cables were needed, some of which were enormous. Anchor cables could be up to 17 inches in diameter (imagine handling such a rope), but the cables for Sir Hugh's ships were probably no more than 8 inches in diameter. Such cables were usually described as from 'Danzic' (Gdansk), or Lynn (King's Lynn) or Bridport. However, there is the possibility that some of the cordage for the expedition ships could have been made in nearby Stepney, as Martha Morris has found a number of wills from that parish of men who described themselves as ropemakers.[29]

Lead was also needed for one of the ships, as it was stated that 'they cover a piece of the keel of the shippe with thinne sheetes of leade. . . . For they had heard that in certaine parts of the Ocean, a kind of worms is bredde, which many times pierceth and eateth through the strongest oake that is.'[30] This was the first recorded instance of the use of metal sheathing by the English as a precaution against the ravages of the teredo worm, though it had been used in Spain since 1514.[31]

SIR HUGH WILLOUGHBY

The commander of the expedition was not a sailor but a soldier. He was Sir Hugh Willoughby, who was chosen by the 'Mysterie and Company of the Marchants Adventurers' from a number of candidates to lead the expedition. Sir Hugh was 'a most valiant gentleman, and well borne . . . both by reason of his goodly personage (for he was of a tall stature) as also for his singular skill in the services of warre'.[32] Sir Hugh had distinguished himself by his energy in the capture of Edinburgh during Henry VIII's invasion of Scotland in 1544, and he had been knighted at Leith by the King's Commander-in-Chief, Edward Seymour, Earl of Hertford; he also defended the castle of Thirlestane in Berwickshire against a fierce siege by the Scots and the French in 1549–50.[33] Sir Hugh seems to have deserved his high reputation as a soldier, but he had no seagoing experience at all. (It was not uncommon for ships-of-war to have soldiers, rather than sailors, as their captains at this time.)[34] He also had connections. He was, for instance, related to Lord Robert Willoughby de Broke, who knew Sebastian Cabot, as he had been instrumental in finding employment for Cabot with the King of Aragon in 1512, and Sir Hugh's older brother, Henry, was Steward of the Royal Household.[35]

As 'Captaine Generall of the fleete' he would usually have been expected to: take overall charge of the organisation; lobby the investors and government officials; organise the finances; arrange terms with the officers and men and the merchants who were to travel with the expedition; supervise discipline and negotiate with the company, the ship-builders and the chandlers.[36] However, in the unique circumstances of this particular enterprise, the overall charge was in Sebastian Cabot's hands, and such tasks as lobbying potential investors probably fell to Sir George Barne and the other 'principall doers' of the company.

RICHARD CHANCELLOR

The second-in-command was Richard Chancellor. A sailor and a gentleman, he was selected to make up for Sir Hugh's lack of any nautical knowledge. He was appointed to be the Pilot Major of the expedition. Chancellor was an experienced and skilful navigator, as well as being 'a man of great estimation for many good partes of wit in him, in whom alone great hope for the performance of this business rested'.[37]

Although originally born in Bristol,[38] Chancellor had been brought up alongside Philip Sidney, in the household of Philip's father, Henry Sidney, who was the nephew of Northumberland, the Regent to Edward VI and the most powerful man in England at the time. He had probably been present at the 'Field of the Cloth of Gold' meeting in 1520 between the Kings of England and France.[39] Chancellor had been one of seventy gentlemen who had sailed under Richard Bodenham on a training voyage organised by Sebastian Cabot to the Mediterranean in 1550. It appears that he learned well on this trip and was singled out by Bodenham for special mention: 'Richard Chancellor, who first discovered Russia, was with me in that voyage.'[40] He and John Dee later collaborated in using a giant quadrant, 5 feet in radius, to take astronomical measurements with which to prepare a set of ephemerides[41] for the 1553 expedition. John Dee was to describe him, some years later, as 'the incomparable Richard Chancellor'. Chancellor took a leading part in the 1553 expedition but his career was prematurely ended by drowning, in 1556.

Chancellor sailed on the largest of the three ships, the *Edward Bonaventura*, of which Stephen Borough was the master. One of the crew was William Borough, Stephen's younger brother, who was just 17 years old at the time and sailing as an ordinary seaman.

CREWS AND CREWING

Other voyages at the time had great problems with finding enough men for their ships. For instance, Windham had to 'press' (press gang) men for his 1553 voyages to Guinea,[42] possibly owing to rumours of the high mortality there. (Windham and many of his men did in fact eventually die there.) Later in the century, there was 'a great lack of sailors'. For instance, Frobisher had to offer wages at twice the going rate for his north-west voyages in 1576–8,[43] and had to use convicts for a voyage in 1579.[44] Men had to be 'pressed' for Gilbert in 1583 and for Raleigh in 1585, and Cavendish and Cumberland's squadrons were reported to be undermanned in 1586.[45]

Lord Clinton, the Lord High Admiral, wrote a letter to the clerk of the Admiralty in May 1553 which authorised the empressment of men for Sir Hugh Willoughby's 'voyage to seke the londe unknowen',[46] but there is no evidence to show that this power was ever used. 'Pressing' may not have been needed for the 1553 expedition: it may have been different from the others in that the prospects of sailing to the riches of the Orient may have attracted more sailors. There was certainly no shortage of men who put themselves forward to be captains on that expedition: it was said that 'many men (and some voyde of experience) offered themselves'.[47]

There is a complete list of the names and positions of the crew members,[48] but no information about their wages or conditions (apart from the mention of 'a jerkyn and a paier of sloppis' (baggy trousers) issued free to each man).[49]

GUNS

The number of guns on the *Edward Bonaventura* can be estimated by comparing her with the *George*, a ship which is included in the *Anthony Roll* of 1546.[50] There were four gunners on the *Edward Bonaventura*,[51] and there were also four gunners on the *George*. The four gunners on the *Edward Bonaventura* probably had a similar quantity of armament to that on the *George*, which was as follows: '1 demi-culverin, 1 saker, 2 porte peces, 1 demi slyng, 8 baessys, 4 hayle shot peces, and 4 handgonnes'. The demi-culverin and the saker were powerful cannon, both of them capable of doing serious damage to other ships. The demi-culverin had a barrel up to 11 feet long and fired a 9lb shot which was 4 inches in diameter. The saker was somewhat smaller; it had a barrel about 9 feet in length and fired a 5lb shot which was 3 inches in diameter. The other pieces were used for shooting at enemy personnel at close quarters.

There were two gunners on the *Bona Confidentia* and only one on the *Bona Esperanza*, so presumably they were both less heavily armed.

SHIPS' EQUIPMENT

Each of the ships would have carried several anchors. A ship called the *Trinitie*, for instance, was listed as having four anchors and four cables when she changed hands in 1539.[52] The anchors in those days resembled the 'Admiralty' pattern anchors of today, and they had cables of tarred hemp up to 100 fathoms long.[53] On one occasion Stephen Borough had to borrow an anchor from a Russian skipper, and he noted that the hawser was 140 fathoms in length.[54] The anchors appear to have worked well: on many occasions they relied successfully on their holding power while riding out storms. They often used their anchors for long periods of time while 'tiding over', that is waiting for the wind, or more often the tide, to be favourable.

SHIPS' BOATS

Each of the three ships had a pinnace and a ship's boat.[55] The actual term 'pinnace' was 'used with a great deal of freedom',[56] but in this instance we are talking about boats of about 25 feet in length, powered principally by several pairs of oars, which could be supplemented by a sail or sails on occasion. Such a pinnace was small enough to be hoisted aboard the mother ship, though recovering a pinnace of such a length onto the waist of a ship perhaps 100 feet long, wallowing in a seaway, must have been a hazardous operation.

Each ship had a ship's boat, in addition to a pinnace,[57] and it may also have been quite sizeable, if the dimensions of some ships' boats in 1570 are anything to go by. Some new ships' boats were ordered in 1570 for two ships in the navy, the *Bull* and the *Tiger*, both of 200 tons. These ships' boats measured 35 feet in length by 8 feet 8 inches in breadth and 3 feet 3 inches in depth.[58] The ships' boats of the 1553 expedition were presumably somewhat smaller, perhaps between about 15 and 25 feet long, in proportion as the three ships (at 160, 120 and 90 tons respectively) were smaller than the *Bull* or the *Tiger*.

PROVISIONS

'Whereas yet it was doubtfull whether there were any passage yea or no, they resolved to victuall the ships for eighteene moneths.'[59] (Another account says that Willoughby's authorisation was for fifteen months.)[60] The provisions seem to have been more or less standardised, not to say monotonous, to judge from the three accounts which follow. The provisions for a ship from Bristol were listed as biscuit, wheat, beans, beer, cider, beef and fish.[61] Sir Jerome Horsey described the provisions of Royal Naval ships as 'bear, bread, bieff, fish, bakon, pease, butter, chese, vinegar, oatmeall, aquavita, wood, water and all other provisions'.[62] The third account is of two ships setting off from Dartmouth to join the fleet mustering at Plymouth against the Spanish Armada in 1588; they were reportedly stocked with biscuit, beer, beef, pork, fish, butter and pease.[63]

The ships carried water, and they used every possible opportunity to replenish their water barrels, but they also carried beer, as water rapidly became undrinkable due to infestation by algae. Frobisher on his expeditions of 1576–8 ordered 8 pints of beer per man per day. However, even the beer did not always last as long as it should have. It is recorded that on one occasion a merchant by the name of Stone promised that his beer would remain good for eight months, but that after only four it proved stinking and undrinkable.[64]

The ships of the 1553 expedition did have trouble with their food going off. Already by the time they reached Harwich Richard Chancellor 'was not a little grieved with the fear of wanting victuals, part whereof was found to be corrupt and putrified at Harwich, and the hoggesheads of wine also leaked and were not stanch'.[65]

The food served up on the ships of the 1553 expedition may have been poorer than those of a ship of a century earlier, by reason of the fact that in the fifteenth century most voyages were made coastwise. This meant that they had ample opportunity to replenish their supplies of fresh food along the way, which a ship on a long-haul voyage into unknown territory would not have had. For instance, during a voyage from London to Bordeaux in 1486, the *Margaret Cely* took on fresh provisions at four places en route, at Plymouth, La Rochelle, the Ile de Rhe and at Blaye.[66]

COOKING STOVES

On big ships, such as the *Mary Rose*, the cooking stoves were in the hold. The *Mary Rose* had a large firebox, with firebars and ashpits, which was built on a large rectangular brick mass in the bottom of the ship, laid across the keelson and the footwales. There were also three large copper cauldrons, each with a substantial brick and mortar support. A metal-lined flue carried the hot air and sparks up through the decks,[67] presumably out through a 'Charley noble' or stove pipe projecting above the deck. (Frobisher's ship, the *Aid*, of 200 tons, had a cooking stove below deck with a faulty stove pipe, which was the cause of a fire in 1577.)[68] The galley of the *Cattewater* wreck is also thought to have been in the hold,[69] but on smaller ships food was cooked, when possible, in a metal frame or cookbox on the deck amidships, in the shelter of the forecastle, with a bed of bricks to provide a base.[70]

Although they were small, the ships of the expedition may have had cooking stoves specially installed in the holds, rather than on deck. Such an arrangement would have made cooking easier in bad weather and it would also help to explain the manner in which the crews of two of the ships met their deaths, as will be touched upon later.

INVENTORIES

A number of ships' inventories of the time still exist, but there is not the space to go into the details of them here.[71]

CLOTHING

The sailors were each issued with 'a jerkyn' (a sleeveless jacket) and a 'paier of sloppis' (baggy breeches).[72] They also wore long woollen hose and a knitted cap, and, in bad weather, a hooded coarse serge gown.[73] Margaret Rule, the director of the *Mary Rose* excavations, found that on the *Mary Rose* they wore long hose (like modern tights, only thicker), a tunic of worsted or leather with or without sleeves (like a sweatshirt reaching as far down as the knees), a leather jerkin and a variety of hats.[74] One might suppose that, heading for the North-East Passage, a sailor would wear all the clothes that he could lay his hands on, and this would mean long hose plus breeches, tunic plus leather jerkin and hooded serge gown (and my guess would be that the gown was oiled or made of untreated sheep's wool for waterproofing).

THE COST OF THE EXPEDITION SHIPS

We do not know the cost of any of the ships of the expedition, but we do know the cost of a few other ships of similar size. There was, for instance, a ship of 150 tons built in Bristol some fourteen years earlier which was valued at £250 in 1539, including the 'hull, mastes, takle, sayles, four ankers, four cables' and 'all them monycions and abyllementes'.[75] Other representative ship prices were £160 for the *Antony Kidman* (eight years old) of 100/105 tons in 1536; £60 for the *Mary* (three years old) of 40 tons in 1538; £133 for the *Michael* (about fourteen years old) of 80 tons in 1559; and £133 for the *Antony* (about nineteen years old) of 100 tons, also in 1559.[76] From these figures it seems that the price per ton of ship was somewhere between about £1 10s and £3.

The ships of the 1553 expedition seem to have been particularly well built and well equipped. Therefore the merchants probably had to spend at least £3 per ton for their ships; as the total tonnage was 370, the total cost of the three ships would probably have been in the region of £1,100 to £1,200.

THE 'ORDINANCES'

On 9 May 1553, the day before the expedition departed from Ratcliffe, Sebastian Cabot produced a set of thirty-three 'Ordinances, Instructions and Advertisements' for its conduct.[77] The Ordinances show every evidence of being the result of a great deal of thought and practical wisdom, some of which no doubt derived from Cabot's own experience of commanding the expedition that reached the River Plate in 1526. Others of them are derived from the combined wisdom of the Casa de Cotractatión at Seville, the organising body behind all the Spanish voyages of discovery and overseas trade, of which Cabot had been in command as 'Grand Pilot of the Emperor's Indies' from 1518 to 1526 and again from about 1533 to 1548.

Many of the 'Ordinances' are excellent common-sense injunctions, such as number 15, which states 'Item, no liquor to be spilt on the balast, nor filthines to be left on boord'. Others may well reflect Cabot's own views rather than those of his erstwhile Spanish masters, for instance number 22 about religion: 'Item, not to disclose to any nation the state of our religion, but to passe it over in silence', and also number 23, about how to get information from the natives: 'Item, it is to be considered how they may be used, learning much of their natures and dispositions, by some one such person, as you may first either allure, or take to be brought aboord your ships, and there to learne as you may, without violence or force'. Another one, number 31, may also be from his own experience: 'Item, there are people that can swimme in the sea, and therefore diligent watch is to be kept both day and night, in some Islands'. There is a brief outline of all thirty-three of the Ordinances in Appendix 3.

CONCLUSION

It is only fair to point out that in the absence of any direct descriptions or pictures of the expedition ships, this chapter has been concerned with making deductions and building up reasonable approximations about their appearances, sizes, shapes and equipment from other sources, such as from the tonnages mentioned by Hakluyt, from the general history of the development of ships, from illustrations of smaller ships of the time, from William Borough's 'Proportion in building of Shyppinge' in combination with Mathew Baker's Old Rule, from archaeological findings and from analogies and extrapolations from other ships of the period. Similarly deductions have been made about the crews, the ordnance, the ground tackle, the ships' boats, the cooking, the provisions and the clothing. Perhaps one day some more direct information may come to light.

CHAPTER 5

Geographical Knowledge

Cosmographers and mathematicians doubt if this passage be practicable,
and cannot agree whether it can or cannot be accomplished.[1]

Very few English people at the time had the slightest interest in the geography
of the further corners of the globe. One of the rare exceptions was Dr John
Dee, the enigmatic polymath, and it was he who provided the expedition with
such geographical information as there was.

There was no help from the maps and charts available, as they, almost
without exception, showed a solid mass of land blocking the proposed route.
There were, however, one or two written accounts of a sea route as far as the
White Sea but beyond the White Sea, the geography was almost pure
conjecture.

It was simply amazing that the merchants of London were willing to fund
an expedition to find a new passage to the Orient when they knew virtually
nothing about what lay ahead.

THE WORLD IS ROUND

The Greeks had shown that the world was round. Indeed, Eratosthenes
(c. 276–194 BC) had measured its circumference, elegantly and accurately, in
stadia.[2] The Romans also knew the world was round: there is, for instance, a
bas-relief in the Roman baths at Bath which shows the earth as a globe. The
knowledge of the sphericity of the earth can be traced from Ptolemy's
Almagest via the work of al-Farghani, the Arab astronomer who died in 861,
to an Englishman who wrote a description of the world as a sphere about
1233. He was John Holywood (Johannes de Sacrobosco). His work, *Tractatus
de Sphera Mundi*, went into many editions in several different languages, and
it became an integral part of Portuguese navigation manuals at the end of
the fifteenth century.[3] It was still recommended by John Dee as the best work
of elementary instruction on the subject as late as 1570.[4]

Christopher Columbus knew that the world was round and he knew of
Eratosthenes's measurement, but there was confusion about the unit of

length (the stadium), and as a result he greatly underestimated the distance to be covered to reach China by travelling westward.[5]

DR JOHN DEE

John Dee (1527–1608) was the expedition's chief source of geographical information. In later life, from about 1568 onwards, he took to alchemy and attempted to converse with angels by means of a crystal globe, activities which largely destroyed his previous reputation.[6] But for the first forty years of his life he was an intellectual giant in mathematics, astronomy and cosmography.[7]

In May 1547 Dee made a visit to Louvain University – 'the fountain-head of all learning', as he described it.[8] He wrote that 'I went beyond the sea . . . to speake and confer with some learned men and chiefly Mathematicians, as Gemma Frisius, Gerardus Mercator, Gaspar a Mirica, Antonius Gogava.'[9]

Frisius (1508–55) and his colleagues at Louvain were cosmographers to Charles V, the Holy Roman Emperor, the most powerful man in Europe. They were well placed to know everything that could be known about the geography of the world. When Dee returned from Louvain to England, he came back with a great deal of information and many manuscripts, as well as a brass astrolabe, an astronomer's staff of brass and two great globes, dated 1537, designed by Frisius and constructed by Mercator.[10] His most prized instrument was a huge cross staff, 10 feet long and 'having the staff and cross very curiously divided into parts equall, after Richard Chancellour's quadrante manner'.[11]

Dee made a second journey to Louvain in 1548, studying there until 1550. He developed a lifelong friendship and correspondence with Mercator, and he also corresponded with the other great cosmographers: Pedro Nunez, Abraham Ortelius and Orontius Finaeus.[12] He returned to England in 1551 and, among many other activities, worked with Richard Chancellor, of whom he had a high opinion, as he referred to him as 'that excellent Mechanician Master Richard Chancellor'[13] and 'the incomparable Richard Chancellor'.[14] Chancellor was the second-in-command of the 1553 expedition, and he and Dee together made observations and constructed a table of ephemerides, for the later use of the expedition, as already mentioned. Dee also drew up what he called a 'Paradoxal Compass', which was a chart of the north polar regions from latitude 50° northwards (although this manuscript did not appear until 1556).[15]

The other men involved with Dee in researching the geography for the expedition were Sebastian Cabot, Richard Hakluyt the Elder and Richard

Eden. Cabot brought with him all the knowledge he had acquired as cartographer from 1513 to 1516 to King Ferdinand of Spain, as grand pilot to the Emperor Charles V from 1519 to 1530 and as examiner of pilots from 1533 to 1547. Richard Hakluyt the Elder (usually referred to as Richard Hakluyt of Eiton, near Leominster, to distinguish him from his nephew, Richard Hakluyt of Oxford, the historian) had meticulously gathered together a great deal of geographical information; and Richard Eden was a linguist and a familiar of Gemma Frisius.

The first to put forward a proposal to explore a north-east passage had been Robert Thorne, an English merchant living in Seville, in 1527. Thorne made his proposal in a letter to a Dr Lee or Ley (later Archbishop of York) who was then on an embassy to Spain, and Thorne followed this up with an address to Henry VIII in 1531.[16] The letter that Robert Thorne sent to Dr Lee included a map (and a footnote which explained that the map had been secretly sneaked from some Spanish source). The map was intended to illustrate his argument for a north-east passage, but it does not really achieve this aim, as the northern parts of Russia and Tartaria are cut off by the upper edge of the map.[17]

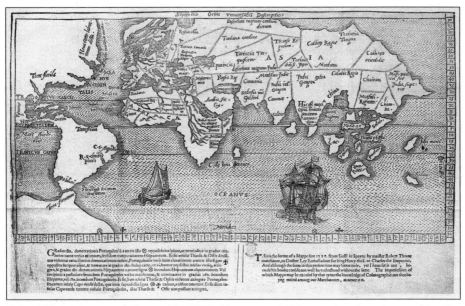

Robert Thorne's map of the world, 1527. Thorne used this map to advocate searching for a north-east passage, even though the map does not extend far enough to show the geography of the far north.

THE RUTTERS AVAILABLE TO THE 1553 EXPEDITION

Rutters (French *route, routier*, 'road') were sea-route books. They included the courses to steer from one headland to the next – for example, 'And who so departeth fro the cape of Cornwayle must sayle eastsoutheast for the double Lezarde for so lyeth the two landes.'[18] They also contained information about the times of high or low water in relation to the direction of the moon, the direction of tidal streams, the soundings and the entrances to harbours. Individual sea captains had compiled their own handwritten rutters for years, such as an anonymous *Rutter of the English Coasts* of 1408.[19] Then, in 1483–4, Pierre Garcie collated into one work all the information available for sailing around the coasts of England and Wales and the coasts of western Europe from the Schelde to the Strait of Gibraltar, the first printed version of which was published in French as *Le routier de la mer* about 1510. The first version in English, translated by Robert Copeland, was published in 1528, as *The Rutter of the Sea*. There were also two rutters of the Scottish coasts, from the Humber round to the Solway Firth, one compiled by Alexander Lindsay in about 1540.[20] The other, a *Rutter of the Northe*, was compiled, also about 1540, by a Richard Proude, who based it on the anonymous *Rutter of the English Coasts* of 1408 already mentioned. From 1540 onwards, *The Rutter of the Sea* incorporated the *Rutter of the Northe*.[21] The expedition of 1553 therefore had detailed information about the coasts of England and Scotland, but there was no published rutter for the coasts of Europe any further north than the mouth of the Schelde river, though there may have been rutters compiled by individual sea captains describing the coasts as far north as Bergen.

ACCOUNTS OF EARLIER VOYAGES TO THE WHITE SEA

The route as far as the White Sea was well known to the Norsemen from the tenth century onwards, and the North Cape of Norway was called Murmansky Nos (which means 'Norseman's Cape') until the English renamed it in 1553. However, the English knew very little about these northern regions, except for the few slender threads of information discussed below.

Dee did know of several voyages along the first part of the hoped-for north-east passage; one of these was 'Ohthere's voyage'. Ohthere (the Anglo-Saxon form of the Norse name Óttarr) had made a voyage to the White Sea at some time in the second half of the ninth century. He later visited King Alfred of

Wessex (849–99) in England at some point between 871 and 899 and gave an account of his voyage to him. In his account, Ohthere describes himself as a native of Hålogaland (in northern Norway) who 'fell into a fantasie and desire to prove and know how farre that land stretched Northward'. He sailed north for six days, 'At the end whereof he perceived that the coast turned towards the East . . . and thence he sailed plain east along the coast' for four days, 'the coast bowed then directly towards the South . . . so that he sailed thence along the coast continually full South as far as he could travaile in 5 dayes' where 'he discovered a mighty river which opened very far into the land' and from where he turned back for 'fear of the inhabitants of the land'. The story shows that Ohthere sailed north, round the North Cape and then east and later south into the White Sea to reach the mouth of the River Dvina, indicating that there was indeed a sea route to the White Sea, but furnishing very little detail.

King Alfred gave orders for this account by Ohthere to be written down and included with a translation of the fifth-century *Historia adversum Paganos* by Paulus Orosius, a treatise about the geography of Europe.[22] A number of manuscript copies were made, and Dee, much later, became the owner of one of them, now in the British Library.[23] Hakluyt also knew of Ohthere's voyage and printed an account of it.[24]

There were later Scandinavian voyages along the same part of the route, several of which were led by kings. Harald Greycloak, for instance, led an expedition to the fur-bearing areas of Hålogaland and onwards to the waters of the White Sea, in about 960–5.[25] *Heimskringla*, a collection of sagas by Snorri Sturluson (compiled *c.* 1220–30) describes another expedition, which started as a trading voyage but turned into a raid on Bjarmaland, the region of the Finns to the west of Gandvík (the White Sea) in 1026.[26] Other kings such as King Harald, *c.* 1070, and King Hákon Thorsfostri *c.* 1090, also sailed to Bjarmaland, to impose a 'tax' of furs by force.[27] *Heimskringla* also reports that King Eirik Blood-Axe and his son, Harald Greycloak, had both sailed to Bjarmaland in person. However, it is possible that all of these accounts stayed in Scandinavia, and there is no actual evidence that Frisius or Dee knew anything about any of them.

An account that Dee very probably did know about was one written by Saxo Grammaticus (*c.* 1140–1206). His *Gesta Danorum* (History of the Danes) was written shortly after 1200.[28] In the Preface he says:

Moreover, the upper bend of the ocean [i.e. the Baltic and the Gulf of Bothnia], which cuts through Denmark and flows past it, washes the southern side of Gothland with a gulf of some width; while its lower channel [i.e. the Arctic Ocean], passing the northern sides of Gothland and Norway, turns eastwards, widening much in breadth, and is bounded by a curve of firm land. This limit of the sea the elders of our race called Gandvík [i.e. the White Sea]. Thus between Gandvík and the Southern Sea, there lies a short span of mainland, facing the seas that wash on either shore; and but that nature had set this as a boundary where the billows almost meet, the tides of the two seas would have flowed into one, and cut off Sweden and Norway into an island [i.e. this described a clear sea route round Scandinavia to the White Sea].

Dee almost certainly also knew of Sigismund von Herberstein's description of the geography of Russia. Von Herberstein was the ambassador to Russia from the Emperor Charles V from 1516 to 1518, and again in 1526. His account, called *Rerum Moscoviticarum Commentarii*, was first published in 1549 in Vienna, and a version in Italian was published in Venice in 1550.[29] As it was dedicated to Emperor Charles's younger brother, Ferdinand,[30] it is extremely unlikely that Frisius, as cosmographer to Charles V, did not know of it, and Dee was at Louvain with Frisius from 1548 to 1550, so he also must almost certainly have known of von Herberstein's work. It is not accurate in every detail, but it does include some information about a voyage made from the White Sea round the north of Norway to Trondheim by a certain Gregory Istoma in 1496.[31] Von Herberstein also reported that a Master David, a Scotsman (whose family name may have been Cocker), acting as a 'herald' from King John of Denmark to the Grand Duke of Muscovy, sailed back by this route in 1506, because of war between Russia and Sweden.[32]

A similar voyage was made a little later by a Russian envoy named Dmitri Gerasimov, and this was included in a work entitled *De Legationes Moscoviticarum* by an Italian, Paulus Jovius (Paolo Giovio), first published in 1525 and republished several times. This work by Jovius was translated into English and published by Richard Eden (a friend of Dee and of Richard Chancellor) in 1555 in his *The Decades of the newe worlde or west India*. Von Herberstein had also referred to Jovius's account of Gerasimov's voyage. According to S.H. Baron, there is good evidence that Eden knew about both Jovius and von Herberstein in 1553, i.e. before the expedition set sail.[33] These several written accounts all indicate that Dee and Chancellor could have known, and almost certainly did know, that a sea route existed, at least as far as the White Sea, though they had virtually nothing to go on in the way of details or description.

CHARTS AND GLOBES

The written accounts mentioned above may have been encouraging about the existence of a possible north-east passage, but the evidence of most of the maps and charts contradicted the written sources. As Richard Eden put it in 1555, 'in the most part of the Globes and Maps they see the continent or firm land, extended even to the North Pole without any such passage'.[34]

There was at the time a renaissance of interest in the work of Ptolemy (c. AD 100–68). He had not shown Scandinavia at all in his *Geographia*, and some later charts were drawn following his example, showing nothing further north than about 60°–65° N.

The few charts that did attempt to show the northern and Arctic regions did so in an almost entirely fanciful manner. (There is a summary in Appendix 11 which shows the geography of the proposed north-east passage area, as depicted in the main maps and charts (and two globes) which had been compiled in the eighty years before the 1553 expedition set out.) Some of the charts showed an enormous promontory extending northwards from Scandinavia. Others showed solid land stretching across to Greenland, either from the north of Scandinavia or from the north of Asia, making the sea to the west of Norway a large closed bay.

At that time, the Scandinavians thought of their sea as the *hafs-botn*, i.e. a bay or gulf of the Atlantic Ocean extending as far east as the far side of Gandvík (the White Sea). The mapmakers knew that the Norse settlements on the west coast of Greenland had been overrun by Eskimos (*skrælingar*) who had appeared from the north, and so, as it was generally agreed that the origin of all human life was in the Middle East, it was deduced that there must be a land bridge somewhere to have enabled the Eskimos to get from the Middle East to Greenland in the first place.[35] A land connection around the end of their *hafs-botn* would also explain how various animals, such as the hare, the wolf and the reindeer, came to be in Greenland.[36]

Very few of the maps, charts or globes showed any evidence of a sea route round the north cape of Norway or across the top of Asia. One of the few that did show such an open route was the *Carta Marina* of 1539 by Olaus Magnus, and Nordenskiold states, though without giving his reasons, that there was a great probability that this map was known in England before 1553.[37]

The best discussion of the various concepts concerning the geography of the north polar regions in the first half of the sixteenth century is that of E.G.R. Taylor.[38] As far as the expedition was concerned, it was the views of John Dee that were significant, and he was optimistic that a sea route would be found.

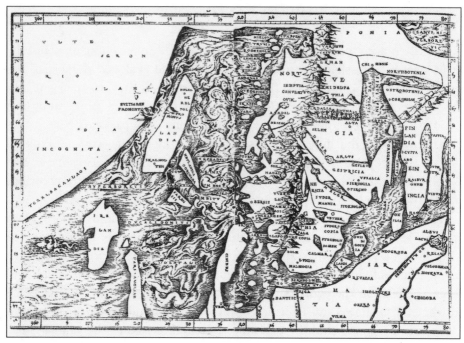

Zeigler's map of northern Europe, 1536. This is one of a number of maps that showed Scandinavia and Greenland connected by a land bridge.

The great whirlpool devouring shipos. This is the Maelstrom, called Moskenstraumen, in the Lotofen Islands.

BEYOND THE WHITE SEA

Dee resorted to ancient sources for information about the route beyond the White Sea, principally the *Historia Naturalis* of Pliny the Elder (AD 23–79) and the work of Abulfeda (or Abu al-fida, AD 1273–1331), the Arab historian and geographer and Sultan of Damascus.[39] Pliny had described a *promontorium Scythicum* or Scythian promontory which was 'totally uninhabitable, owing to the snow, and the regions adjoining are uncultivated on account of the savage state of the nations which dwell there. Here are the abodes of the Scythian Anthropophagi, who feed on human flesh.'[40] (When the Tudor explorers did eventually reach the regions far to the east of the White Sea, 'about the river of Pechere', they encountered people called the Samoeds, or Samoyeds, who were indeed reported to be cannibals: 'the wilde Samoeds will not suffer the Russes to land out of the Sea, but they will kill them and eate them'.[41] The great Pliny seems to have been remarkably well informed.)

In 1549 Dee saw a copy of Abulfeda's *Cosmography*, which had been brought from Constantinople, and concluded that it showed the northern coast of Asia trended uniformly towards the south and east. (This conclusion was, according to E.G.R. Taylor, based on a faulty reading of the text.)[42] A few years later, Dee wrote that 'none of our Tripartite mayn land is more to the North than the Cape . . . named the North Cape, in the coast of Norway, to which, from the Russie coast confines, he noteth the course to lie near north west'.[43]

In other words, Dee thought that once the expedition got round the North Cape, the route to the Orient would be east and south all the way. Dee was obviously delighted with Abulfeda's account, as it appeared to confirm the possibility of a north-east passage, and he commented in the margin that this information was 'A record worthy to be printed in gold'.[44]

Dee's surmise was that the northernmost extremity of Asia, Pliny's Cape Tabin (the *promontorium Scythicum* mentioned above), which Ptolemy had placed at 80°N,[45] was not in fact any further north than 70° (i.e. two degrees less far north than the North Cape of Norway). The route to Cathay therefore would be south of east and, as he described it, 'You shall fall in with the famous river Oechardes, which I conjecture to Pass by the renowned city of Cambalu . . . and then, in lat. 46°, you may enter Quinsay haven.'[46]

As mentioned earlier, Dee had almost certainly seen the accounts of von Herberstein and Jovius. Both of these works included suggestions that one could reach Cathay by sailing eastward from the White Sea along the north coast of Asia and then up the River Ob.[47]

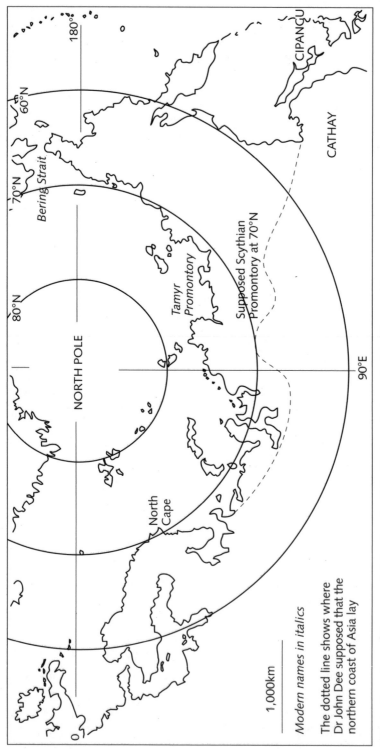

The Arctic regions of Europe and Asia, showing John Dee's conjecture of where the coast lay.

A modern map shows that the mouth of the Ob is about 750 miles east of the entrance to the White Sea. To reach it, one would have to sail east through the Kara Strait, across the Kara Sea (usually filled with ice) and round the long Yamal Peninsula. One might then sail up the Ob for a long way but one would still be left with an overland journey of 2,000–2,500 miles eastwards to reach China.[48]

The sea route beyond the Yamal Peninsula involves rounding a formidable promontory. It is the *Poluostrov Taymyr* (Taymyr Promontory), which extends to 77° 43'N, with *Mys Chelyuskin* (Cape Chelyuskin) at its northernmost point, the most northerly point in the mainland of Eurasia.[49] It extends almost as far north as Pliny had said it did in his *Historia Naturalis*.

Even in those few maps that showed a clear water route from western Europe to the seas to the north of Asia, there was seldom any definite indication of a route from there to Cathay (China). In the 1540s and '50s, Gemma Frisius held the view that the Arctic Ocean was a landlocked sea, and this view seems to have been generally accepted by the relatively few people who gave much thought to the matter. It was not until 1569 that the concept of a strait between Asia and the Americas began to be promulgated by Mercator, Frisius's erstwhile pupil. Mercator showed it as the 'Strait of Anian' in his world map (it would have been very approximately where the Bering Strait is now). Dee discussed the possible existence of this strait at some length in 1577, but it was much too late for the 1553 expedition, and the arguments were all completely hypothetical.[50] One version of this concept may be found in Sebastian Munster's edition of Ptolemy's *Geographia*, published in Basel in 1540, which includes a map 'Typus orbis universalis' which shows *Terra noua siue de Bacalhos* (Labrador) attached by land to *Islandia* (Iceland), itself attached to Scandinavia, leaving only the North-West Passage as a possible route to Asia.[51]

The 'Vínland Map' of 1440–8 is one of the exceptions that does show a clear water route from western Europe across the top of Asia and down to Cathay. The route goes past Rex Norvicorum (Scandinavia), Frigidum Pars (northern Asia), and then Ultima Thule, Tatazrata fluvius, Kitaius and then into the Oceanum Orientale, i.e. a clear water route.[52] However, it would appear from its history that this map was most unlikely to have been known by the western European cosmographers. (Scammell and many others dismiss the 'Vínland Map' as a fake, but other experts such as Quinn and Skelton regard it as genuine.)

In conclusion, therefore, it appears that Dee did have some written accounts that indicated there was a sea route as far as the White Sea, even though nearly all the charts showed solid land in one form or other blocking the way. Dee also believed, based largely on his reading of Abulfeda, that a sea route continued beyond the White Sea all the way to 'the country of the great Chamchina (the Great Khan)'.

The expedition was intended to sail to Cathay and the Orient. There was no mention of Russia in any of the instructions, which is not surprising, as knowledge of Russia was extremely vague. For instance, Roger Barlow in his *Brief Summe of Geographie*, written about 1541, can only place Russia by saying that it is 'hard by the mountaynes sarmaticos and riscos' and 'by the mountains of ercynia'.[53]

MISINFORMATION

There was also a vast amount of misinformation that Dee, Cabot, Chancellor and the other planners had to contend with, far too much to be described here, but I cannot resist mentioning the boronets or 'vegetable lamb', which was said to be found in Russia. This was a creature having the exact shape and appearance of a lamb but which grew like a plant on a stalk attached to its stomach. When it had devoured all the grass which the stalk permitted it to reach, it died. This charming conceit seems to have originated in the travels of Sir John Mandeville, but belief in it seems to have persisted until at least the end of the seventeenth century.[54]

MONSTERS AND OTHER HAZARDS

In *The Faerie Queene* Edmund Spenser describes some of the hazards that his hero, Guyon, had to face, in addition to the normal run of tempests, rocks, shoal water, mermaids and the like.[55] Some of them would have been considered as entirely fanciful by any experienced mariner, including the 'Spring-headed Hydraes' (well-known multi-headed monsters from classical times); 'the grisly Wasserman', that pursued ships; 'the dreadfull Fish, that hath deserved the name of Death'; the 'Sea-satyre'; and the 'huge Ziffius'.

However, cautious mariners might well have kept an open judgement on some of the other monsters that Spenser mentioned. For instance, they might have related the 'Mighty Monoceroses' in their minds to the reports of rhinoceroses and hippopotamuses. Spenser's 'Greedy Rosmarines with visages deforme' did have some semblance to reality: they were reputed to have been walruses and were said to climb with their tusks to the tops of rocks to feed on the sea dew;[56] and his 'Scolopendraes' are a form of fabulous sea fish, though there are some formidable centipedes that have the same name.

Some of the other monsters that Spenser mentions were taken much more seriously, such as the 'sea-shouldring Whales'. Stephen Borough and his crew were very alarmed by 'a monstrous whale aboard of us, so neere to our side that we might have thrust a sword in him which we durst not doe for feere he should have overthrowen our shippe'.[57]

Spenser also talks of 'Great whirlpools'. There is indeed a mighty whirlpool called the Maelstrom in the Lofoten Islands off the coast of Norway. It was described and illustrated in an encyclopedia written by no less an authority than Olaus Magnus, the Bishop of Oslo, and Stephen Borough may well have heard about it, even though the book was not actually published until 1555.[58] The illustration in Magnus's encyclopedia (see page 48) shows a ship being swallowed up by the whirlpool.

There was another dreadful hazard that was believed to live in the sea off the coast of Norway, and that was 'the Kraken', a sea monster of enormous size. It was described in great detail by the same Olaus Magnus who had described the Maelstrom, though he did not use the name 'Kraken'. The creature had skin that looked just like gravel on a seashore, so that men were tempted to think it was an island and to land on it and make fires on its back to cook their victuals. It has been variously depicted as a devouring whale, a huge sea serpent or as a giant octopus. Olaus Magnus included in his book detailed descriptions of a number of other terrifying creatures of the deep.[59]

As far as Stephen and his crew were concerned, they were setting off on a voyage into unknown seas. They knew that they faced a great number of physical dangers, some known and others unknown, and they may well have suspected that they might encounter other uncertain hazards such as monsters. Their response was to commit themselves to God's good deliverance and to make their departure.

CHAPTER 6

'The Haven of Death': Sir Hugh Willoughby's Account of the 1553 Voyage

The three vessels . . . will follow a northerly course and navigate by the Frozen Sea towards the country of the great Chamchina, or the neighbouring countries . . . they believe the route to be a short one and very convenient for the Kingdom of England for distributing carsees in those far countries, bringing back spices and other rich merchandise in exchange. I asked him [Captain Cabot] if the said voyage was as certain as it seemed. He replied Yes it was.[1]

Sir Hugh Willoughby and all the men in two of his ships were to perish in the Arctic winter in January 1554. Luckily for posterity, however, he did keep an account of his voyage which was later found in the desolate remains of his ship. He had scribbled 'the Haven of Death' in the margin, and much of what follows here is based on his 'Haven of Death' account.[2] This chapter, then, tells the story of Sir Hugh's voyage, about the three ships that sailed together to the north of Norway, and about the two of them that were lost. The story of the third ship, the one that survived, is related in Chapter 7.

The drama of the voyage started with the heartfelt farewells: 'They having saluted their acquaintances, one his wife, another his children, another his kinsfolkes, and another his friends dearer than his kinsfolkes, were present and ready at the day appoynted: and having wayed ancre, they departed with the turning of the water.'[3]

The three ships, Sir Hugh's vessel the *Bona Esperanza*, the *Edward Bonaventura* with Richard Chancellor and Stephen Borough on board, and the *Bona Confidentia* set out from Ratcliffe on the ebb tide on 10 May 1553. They carried with them Edward VI's letters addressed to 'Kings, princes and other potentates inhabiting the north-east parts of the world toward the mighty Empire of Cathay', written in Greek and several other languages.[4] The three ships 'valed unto Detford', that is to say that 'The greater shippes are towed down with boates, and oares, and the mariners, being all apparelled in Watchet or skie coloured [sky blue] cloth, rowed amaine and made way with diligence.'[5]

The Muscovy Company had issued the uniforms to the crews, but they were only to be used on special occasions.

The next day they passed Placentia, the royal palace at Greenwich.[6] There was tremendous excitement there:

> where the Court then lay. . . . The Courtiers came running out, and the common people flockt together, standing very thicke upon the shoare: the privie Counsel, they lookt out at the windowes of the Court, and the rest ranne up to the toppes of the towers: the shippes hereupon discharge their Ordinance and shoot off their pieces after the maner of warre, and of the sea, insomuch that the tops of the hilles sounded therewith, the valley and the waters gave an Echo, and the Mariners, they shouted in such sort, that the skie rang againe with the noyse therof. . . . To be short it was a very triumph.[7]

This artillery salute, in honour of King Edward at Greenwich, was almost the only time on this expedition that the guns were fired. This is remarkable: it must have been almost the only expedition of Tudor times in which the heavy guns were not used in battle. 'But (alas) the good King Edward [in respect of whom principally all this was prepared] hee onely by reason of his sicknesse was absent from this shewe.'[8] The young Edward VI (1537–53) was already dying. He had become king at the age of 9 in January 1547, but his health began to fail in 1552 and he died, probably of tuberculosis, on 6 July 1553, two months after the expedition had departed.[9]

The great send-off reflects the importance of the venture. It was an undertaking of great national interest, not only to the London merchants, but also to many of the high officers of state who had invested money in it, and many of the best minds in the land had put a great deal of effort into the organisation and the preparations for the voyage.

Progress down the Thames was slow. They appear to have moved down in a series of short stages, working the tide, using the ebb to help carry them down as far as they could before anchoring again and 'tideing over'. On some days they did not make a great deal of progress. On 10 May, for instance, the ships moved from Ratcliffe to Deptford, down Limehouse Reach, which is only about 2 miles. On the following day their progress was little better: Deptford to Blackwall is again only about 2 miles, and when they did reach Blackwall, they stayed there for six nights. In the next few days they made a little more progress, Blackwall to Woolwich, about 5 miles; the following day, Woolwich to Heyrith (modern Erith), about 7 miles, and then Erith to Gravesend, about 8, and here again they stayed for two nights. Gravesend was traditionally the last port of call on the way out to sea, where the last mail or messages were exchanged. However, even after Gravesend, where the Thames Estuary widens out, progress continued to be slow, and they may have had to continue using the tow boats, due to contrary or fickle winds, to enable them to reach Tilbery Hope (the Lower Hope near Stanbury-le-Hope), where they stayed two nights, and Hollie haven (Hole Haven, where Shellhaven now stands, to the west of Canvey Island), and the next day on to Lee (Leigh on Sea, just to the west of Southend).[10] By this time it had taken them fourteen days just to reach Lee, a total distance of no more than 40 miles. This must have been very frustrating, but it demonstrates the kind of delays that they had to put up with.

The expedition almost certainly used a copy of the chart of the Thames Estuary that Richard Caundish (or Cavendish) had drawn up in about either 1533 or 1547.[11] His chart was executed in colour, with green for land, yellow for sand and brown for mud, and it clearly shows the principal navigable channels, like the King's, the Black Deep and the Swoene (the Swin, the channel that the Expedition used) and also the mudbanks on either side of the Swin, with such names as the Dodman, Black Tayle, Shoo, Myddelgrounde, Nase ege, Spit of Monoch and Nase Baronoce. (These are all names with which a modern-day east-coast yachtsman would be familiar.)

There was also a set of written directions, a rutter for the voyage from Harwich to London (i.e. in the opposite direction to the one in which they were sailing).[12] For instance, the rutter instructs the mariner to 'Go oute of Orwell Waynys to the Naisse . . . go south west fro the Nasse to the merkis of the Spetis . . . than go your cours on the spetis south till ye come to X ffadome or xij, than go your cours with the horse shoo south southwest.'[13] The rutter refers to the seamark at the Spits and to several other buoys and beacons (at the Whitaker and the Shoe, for instance). These marked the approaches to the Thames from the north, and were referred to in the rutter of 1408, though Cavendish did not show any of them on his chart drawn in the 1530s or '40s.[14] Perhaps they had disappeared in the interim.

They made good progress northwards, only to be followed (as we shall see) by two successive setbacks. For the next three days they had favourable winds and could sail north-east. They sailed from Lee, doubtless keeping outside the Maplin Sands, then over the Spits to reach St Osyth (near the mouth of the River Colne), where they anchored overnight, and then on to the Nase (on the south side of the Stour and Orwell Estuary), 'and there abode that night for wind and tide'. They continued north in this fashion, anchoring up each night, first at Orwell Wands (at the mouth of the Orwell, and within a mile or so of Harwich), then at Walsursye (?Walberswick),[15] and the next night at Holmhead (Holmys hede, the head of Holm Sand off Lowestoft),[16] and on to spend another night at anchor 3 leagues[17] out to sea off Yarmouth (Great

Yarmouth), and on 31 May 'into the sea six leagues Northeast, and there taried that night, where the winde blew very sore'.[18] These two nights when they were riding out the storm off Yarmouth show the effectiveness of their anchors and cables.[19]

The next day, 1 June, they suffered the first setback: 'the wind being at North contrary to us, wee came back again to Orwell, and remained there untill the 15. Day, tarying for the winde, for all this time the winde was contrary to our purpose'.[20]

Incidentally, the latitude of Orwell, which had probably been determined by Richard Chancellor, is given as 52°, which agrees exactly with the modern Ordnance Survey map which shows the latitude of the Orwell, about a mile in from the entrance, as 52°.

On 16 June, they made a little forward progress to Allburrough (Aldeburgh), but on the following day they had the second setback, when they were forced to drop back to Orfordness, where they spent two nights. On 19 June they went back to the Orwell, for the third time, where they were delayed again. It was here that two men were discharged, one because of sickness; and the other man, Thomas Nash, was 'for pickerie ducked at the yards arm, and so discharged'.[21] (Nash was fortunate. He lived, but all the other crewmen of two of the ships were to die within a few months.)

It was here at Harwich that Richard Chancellor noticed that some of their food supplies had gone off. He was 'not a little grieved with the feare of wanting victuals, part whereof was found to be corrupt and putrified'.

It was not until 23 June, six weeks and two days after departing from Ratcliffe, that they managed at last to get away from the East Anglian coast. Their departure from Orwell is described thus:

at the last with a good winde they hoysed up saile, and committed themselves to the sea, giving their last adieu to their native Countrey, which they knewe not whether they should ever return to see again or not. Many of them looked oftentimes backe, and could not refraine from teares, considering into what hazards they were to fall, and what uncertainties of the sea they were to make triall of.[22]

As to Richard Chancellor, the pilot major, his 'naturall and fatherly affection . . . troubled him, for he left behinde him his two little sonnes, which were in the case of Orphanes if he spedde not well'.[23]

Weighing anchor for the last time in home waters would have been an occasion for a shanty. There is one surviving from 1548, which they could have used:

> Veyra veyra, veyra veyra, gentil gallandis, gentil gallandis,
> Veynde, I see him, veynde I see him, Pourbossa, pourbossa,
> Haul all and one, Haul all and one
> Haul hym up to us, Haul hym up to us.[24]

With a favourable south-westerly wind at last, they sailed north-east to Orfordness, and then 10 leagues further north-east to clear the offshore sandy shallows, then 6 leagues north-north-east, and later north for three days.

The sea, of course, has not changed since those days and I do not suppose that the movement of a ship on the water has changed much either, though one may well believe that Tudor ships had a tendency to roll more than sailing ships nowadays. One can imagine that every sailor in the three ships was heartened by the free movement of his ship on the water, out on the open sea for the first time after weeks of delays: the lift of the stern as a swell comes up from behind, then she rolls and the stern settles and the bow lifts, as the swell rolls under and the bow slews a little to the lee side, the helmsman checking the swing until the next swell comes up from behind. It is an age-old rhythm.

They headed north-north-west for 42 leagues in the hope of reaching Scotland, but the wind turned westerly, and they found that they could not head any better than north and by west, and later north-north-west, and even south-east for a while, owing to contrary winds. Eventually, on 14 July, after twenty-two days at sea, they saw land to the east: 'We discovered land Eastward of us, unto which we sayled . . . and found little houses to the number of thirty . . . but the people were fled away, as we judged, for fear of us. The land was all full of little Islands, and that innumerable, which were called (as we learned afterwards) Aegeland and Halgeland.'[25]

The modern map of Norway shows that the region of Helgeland extends from about Namsos north to about Bodø, i.e. from about 64° 30' to about 67° 30' N.[26] The coast here was described from a yacht on the sea in 1990 as 'green islands with fields and woods and white villages, and a snowy backdrop of the mountains, sometimes far away and some times close on our starboard side . . . the travel brochures had said that it was the most beautiful coast in the world'.[27]

This first landfall cannot be exactly identified. It lay apparently 12 leagues (36 nautical miles) south-east of the Isles of Røst.[28] It was probably some-where south of present-day Bodø.

The expedition estimated that they were 250 leagues north and by east from Orfordness (the actual distance by the modern map is more like 310 leagues). Be that as it may, they had already sailed over halfway up the coastline of Norway, which is well over 1,000 miles long and runs north-east to south-west. They did not stop at their first landfall but sailed 12 leagues north-west to reach the Isles of Røst. There they found:

> people mowing and making of hay, which came to the shore and welcomed us. In which place were an innumerable sort of Islands, which were called the Isles of Rost, being under the dominion of the king of Denmarke . . .[29] the winde being contrary, we remayned there three dayes . . . there was an innumerable sort of foules [birds] of divers kinds, of which we took very many.[30]

The Isles of Røst dangle at the very tip of the island chain of the Lofoten and Vesterålan Islands, which stick out some 115 miles from the mainland coast of Norway. Most of the Lofotens consist of granite crags rising sheer out of the sea, but the Isles of Røst are pancake flat, with dozens of lakes and lonely farmsteads dotted about. The weather here is uncommonly mild, and sheep can graze on the meadows throughout the year.[31]

Nowadays there are boat trips to the islets to the south-west of Røst, where the jagged cliffs harbour seabird colonies that are internationally famous. There were, until 2002, nearly half a million pairs of puffins, not to mention large numbers of auks, kittiwakes, guillemots, cormorants, gannets and fulmars, and lesser numbers of storm petrels and some sea eagles.[32] Since then, and particularly in 2004, there has been a disastrous drop in seabird numbers, especially puffins, due largely to a shortage of sand eels, which in turn may be due to overfishing, pollution or to warming of the Norwegian Sea.

Røst's position at the tip of the projecting island chain meant that it was often the first place to receive visitors from the sea. One of the strangest of these was an Italian castaway called Piero Quirino in 1431.[33] Very briefly, Quirino was the master of a ship from Venice. The ship set out from Candia (now Iraklion) in Crete, bound for Flanders with a crew of 68 men and a cargo of over 700 buttes of wine and spices. They sailed out of the Mediterranean and up the Atlantic coast of Europe to reach 'the channels of Flanders', when a storm caught them and blew them far out into the Atlantic, where twenty-six men died. The ship was reduced to a wreck and the survivors were carried eventually, after two months at sea, to a rock called the Isle of Saints, some 5 miles off Røst. Astonishingly, eleven of the original crew, including Quirino himself, survived the ordeal.

Another unplanned visit was made by Princess Elisabeth of the Netherlands in 1520. She later donated a fine altar screen to the church at

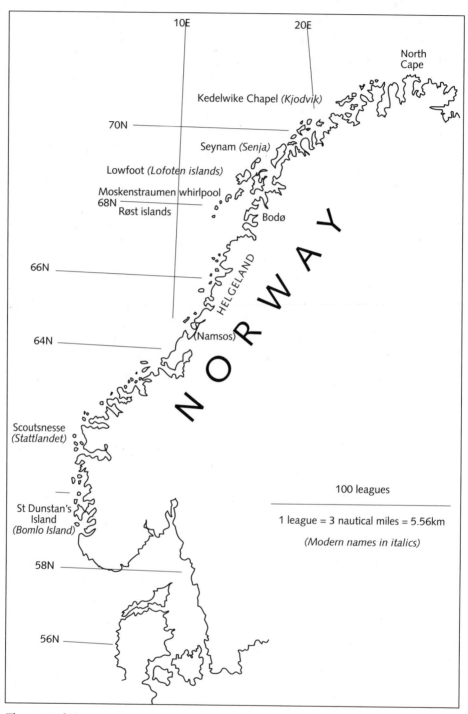

The coast of Norway.

Røst, 'in heartfelt thanks for surviving a stormy voyage' – a very under-
standable sentiment.[34]

The leaders of the 1553 expedition had almost certainly heard about the
great whirlpool, or Maelstrom, before they departed from England, and been
suitably terrified. Their route took them not far from it, though Sir Hugh does
not mention it in his journal. It is called the Moskenstraumen, and it is in the
sea near the southern end of the island of Moskenesøya, just north of Røst. It
was first described in an account of a voyage in 1360 towards the North Pole
by Nicholas de Lynn. He reported that 'Foure Indraughts were drawn into an
inward gulfe or whirlepoole, with so great a force, that the ships which once
entered therein, could by no meanes be driven backe againe.'[35] It was
described again, in 1555, by Olaus Magnus, the Bishop of Oslo, who wrote
that between Røst and Lofoten 'there is in the sea such a great chasm or
whirlpool, that when mariners approach it carelessly their helmsman is
deprived of his strength and resourcefulness, and they are swallowed up in an
instant by the sudden swirl of the water'. Magnus went on to say that:

> Navigation upon this sea is extremely perilous, for those who sail at the
> wrong time are suddenly snatched down into the spiralling abysses. The
> debris of shipwrecks is very seldom cast up and, if it is, the timbers are so
> battered by being dashed against the rocks that they look as though they
> have been wrapped in fluff and smashed to pieces. Here the might of
> nature may be plainly seen outdoing the mythical Sympleglades, the
> dreaded Cape Malea, Charybdis of Sicily and other great marvels.[36]

This famous whirlpool has also featured in the works of Edgar Allan Poe and
Jules Verne. Perhaps Sir Hugh and Richard Chancellor, if they did know about
the Maelstrom, decided not mention it to their men because they thought it
would terrify them.

The voyage continued:

> The 22 day [of July] . . . we departed from Rost, sailing Northnortheast,
> keeping the sea untill the 27 day, and then we drew neere unto the land,
> which was still east of us . . . and found many good harbours, of the which
> we entered into one with our shippes, which was called Stanfew, and the
> land being Islands, were called Lewfoot or Lofoot . . . being in latitude
> 68 degrees and from the foresaid Rost about 30 leagues Northnortheast.

'Stanfew' has been identified as Svolvær, or alternatively as Stamsund or
Steenfjord.[37] The settlement at Svolvær has existed since the Middle Ages, when

a certain King Oystein ordered fishing huts and a church to be built there, and today it is the biggest town in the Lofoten Islands.[38] It is about 80 sea miles north-east of the Røst Islands, which agrees well enough with the 30 leagues (90 sea miles) north-north-east of the original account, and its latitude is 68° 14', which also agrees well with the 1553 measurement, which was 68°.

From Stanfew, they sailed 'along these islands Northnortheast, keeping the land in sight . . . to the Island called Seynam', which was in latitude 70°, and 30 leagues from Stanfew, where the only merchandise was dried fish and train oil (whale oil). Seynam has been identified with Senja Island.[39] The true latitude of Senja is between 69° and about 69° 40'N.

Anthony Jenkinson, on his voyage up this coast in 1557, wrote of Zenam (Senja) that 'About this Island, we saw many whales, very monstrous, about our ships, some by estimation of 60 foote long.'[40] It is interesting to note that the whales are still there and that there is now a Whale Watching Safari base on the nearby island of Andøya, about 20 miles to the west of Senja.[41]

It was here or hereabouts that:

> Sir Hugh Willoughby . . . erected and set out his flagge, by which he called together the chiefest men of the other shippes . . . who being come together accordingly, they conclude and agree, that if any great tempest should arise at any time, and happen to disperse and scatter them, every shippe should indevour his best to goe to Wardhouse, a haven or castell of the same name in the kingdome of Norway, and that they that arrived there first in safetie should stay and expect the comming of the rest.[42]

When they were off 'Seynam' (Senja Island) on 30 July 1553, they spoke to a man in a skiff and asked him if they could get a pilot to take them to 'Finmarke', the region of land round what is now known as the North Cape of Norway. Sir Hugh Willoughby, on the *Bona Esperanza*, described what happened next:

> He [the man on the skiff] said, that if we could beare in, we should have a good harbour, and on the next day a pilot to bring us to Finmarke, unto the Wardhouse, which is the strongest hold in Finmarke. . . . But when we would have entered into an harbour, the land being very high on every side, there came such flawes of winde and terrible whirlewinds, that we were not able to beare in, but by violence were constrained to take the sea agayne, our Pinnesse [pinnace] being unshipt: we sailed North and by East, the winde increasing so sore that we were not able to beare any saile, but took them in, and lay a drift, to the end to let the storm over passe. And

that night by violence of winde, and thicknesse of mists, we were not able to keepe together within sight, and then about midnight we lost our pinnesse, which was a discomfort unto us.[43]

The same incident was seen from the *Edward* and described by Richard Chancellor:

In the afternoone, about foure of the clocke, so great a tempest suddenly arose, and the Seas were so outragious, that the ships could not keepe their intended course, but some were perforce driven one way, and some another way, to their great perill and hazard: the generall [Willoughby] with his loudest voyce cried out to Richard Chanceler, and earnestly requested him not to goe farre from him: but hee neither would nor could keepe companie with him, if he sailed still so fast: for the Admirall [the ship, the *Esperanza*, rather than the man] was of better saile than his shippe. But the Admirall (I knowe not by what meanes) bearing all his sailes, was caried away with so great force and swiftnesse, that not long after hee was quite out of sight, and the third ship [the *Confidentia*] also with the same storme and like rage was dispersed and lost to us. The shippe boate of the Admirall (striking against the shippe,) was overwhelmed in the sight and viewe of the Mariners of the *[Edward] Bonaventura*.[44]

Thus the *Bona Esperanza* (Willoughby's ship) and the *Confidentia* (the smallest ship of the three) were literally blown away, completely out of sight of the *Edward*. I suspect that the reason the *Edward* did not suffer the same fate as the other two ships was because her master, Stephen Borough, noticed the commotion of the sea made by the approaching squall and managed to get enough of the sails off his ship in time, before the storm struck.

These are the same stormy waters that the Arctic convoys sailed in the Second World War. Those convoys would assemble in a Scottish loch or in Reykjavík Harbour and then sail together, well to the north of the North Cape, to Murmansk or Archangel'sk. Some of the storms that they encountered were legendary. As Paul Kemp rather drily puts it, 'The latitudes through which the convoys sailed are notorious for gales and blizzards of great intensity.'[45]

One such storm, in these same waters, was described by Alistair MacLean in his fictional story *HMS Ulysses*:

It struck with a feral ferocity, with an appalling savagery that smashed minds and bodies into a stunned unknowingness . . . its voice was the devil's orchestra, the roar of a great wind mingled with the banshee shrieking of tortured rigging, a requiem for fiends: its weight was the crushing power of the hurricane wind that pinned a man helplessly to a bulkhead fighting for breath, or flung him off his feet to crash in some distant corner, broken limbed and senseless . . . it goaded the cruel sea into homicidal alliance and flung itself, titanic in its energy, ravenous in its howling upon the cockleshell that was the Ulysses.[46]

This is admittedly a fictional account, and HMS *Ulysses* was some 200 miles or so further north than the expedition ships were, where the weather can be even worse, but it does not take a great deal of imagination to see what effect such a storm could have had on Sir Hugh's ships. The *Ulysses* was a powerful, twentieth-century destroyer, not a small, wooden, sixteenth-century sailing ship.

The crews of the *Bona Esperanza* and the *Confidentia* were never seen alive again. The only way we know what happened to them was from Sir Hugh's journal of their wanderings, which was discovered a year or so later. This was the 'Haven of Death' account, written by Sir Hugh Willoughby himself before his demise. His account tells how the *Bona Esperanza* took in her sails and:

lay adrift to the end to let the storme overpasse. . . . At the last we descried one of our shippes to Leeward of us: then we spread an hullocke[47] of our foresaile, and bare roome with her, which was the *Confidence*, but the *Edward* we could not see. Then the flaw something abating, we and the *Confidence* hoysed up our sailes the fourth day, sayling Northeast and by North, to the end to fall with the Wardhouse, as we did consult to doe before, in case we should part company.[48]

From then on, the 'Haven of Death' account gives a somewhat incomplete account of the courses they sailed. On several days there is no indication of what their course was at all. At one stage Willoughby comments, perhaps a little wistfully, that 'The land lay not as the globe made mention.' (This was almost certainly Mercator's globe, or a copy of it, which in these northern parts was almost purely conjectural.)

A number of authors believe that Sir Hugh and his two ships could have discovered Novaya Zemlya in their wanderings.[49] T. Rundall, in particular, argues the claim that Sir Hugh discovered Novaya Zemlya. Rundall quotes Samuel Purchas, writing in 1625, though Purchas seems to have been particularly vague as to where Sir Hugh might have got to, describing it thus:

'this is the land which is now called GREENLAND, or King James his new land, and is known to the Hollanders by the name of SPITZBERGEN'.[50]

Nordenskiold, from personal experience in these waters, formed the opinion that Sir Hugh had reached, not Novaya Zemlya, but the shoals off Kolguev Island.[51] Sir John Barrow, writing in 1818, came to the conclusion that 'The brief journal of Sir Hugh Willoughby by no means sanctions such a supposition, that this ill-fated commander was ever within many degrees of Spitzbergen', adding 'the discovery of this land is certainly due to the Dutch'.[52] However, Rundall dismisses Sir John Barrow's scepticism and forcefully puts the case for Sir Hugh.

In an attempt to resolve this debate, the courses that Sir Hugh recorded in his journal have been tabulated and plotted in Appendix 5 (as far as is possible to do so in view of the several omissions and inconsistencies in his account), and as a result, the conclusion reached by the present author is that Sir Hugh did indeed see the coast of Novaya Zemlya on 14 August 1553. However, he can hardly have claimed to have been the 'discoverer' of Novaya Zemlya, as he appears to have had very little idea where he was, and also he

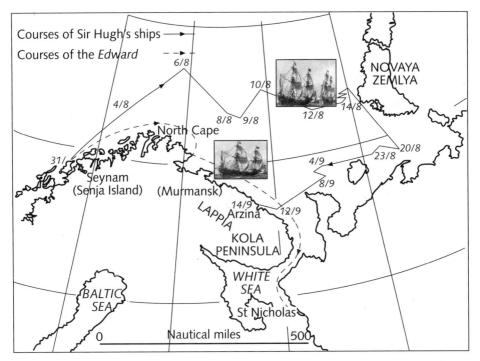

The course sailed by Sir Hugh and his ships, the *Bona Esperanza* and the *Bona Confidentia*, and that taken by Richard Chancellor and Stephen Borough in the *Edward Bonaventura* in 1553, after the storm had separated them at Seynam (Senja Island).

did not live to tell the tale, so he was unable to 'discover', or report on his findings to anyone else.

Novaya Zemlya is the summer breeding ground for large numbers of geese, and the part of the coast that Sir Hugh and his company almost certainly saw is now called Gusinaya Zemlya (Goose Land) in Russian.[53]

After their sighting of what was almost certainly Novaya Zemlya, the two ships sailed on many different courses, but generally in a westerly direction, until they reached more land, where they spent what were to be their last days, which were described in Sir Hugh's account:

> the 18 of September, we entered into the haven, and there came to an anker at 6 fadoms. This haven runneth into the maine, about two leagues, and is in bredth halfe a league, wherein were very many seale fishes, & other great fishes, and upon the maine we saw beares, great deere, foxes, with divers strange beasts, as guloines [elk], and such other which were to us unknowen, and also wonderful.
>
> Thus remaining in this haven the space of a weeke, seeing the yeare farre spent, & also very evill wether, as frost, snow, and haile, as though it had beene the deepe of winter, we thought best to winter there. Wherefore we sent out three men Southsouthwest, to search if they could find people, who went three dayes journey but could finde none: after that, we sent other three Westward foure daies journey, which also returned without finding any people. Then sent we three men southeast three dayes journey, who in like sorte returned without finding of people, or any similitude of habitation.

Hakluyt added his own comments: 'The river or haven wherein Sir Hugh Willoughbie with the companie of his two ships perished for cold, is called Arzina in Lapland, neere unto Kegor. But it appeareth by a Will found in the ship that Sir Hugh Willoughbie and most of the company were alive in January 1554.'[54] Samuel Purchas retold this story, at the end of which he printed this marginal comment: 'Heere endeth Sir Hugh Willoughby his note, which was written in his owne hand.'

There have been several theories as to the cause of death of Sir Hugh and his two crews. Hakluyt, who printed the first account of Sir Hugh's voyage, stated that they 'perished for cold'. Some years later, in 1576, it was stated that the entire crews of the two ships 'for lacke of Knowledge were frozen to death'.[55] Henry Lane, in about 1584, gave it as his opinion that 'all to the number of seventy persons perished which was for want of experience to have made caves and stoves'.[56] Nordenskiold, the explorer and cartographer who, in 1878, was the first to navigate the whole of the

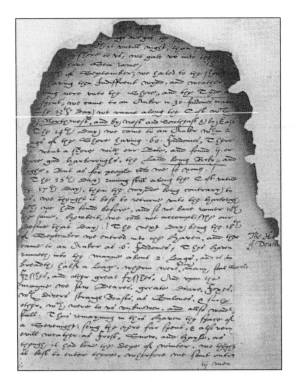

The 'Haven of Death' entry in Sir Hugh Willoughby's journal. The journal was eventually taken back to London, where it was subsequently charred round the edges, but it is still possible to read 'The Ha . . . of Death' in the right-hand margin.

North-East Passage, stated unequivocally that all the members of the expedition had died of scurvy.[57]

However, there is an intriguing letter that sheds a little more light on the matter. It was written by the Venetian ambassador in London, Giovanni Michiel, to his master, the Doge, in Venice, on 4 November 1555. He reported that the two vessels of the first voyage had been found on the Muscovite coast and that:

> the mariners now returned from the second voyage narrate strange things about the mode in which they were frozen, having found some of them seated in the act of writing, pen still in hand, and the paper before them; others at table, platters in hand and spoon in mouth; others opening a locker, and others in various postures, like statues, as if they had been adjusted and placed in these attitudes. They say that some dogs on board the ships displayed the same phenomena. They found the effects and merchandise all intact in the hands of the natives.[58]

Giovanni Michiel's letter has led Gordon to conclude that the most probable cause of death was carbon monoxide poisoning, due, in her opinion, to battening down all the hatches to keep out the cold and then using sea coal for the first time instead of wood to prepare a meal.[59] This conjecture does indeed seem very plausible. The men of the van Heemskerck and Barents' expedition to the Arctic in 1596 were likewise very nearly all killed by the same cause when they gathered in the wooden hut they had built on the shore. They closed the door and blocked the chimney before building a fire of sea coal in a desperate effort to keep themselves warm on a bitter night in December. They became dizzy and fainted and were only saved by one of them throwing open the door before he also collapsed.[60] Other explorers have had similar problems, including Byrd in Antarctica in 1930.[61] Mountaineers and explorers today are all very alert to the potential hazards of carbon monoxide poisoning in their huts and tents.

The missing ships and all of the sixty-three dead crew men were discovered in the following spring, in 1554, by a Russian fisherman.[62] The tsar ordered the Governor of Dwina, Prince Semen Ivanovitch Mikulinsky Punkoff, to have the two vessels conveyed to Cholmogora, under seal, and this was done, the following year, in the spring of 1555.[63]

Commenting on Sir Hugh's voyage, Nordenskiold wrote, 'Great geographer or seaman Sir Hugh Willoughby clearly was not, but his and his followers' voluntary self-sacrifice and undaunted courage have a strong claim on our imagination.'[64]

The Arzina river is still a harbour; it is now one of the two big Russian submarine bases on the Kola Peninsula (the other is at Murmansk). The 'Haven of Death' letter eventually found its way into the Cotton Collection of manuscripts in the British Library.[65]

CHAPTER 7

The Voyage of the Edward (1553)

The strange and wonderful discoverie of Russia.[1]

After the *Bona Confidentia* and the *Bona Esperanza* were blown away in the storm at Seynam on 30 July 1553, the *Edward Bonaventura* was left all alone: 'Nowe Richard Chanceler with his shippe and company being thus left alone, and become very pensive, heavie, and sorowful, by this dispersion of the Fleete, hee [according to the order before taken] shapeth his course for Wardhouse in Norway, there to expect and abide the arrivall of the rest of the shippes.'[2]

THE NORTH CAPE

There is no description of how the *Edward* managed to survive the storm or of how they reached Wardhouse (modern Vardø). The only statement that was made on this part of the journey was made some three years later, in 1556, by Stephen Borough, when he was once again sailing these waters. He then commented that they were athwart 'the North Cape (which I so named the first voyage)'.[3] He was indeed later credited with having named the North Cape,[4] despite the fact that the cape was already known as 'Murmansky Nos'. Be that as it may, the *Edward* successfully sailed round the North Cape, the most northerly point in Europe.

Nowadays the cape has a large visitors' centre, with an exhibition that includes details of these first voyages of exploration.[5]

WARDHOUSE

The *Edward* stayed in Wardhouse for a week, waiting for the other two ships to arrive, but of course they never did. 'Wardhouse' is the anglicised form of Vardøhus, meaning the fortified house or castle on the small island of Vardø, a little over 100 nautical miles east of the North Cape. Despite the site's remoteness, the first church was consecrated there in 1307 and the first fortress built there at about the same time. It was the furthest outpost of the kingdom of Denmark. As Richard Johnson described it in 1556: 'Wardhouse

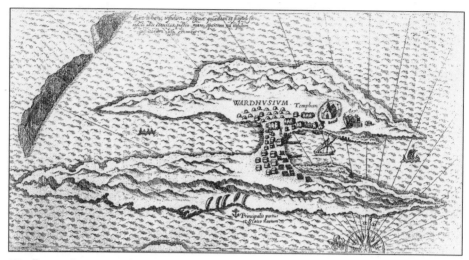

Wardhouse, from a Dutch drawing of 1594.

is a castle and the King of Denmark doth fortify it with men of war: and the Russes may not go to the westward of that castle.'[6] In 1557, Anthony Jenkinson added that 'the inhabitants of the three islands live onely by fishing, and make much stockfish which they dry with frost . . . [they have] small store of cattell which they feed also with fish'.[7]

Astonishingly, Vardø is further east than both Istanbul and Alexandria.[8] It still has a fortress, although of later origin, constructed in 1734–8. Much of Vardø was destroyed by Russian bombers or by retreating Germans in the Second World War, but it has since then been rebuilt, and the island now has a population of some 3,000. The midnight sun shines there from 20 May until 20 July, and darkness lasts for two months in the winter, from 20 November until 20 January. There is now (since 1983) a tunnel that runs under the sea for over a mile to connect the island to the mainland.[9]

The crew of the *Edward* came across some Scotsmen at Vardø, as the following narrative relates:

And being come thither [to Vardø], and having stayed there the space of 7. dayes, and looked in vaine for their comming, hee [Chancellor] determined at length to proceede alone in the proposed voyage. And as hee was preparing himselfe to depart, it happened that hee fell in company and speech with certaine Scottishmen: who having understanding of his intention, and wishing well to his actions, beganne earnestly to disswade him from the further prosecution of the discoverie, by amplifying the dangers which he was to fall into, and omitted no reason that might serve to that purpose. But hee holding nothing so ignominious and reprochfull, as inconstancie and levitie of minde, and perswading himselfe that a man of valour coulde not commit a more dishonourable part then for feare of danger to avoyde and shunne great attempts, was nothing at all changed or discouraged with the speeches and words of the Scots, remaining stedfast and immutable in his resolution: determining either to bring that to passe which was intended, or els to die the death.[10]

It is not surprising that there were Scotsmen at Vardø, as there had long been amicable connections between Scotland and Scandinavia.[11] There is, however, no information about what the Scotsmen were doing there. Fox Bourne describes them as traders,[12] but there is not a scrap of evidence for this assertion. It seems to me that they could just as easily have been sailors or mercenary soldiers. There is also no evidence as to why the Scotsmen were so anxious to discourage Chancellor and his expedition from going further east. It may have had something to do with the tsar's reputation as a belligerent despot: he did indeed attack Sweden five years later, in 1558, and took the Baltic port of Narva from them.

However, Richard Chancellor and Stephen Borough were not put off by the warnings of the Scots and went on with their voyage:

And as for them which were with Master Chanceler in his shippe, although they had great cause of discomfort by the loss of their companie (whom the foresaid tempest had separated from them), and were not a little troubled with cogitations and perturbations of minde, in respect of their doubtfull course: yet notwithstanding, they were of such consent and agreemint of minde with Master Chanceler, that they were resolute, and prepared under his direction and government, to make proofe and triall of all adventures, without all feare or mistrust of future dangers. Which constancie of minde in all the companie did exceedingly increase their Captaines carefulnesse: for hee being swallowed up with like good will and love towards them, feared lest through any errour of his, the safetie of the companie should bee indangered. To conclude, when they sawe their desire and hope of the arrivall of the rest of the shippes to be every day more and more frustrated, they provided to sea againe, and Master Chanceler held on his course towards that unknowen part of the world.[13]

One senses in this passage a certain feeling of community and common cause between the officers and men on the *Edward*. This is very different from the atmosphere in the 1750s, when officers dominated their crews and discipline was severe, the punishments often being brutal. In Tudor times, in contrast, it was customary for the crew to be paid in shares of the profits of the voyage and for discipline to be a matter more of cooperation than of enforcement. The shipmaster, in Tudor times, had considerable power, but not as much as those in later centuries. As Scammell points out: 'In moments of crisis he had, like a medieval captain, to consult his men.'[14]

Chancellor sailed east from Vardø into a 'huge and mighty sea': 'Master Chanceler held on his course towards that unknowen part of the world, and sailed so farre, that hee came at last to the place where hee found no night at all, but a continuall light and brightnesse of the Sunne shining clearely upon the huge and mighty Sea.'[15]

The narrative must be wrong about the midnight sun shining on them in this particular part of the voyage, as it was already nearly the middle of August. By then, the *Edward* could still have benefited from the long, drawn-out twilight, but it must have been somewhat earlier in their voyage that they actually saw the midnight sun.[16]

They sailed on and 'At length it pleased God to bring them into a certaine great Bay, which was of one hundred miles or thereabout over. Whereinto they entred, and somewhat farre within it cast ancre.'[17] This bay, as it turned out, was the Dvinskaya Guba (Dvina Bay) of the Beloye More (White Sea). They had sailed past present-day Murmansk, and along the coast of the Kol'skiy Poluostrov (the Kola Peninsula) and reached the White Sea. After the 1,000-foot-high cliff of the North Cape, the coast on their right-hand side had been mostly low and empty tundra with few features, except for Nokujeff Island, which is elevated.[18] They had sailed about 500 nautical miles since passing the North Cape, and through some 16 meridians of longitude, as the meridians are much closer together nearer to the poles.

They espied a farre off a certaine fisher boate, which Master Chanceler, accompanied with a fewe of his men [probably in the pinnace or in the ship's boat], went towards to common with the fishermen that were in it . . . but they being amazed with the strange greatness of his shippe . . . began presently to avoid and to flee: but hee . . . at last overtooke them, and being come to them, they (being in great feare as men half dead), prostrated themselves before him, offering to kiss his feete: but hee (according to his great and singular courtesie), looked pleasantly upon them, comforting them by signes and gestures. . . . It is strange to consider howe much favour afterwards in that place, this humanitie of his did purchase to himselfe . . . the common people came together offering to these newe-come ghests victuals freely.[19]

The fishermen were accustomed to seeing the local single-masted ships, called lodias, which were used for fishing and for travel along the coast. They had never seen a three-masted ship before, and the *Edward* might well have had its cannon at the ready, so it is not surprising that the fishermen were frightened.[20]

Hakluyt's report continues, 'Our men learned that this Countrey was called Russia, or Moscovie, and that Ivan Vasiliwich (which was at that time their king's name) ruled and governed farre and wide in those places.'[21] This was a complete surprise: there had been no mention of Russia in any of the instructions or ordinances that they had received before they had set out on this voyage. There had been a good deal of speculation before they set out as to whether or not a north-east passage might be feasible, but no one had even considered the possibility of reaching Russia by this route.

It was now the end of August 1553, and the northern winter would soon be upon them. They were forced to review their options, and at least for the present to abandon any further attempt to find a north-east passage.

The *Edward* moored up at the mouth of the Dvina, a great river that flows into the White Sea. It is about 10 miles wide at its mouth, where several islands divide the stream into four channels. The ship's mooring was at the mouth of the southernmost of these channels, to the east of a place called Nenocksa, near to the convent of St Nicholas.[22] This place became known to the English as St Nicholas or Rose Island, from the wild roses that grew there.[23] Richard Chancellor reckoned that it was about 750 leagues from London to St Nicholas (2,250 sea miles), which is about right.[24]

The Russian archives recorded the arrival of the *Edward* in the *Dvina Chronicle*: 'Aug. 24 [1553], a ship arrived and anchored in the Dvina mouth, when one named Ritzert [Richard], envoy of the English King Edward came to Kholmagora in boats, saying he was going to the Great Sovereign the Czar.'[25]

Some 10 miles from where the *Edward* moored, on the other side of the Dvina river, is where the city of Archangel'sk was founded in 1584. This was on the mainland shore on the north side of the northernmost of the four mouths of the great river.[26]

In 1944 there was a port on the south shore of the estuary of the Dvina river, then called Molotovsk (now called Severodvinsk), which was used by some of the Arctic convoys in the Second World War. It was not far from the site where the *Edward* moored up. My informant, Jim Row, was ice-bound there in a tanker, the MV *Daphnella*, in February and March 1944. He remembers seeing a group of political prisoners there, being marched out across the sea ice in the darkness each morning, at seven o'clock, to do forced

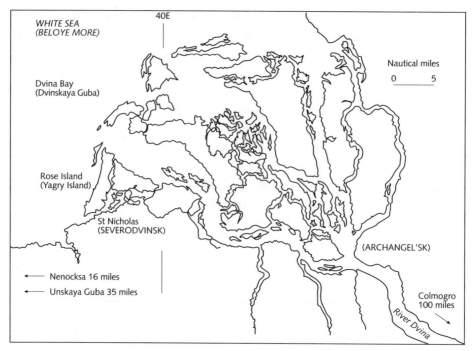

The mouths of the Dvina river.

labour on one of the islands, possibly Rose Island.[27] Presumably they had fallen foul of Stalin's secret police.

Severodvinsk was, for many years, the most secret of all cities. The Admiralty Chart still marks the whole area 'Entry Prohibited', and does not show Severodvinsk at all. During the Soviet era it was the centre for the production of nuclear submarines for the Russian Navy. It was also the mainland base for the above-ground nuclear testing ranges on the Novaya Zemla Islands, 500km to the north (no longer in use). The city was eventually opened to foreigners in 1991, on the fiftieth anniversary of the first allied supply convoy in the Second World War.[28]

When Chancellor and Stephen Borough arrived there in the *Edward*, the ruler of Russia was Ivan Vassilivich, Ivan IV (1533–84), who later earned the soubriquet 'the Terrible'. Ivan seems to have been morbidly suspicious, though more or less mentally stable for the first half of his life, but to have become more irrational and terrifying from middle age onwards.[29] The Tsar's rule was always autocratic, so much so that even at a distance of some 600 miles from Moscow, little could be done without his permission.

The Englishmen from the *Edward* informed their Russian contacts that they had:

certaine things to deliver to their King, and seeking nothing els but his amitie and friendship . . . Master Chanceler intreated victuals for his money of the governour of that place (who together with others came aboord him) . . . to whom the governours answered that they knewe not in that case the will of their king, but yet were willing in such things as they might lawfully doe, to pleasure him: which was as then to affoord him the benefit of victuals.[30]

It appears that the Governor of Dvina[31] was willing to allow the local people to give victuals to the crew of the *Edward* but he would not allow them to trade with the *Edward* until he had the consent of the Tsar.

Nowe while these things were a doing, they [probably the Governor of Dvina] secretly sent a messenger unto the Emperour, to certifie him of the arrivall of a strange nation, and withall to knowe his pleasure concerning them . . . hee graunted libertie to his subjects to bargaine, and to traffique with them: and further promised, that if it would please them to come to him, hee himselfe would beare the whole charges of poste horses. In the meane time the governours of the place differed [deferred] the matter from day to day, pretending divers excuses . . . to protract the time, untill the messenger (sent before to the king) did returne with relation of his will and pleasure. But Master Chanceler (seeing himselfe held in this suspense with long and vaine expectation) . . . tolde them that he would depart and proceede in this voyage. So that the Muscovites (although as yet they knew not the minde of their king) . . . at last resolved to furnish our people with all things neccessarie, and to conduct them by land to the presence of their king. And so Master Chanceler beganne his journey, which was very long and most troublesome, wherein hee had the use of certaine sleds, which in that Countrey are very common . . . the cause whereof is the exceeding hardnesse of the ground congealed in the winter time by the force of the colde, which in those places is very extreme and horrible.[32]

To cut a long story short, Richard Chancellor and his small party did eventually reach Moscow, which they reported to be 'in bignesse as great as the Citie of London, with the suburbes thereof. There are many and great buildings in it, but for beautie and fairnesse, nothing comparable to ours.'[33] They were well looked after there and managed to get an audience with the Tsar, who wore: 'a long garment of beaten gold, an imperial crown upon his head, a staff of crystal and gold in his right hand'. Chancellor and the members of his party ate roast swan off solid gold plates and drank wine from a massive gold cup.[34]

Eventually, the party returned to St Nicholas, with a letter from the Tsar dated February 1554 (in Cyrillic script and with a copy in Dutch) inviting the English to send ships to Russia as often 'as they may have passage', with merchants who 'shall have their free Marte with all free liberties through my whole dominions with all kindes of wares, to come and go at their pleasure'.[35]

Meanwhile, Stephen Borough and his men in the *Edward* had been directed by the magistrates to spend the winter at Unskaya Guba, a sheltered bay some 35 miles west of St Nicholas.[36] They 'had ayde of the people at a village called Newnox' (Nenoksa).[37]

The *Edward* sailed back to London in 1554. She had the misfortune to be 'homeward robbed by Flemings',[38] but otherwise completed the voyage without mishap. As soon as they arrived in London, the crew of the *Edward* were busy 'shewing their entertainments and discoverie of the countries', as the chronicler Purchas put it.[39]

They had started out with three ships in search of a route to the riches of the Orient. Only one ship had returned, and she had no gold, no spices and no silks. She had not even reached the Orient or anywhere near it, and she had little information about any possible route there. But, to everyone's surprise, she did have some letters from the ruler of Russia, inviting the English to trade there free of any customs dues.

It looked as though the whole expedition had been a disaster. Or had it? The merchants of London were left in a quandary.

CHAPTER 8

The Voyages of the Serchthrift

PART 1: 1556 – THE EXPLORATION

The Navigation and discoverie toward the river of Ob, made by Master Steven Burrough, Master of the Pinnesse called the Serchthrift, with divers things worth the noting passed in the yere 1556.[1]

The voyage of the *Serchthrift* in 1556 was Stephen Borough's epic voyage, in which he made a second attempt to find a north-east passage.[2]

The first expedition to find the North-East Passage had been in 1553, in the course of which Sir Hugh Willoughby and the entire crews of two of the three ships had perished, though the *Edward Bonaventura* survived and, with Richard Chancellor and Stephen Borough in charge, reached St Nicholas in Russia, returning to London in 1554.[3] (There had been another voyage to Russia in 1555, but this was a trading voyage, not an exploration, the first trading voyage of the newly formed Muscovy Company, to Wardhouse and St Nicholas and back, and it is described in Chapter 10.)

For the voyage in 1556, the fleet consisted of two ships: the *Edward Bonaventura* and the *Philip and Mary*, and a pinnace called the *Serchthrift*.[4] The *Edward Bonaventura* had Chancellor on board and John Buckland, and also, as far as Wardhouse, Stephen Borough. At Wardhouse he was to change ship into the much smaller *Serchthrift*, and in her he was to explore the North-East Passage as far as he could. The *Edward Bonaventura* and the *Philip and Mary* were to sail to St Nicholas and then back to London. They carried two extra crews on board, who were to sail back to London in the two ships that Sir Hugh Willoughby and his crews had died in on the Arzina river, the ships having been found and taken round to St Nicholas.[5]

We know very little about the *Serchthrift*, apart from the fact that she had a crew of ten men, which included Stephen Borough as master, together with Stephen's younger brother, William, and also Charles Pet, who was to make another attempt to find the North-East Passage twenty years later, and a certain Richard Johnson, who later went on to write about his experiences with the 'wild Samoyedes'.[6] We do know that the *Serchthrift* drew no more than 5 feet of water, as there was only 5 feet depth of water when she sailed over the bar of the Pechora river.[7] We also know that she had a mizzen mast, as Stephen Borough mentions on one occasion that his 'Pinnesse bare her missen mast overboorde with flagge and all, but God be praised they were saved'.[8]

She must therefore have had at least two masts, a main mast and a mizzen, and she could possibly also have had a fore mast. The fact that the *Serchthrift* was described as a 'pinnace' (a term that embraced a wide range of vessels, from those of over 100 tons down to the larger ships' boats, as already alluded to in Chapter 4, note 56) suggests that she was somewhat more slender than the average ship of the time.[9]

The measurements of the *Serchthrift*, at perhaps about 20 tons, might thus have been, very approximately, 44 feet in length of keel and 10½ feet in maximum breadth, and with no more than about 4½ feet height between the lower side of the deck beams and the top of the keelson in the waist of the ship, though with more headroom in the forecastle and sterncastle.[10]

The small fleet departed from Ratcliffe on 23 April 1556 and took only four days to reach the mouth of the Thames at Gravesend, where Sebastian Cabot paid them a visit. He had been the chief instigator, planner and organiser of the 1553 expedition, and he had been instrumental in setting up the Muscovy Company, of which he was Governor for life. He was now 82 years old, but still highly respected. Sebastian Cabot

came aboord our Pinnesse at Gravesende, accompanied with divers Gentlemen and Gentlewomen, who after they had viewed our Pinnesse, and tasted of such cheere as we could make them aboord, they went on shore, giving to our mariners right liberall rewards: and the good olde Gentleman Master Cabota gave to the poore most liberall almes, wishing them to pray for the good fortune, and prosperous successe of the *Serchthrift*, our Pinnese. And then at the signe of the Christopher, hee and his friends banketted, and made me and them that were in the company great cheere: and for very joy that he had to see the towardness of our intended discovery, he entred into the dance himselfe, amongst the rest of the young and lusty company: which being ended, hee and his friends departed most gently, commending us to the governance of almighty God.[11]

Tuesday [28 April 1556] we rode still at Gravesend, making provision for such things as we wanted.

Wednesday in the morning we departed from Gravesende, the winde being at southwest, that night we came to an anker thwart our Lady of Hollands.[12]

Thursday at three of the clocke in the morning we wayed, and by eight of the clocke, we were at an anker in Orwell wannes, and then incontinent I went aboord the *Edward Bonaventura*, where the worshipfull company of marchants appointed me to be, untill the sayd good ship arrived at Wardhouse. Then I returned againe into the pinnesse.[13]

Stephen Borough sailed in the pinnace *Serchthrift* as far as Orwell Wands (near Harwich), where he swapped ship and sailed aboard the *Edward Bonaventura* until he swapped back again into the *Serchthrift* west of Wardhouse. The other two ships of the fleet then proceeded to St Nicholas, while he and the *Serchthrift* parted from them to explore further east.

There is no doubt that it is indeed Stephen Borough's own account of the voyage, as it was described very much from his own viewpoint. The evidence is in the narrative: for instance, on the voyage north, he several times makes such comments as 'we lost sight of the pinnesse', implying that he was at that time on board the *Edward*. But, after Corpus Christi Bay (to the east of North Cape), he comments, 'we heard a piece of ordinance, which was out of the *Edward*, which bade us farewell', clearly indicating that by this time he was back aboard the *Serchthrift*.[14]

The fleet sighted the coast of Norway on 15 May 1556, at a point much further south than on the previous journey. This time they were in latitude 58½° N, on the south-west corner of Norway, a little to the south of present-day Stavanger. They followed the line of the coast north-east, past 'St Dunstans Island, which island I so named', at 59° 42',[15] past a headland they called 'Scoutsnesse',[16] and onwards north and north-east past 'the Chappel, which I suppose is called Kedilwike',[17] 9 leagues to the west of North Cape, and round the North Cape until, on 1 June, they were at anchor in 'Corpus Christi Bay'.[18] From Corpus Christi Bay onwards Stephen Borough was on board the *Serchthrift*. When they had gone 20 leagues to the south-east and by south from Corpus Christi Bay, they found themselves in mist and with much ice out of a bay, and it was here that they heard the gun from the *Edward* bidding them farewell, to which they replied in kind. They sailed on, generally south-eastward, past the Isle of Crosses,[19] Point Lookout, Cape Good Fortune, and Saint Edmond's Point (none of which can now be positively identified) to the mouth of the River Kola. Stephen Borough states that 'the latitude of the mouth of the river Cola is sixtie five degrees, fortie and eight minutes', though the modern chart shows it to be 69° 20' N. This was his biggest discrepancy, unless it was a mistake in copying his manuscript.

It was while at anchor in the mouth of the River Kola, near where Murmansk now stands, that they met up with the first lodias. These were

Russian fishing boats with twenty-four or more men in each, a single sail and twenty oars.[20] Stephen Borough became friendly with several of their skippers: he mentions Pheodor and Keril by name, and he became particularly friendly with one named Gabriel and later another called Loshak, both of whom gave him considerable assistance.[21] Early on in their friendship Gabriel gave the *Serchthrift* a barrel of mead and another of beer; Stephen Borough noted that the Russians had had to carry the barrel of beer for over 2 miles on their backs to bring it to him.

It is interesting to notice how much the English and the Russians managed to communicate with each other. At no point is there any mention of any difficulty due to language, although, at this stage, the English can only have had the most rudimentary Russian, and the 'Russes' had no English at all and were most unlikely in this area to have had any Latin or German either. A year later, Stephen Borough went so far as to compile a list of Russian words, together with their English equivalents. He learned them from a party of Lapps, some of whom spoke Russian. His list of over eighty words starts with 'Cowghtie coteat, what call you this', and it includes 'Iomme lemaupes, I thank you' and 'Avanchy thocke, get thee hence'.[22]

EASTWARDS FROM THE RIVER KOLA (modern-day Murmansk)

The *Serchthrift* departed from the mouth of the River Kola on 22 June, in company with Gabriel and a number of other lodias. They rounded Cape Saint Bernard[23] and soon discovered that the lodias could sail faster before the wind than they could, but Gabriel and his friends often went more slowly in order to keep them company. They had much work with anchors and cables in and around the shoals off Cape Saint John.[24] On one occasion they had to borrow two anchors off Gabriel in a hurry, when they found they were drifting onto a lee shore.[25]

The *Serchthrift* kept company with the fleet of lodias as best she could, though the lodias drew less water and on three different occasions, north of Cape Saint John, the lodias used creeks for shelter that were too shallow for the *Serchthrift*.[26]

CAPE KANIN, TO THE EAST OF THE ENTRANCE TO
THE WHITE SEA

By 7 July, they had reached Cape Caninoz (Cape Kanin Nos[27] or Cape Kanin).[28] They had crossed the entrance to the White Sea and were starting out to explore further east than they or anyone else from western Europe had ever been before. The *Serchthrift* was at anchor here, against a lee shore, when they saw a storm approaching. It was misty, and while Stephen Borough was trying to decide what to do, he saw Gabriel come out of a nearby harbour to help them. Gabriel indicated to them to sail eastwards, and they followed him some 30 leagues (90 nautical miles) to a harbour called Morgiovets (Morjovets Island).[29]

'In this place we found plenty of young foule, as Gulles, Seapies [oyster catchers] and others, whereof the Russes would eate none, whereof we were nothing sory, for there came the more to our part.'

The crew of the *Serchthrift* spent two days at Morjiovets Island, collecting driftwood from the shore, fresh water in barricoes and stones to increase the ballasting of the vessel. Gabriel brought a young Samoyed man to meet them, whose 'apparell was then strange to us, and he presented me with three young wild geese, and one young barnacle' (presumably a barnacle goose).[30]

They sailed on further east another 25 leagues and saw an island to the north of them called Dolgoieve (Kolguev Island)[31] and a headland called Swetinoz (Mys Svyatoy Nos).[32]

THE PECHORA RIVER

On Wednesday 12 July 1556 'we went in over the dangerous bar of the Pechora [river], and had upon the barre but one fadome of water'. Here, as at many other places along the route, Stephen Borough made his observations:

I went on shoare and observed the variation of the Compasse, which was three degrees and a halfe from the North to the West: the latitude this day was sixtie nine degrees ten minutes. From two or three leagues to the Eastward of Swetinoz, untill the entering of the river Pechora, it is all sandy hilles, and towards Pechora the sandie hilles are very low. It higheth on the barre of Pechora foure foote water, & it floweth there at a Southwest moone a full sea [i.e. the range of the tide, from low to high water, is 4 feet, and high tide occurs when the moon is in the south-west].[33]

When they went out again over the bar, still in the company of the Russians, they found that they only had 5 feet of water and 'we thanke God that our ship did draw so little water'. Just outside the bar, 'the wind scanted upon us, and was at Eastsoutheast, insomuch that we stopped the ebbes, and plyed all the floods to the windewards, and made our way Eastnortheast'.[34]

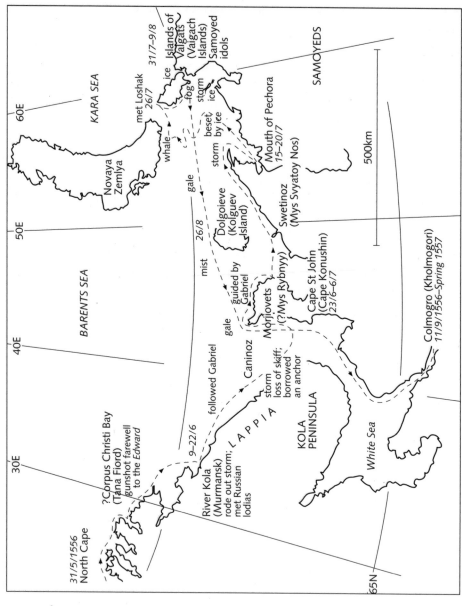

The *Serchthrift* sailed from London in 1556, past the entrance to the White Sea, and then sailed 800km further east than any western European had been before. Eventually ice, storms, fogs and the onset of winter forced her to retire to Colmogro.

ICE

Their first serious encounter with ice occurred just a little to the east of the entrance to the Pechora river. As Borough recorded:

> We thought that we had seen land at East, or east & by North of us: which afterwards prooved to be a monstrous heape of ice.
>
> Within a little more than halfe an houre after, we first saw this ice, we were inclosed within it before we were aware of it, which was a fearefull sight to see: for, for the space of sixe houres, it was as much as we could doe to keepe our shippe aloofe from one heape of ice, and beare roomer from another, with as much wind as might beare a coarse. And when we had past from the danger of this ice, we lay to the eastwards close by the wind.
>
> The nexte day we were again troubled with the ice.
>
> We had not runne past two houres Northwest . . . but we met againe with another heape of ice: we weathered the head of it, and lay a time to the seawards.[35]

A MONSTROUS WHALE

The explorers were terrified of whales, as became apparent on 22 July:

> On S. James his day [22 July] . . . there was a monstrous Whale aboord of us, so neere to our side that we might have thrust a sworde or any other weapon in him, which we durst not doe for feare hee should have overthrowen our shippe: and then I called my company together, and all of us shouted, & with the crie that we made he departed from us: there was as much above water of his backe as the bredth of our pinnesse [about 8 or 9 feet], and at his falling downe, he made such a terrible noyse in the water, that a man would greatly have marvelled, except hee had knowen the cause of it: but God be thanked we were delivered of him.[36]

This must have been a Northern Right whale, a species that was numerous in those waters before being almost exterminated by the whaling industry in the following century. The adults are, on average, about 50 feet long,[37] longer than the men's pinnace (about 44 feet), so it is not surprising that they were terrified of it. At that time, the sailors knew nothing of the usually very peaceful habits of whales; they had been brought up on tales of monsters of the deep. Before the first expedition in 1553, Henry Sidney, Chancellor's patron, had referred to the perils from whales and monsters of the deep in his speech to the merchants when he said 'he [Chancellor] shall hazard his life amongst the monstrous and terrible beastes of the Sea'.[38]

It is interesting to note how rapidly attitudes to the whale changed: in the sixteenth century the whale was seen as a terrifying monster of the deep, but early in the following century it was a quarry to be hunted down and turned into train oil for profit.[39]

NOVAYA ZEMLYA

On 25 July 1556 the *Serchthrift* met up with one of the lodias that they recognised from a previous meeting in the Kola river. Its captain was called Loshak, and he told them that the land that they had reached was Novaya Zemlya, or the 'New Land'. He gave them directions how to go further to the east, towards the River Ob, and he also told them that the highest mountain in the world was on Novaya Zemlya, though, as Stephen Borough says, 'I saw it not.'[40]

THE ISLANDS OF VAIGATS

For the next three days 'we plied to the eastwards' and reached the Islands of Vaigats. These islands are in the Straits of Kara, the entrance to the Kara Sea. Here they met up with two other lodias, the crews of which were killing 'morse' (walruses), and they also watched one group chasing and killing a polar bear.[41]

ICE AND STORMS

While they were at anchor among the Islands of Vaigats, they had 'a great gale of wind at North, and we saw so much ice driving a seaboord, that it was then no going to sea'. The following night 'there fell a cruell storm, the wind being at West', and the day after that 'we had very much winde, with plenty of snow, and we rode with two ankers a head'.[42]

SIGNS OF THE SAMOYEDS

While they stayed there, trapped by the storms, they went ashore and met Loshak again, who told them about the local people, the Samoyeds:

who have no houses, but onely coverings made of Deersskins, set over them with stakes: they are men expert in shooting, and have great plenty of Deere . . .

their boates are made of deers skins, and when they come on shoare they cary their boates with them upon their backes: for their cariages they have no other beastes to serve them, but Deere only. As for bread and corne they have none, except the Russes bring it to them: their knowledge is very base, for they know no letter . . . they will shoot at all men to the uttermost of their power, that cannot speake their speech.

The Englishmen were shown some of the Samoyeds' idols, 'above 300 of them, the worst and most unartificiall worke that I ever saw: the eyes and mouthes of sundrie of them were bloodie, they had the shape of men, women and children, very grossly wrought, & that which they made for other parts, was also sprinckled with blood'.[43]

The Samoyeds lived over a large area in the north of Russia, extending from where Archangel'sk is now in the west to the Pechora river and far beyond it to the remote Yamal Peninsula in the east.[44] Richard Johnson later gave Hakluyt an account of them and their 'develish rites'. He described how, 'they lie in tentes made of Deere skinnes, and they use much witchcraft, and shoot well in bowes'. He went on to describe their sacrifices and other practices in gruesome terms.[45] These people are now called the Nenets. They still live in tents made from deer skins, which are called 'chums', and they still live very much off deer, and in the summer off wild birds and fish.[46]

MORE ICE

On Wednesday 5 August, the *Serchthrift* was still at the Islands of Vaigats when 'we saw a terrible heape of ice approch neere unto us, and therfore wee thought good with al speed possible to depart from thence, and so I returned to the Westwards againe, to the Island where we were the 31. of July.'

The following day Borough went ashore to take the latitude, and while there he noticed Loshak departing very suddenly, over some shoals 'where it was impossible for us to follow them. But after I perceived them to be weather-wise.'[47]

STORM-BOUND IN THE ISLANDS OF VAIGATS

Indeed they found themselves storm-bound for another two days. On the Friday 'We rode still, the winde being at Northnortheast, with a cruell storme. The ice came in so abundantly about us at both ends of the Island that we rode under, that it was a fearfull sight to behold: the storme continued with snow, raine, and hayle plenty. Saturday [8 August] we road still also, the storme being somewhat abated, but it was altogether misty, that we were not able to see a cables length about us.'[48]

FOG AND MORE FOG

They managed to get away early on the Sunday morning, 9 August, but then 'it came so thick with mistes, that we could not see a base shotte from us. Then we took in all our sailes to make little way.' It cleared for a while but then 'at a west sunne [about 6 p.m.] we tooke in our sayle againe because of the great mist and raine'. The mists persisted through the next two days, but it cleared on the Wednesday and eventually they anchored 'under the Southwest part of the said Vaigats, and then I sent our skiffe to shoare with three men in her, to see if they might speake with any of the Samoeds, but could not'.[49]

They stayed there for the whole of the next week, owing to mists or contrary winds. Fog and mist are still very common in Arctic waters in the summer.[50] They did manage to make a little progress through the mist on the 13th, as 'we followed the shore by our lead'.

THE WORST OF ALL THE STORMS

Eventually they did get away in a south-easterly direction, intending to explore the mainland coast, but they were assailed by further storms.

At a Northwest sunne we took in our maine saile, because the wind increased, and went with a foresaile Westnorthwest, the winde being at Eastnortheast: at night there grewe so terrible a storme, that we saw not the like, although we had endured many stormes since we came out of England. It was wonderfull that our barke was able to brooke such monstrous and terrible seas, without the great helpe of God, who never fayleth them at neede, that put their sure trust in him.

Thursday at a Southsouthwest sunne, thanks be to God, the storme was at the highest, & then the winde began to slake.[51]

For the next two days they made little progress, as they had light winds and heavy seas.

A WALL OF ICE ACROSS THE HORIZON

On Saturday 22 August Borough records: 'This present Saturday we saw very much ice, and were within two or three leagues of it: it shewed unto us as though it had beene a firme land as farre as we might see from Northwest off us to the Eastwards.'[52]

Such a solid wall of ice, extending right across their route and completely impassable, totally put an end to any hope of exploration further east that year.

THE RETREAT TO COLMOGRO

And thus we being out of al hope to discover any more to the Eastward this yeere, wee thought it best to returne . . . this afternoone the Lord sent us a little gale of wind at South, so that we bare cleere off the Westernmost part of it, thanks be to God.[53]

Stephen Borough listed three reasons for his retreat: firstly the 'continuall Northeast and Northerly winds', more powerful here than in any other place he knew,[54] and secondly the 'great and terrible abundance of ice which we saw with our eies, and we doubt greater store abideth in those parts: I adventured already somewhat too farre in it, but I thanke God for my safe deliverance from it'. The third reason was 'because the nights waxed darke, and the winter began to draw on with his stormes'.[55]

They made their way westward, often against contrary winds, past Colgoieve Island (Kolguev Island) and Caninoz (Kanin Nos), and on 11 September eventually reached the River Dvina and Colmogro (Kholmogori), where they spent the winter.

They had done well to survive. They had faced violent storms; several encounters with the ice, any one of which could have been their last; many days of fog and mist, not to mention the shoals and all the hazards of not knowing anything about where the land lay; and all this in a small boat only about 44 feet long, cold, wet and clammy, and devoid of any modern amenities, in a dreary and desolate landscape where the very few people that they met spoke what was to them a very strange language.

This was the first epic voyage of exploration by the English, and a very worthy one, for not only had the seamen survived, they had also managed to keep a careful record of their navigation and their discoveries, a feat in itself considering the conditions of danger and discomfort that they were in.

PART 2: 1557 – SURVEYING THE COAST
OF LAPPIA

At the end of his great voyage of exploration in 1556, Stephen Borough had written 'and there [at Colmogro] we wintered, expecting the approch of the next Sommer to proceede farther in our intended discoverie for the Ob: which (by reason of our imploiments to Wardhouse the next spring for the search of some English ships) was not accordingly performed'.[56]

He had been expecting to try to explore further east in the *Serchthrift* in 1557, but instead he sailed west to try to find the ships that were missing from the 1553 expedition.[57] The 1557 voyage was therefore from Colmogro westwards to Wardhouse, following the coast as much as possible.[58] The missing ships were the *Bona Esperanza*, the *Bona Confidentia* and the *Philip and Mary*. They had all left St Nicholas on 20 July 1556 to sail to London, but none of them had been heard of since.[59] (As it turned out, the *Philip and Mary* had overwintered in Dronton (Trondheim) and left there in March 1557, eventually reaching London but not until April 1557.)

Stephen Borough was obliged to retrace his steps towards Wardhouse, and so he used this opportunity to make as many cartographic observations as he could. His account of this journey is very detailed. It includes notes of all the headlands from the mouth of the Dvina river northwards and westwards to Wardhouse, with a note of the distance and the direction from one to the next, and it forms a complete catalogue with only two small gaps. (See Appendix 7.)

He also includes a great deal of additional information on depths, currents, tide times, safe anchorages, latitudes, magnetic variation and the like. For instance, right at the start of the voyage, he sent out two skiffs to sound the best depth that they could find at the bar of the Berozova Guba.[60] He describes the appearance of the coast in different places. He notes the nature of the bottom carefully when he takes soundings, finding 'faire sand, and amongst the sand little yong small limpets' in one place, 'broken cocle shels, with brannie sand' in another, and 'oazie sand' in a third.[61] He comments in particular on several possible anchorages along the way, how to get into them and their suitability in different wind directions – at Tri Ostrove, for instance, and at St John's Islands, and also at the southernmost of the St George's Islands and St Peter's Islands.

His account is effectively a rutter: the distances and directions are carefully measured and recorded, together with much other information, to make it a very useful document for any other shipmaster sailing along this coast at some later date. The information that was recorded was so accurate that his brother William could later make a chart of the whole area that closely resembles modern charts.[62]

The *Serchthrift* sailed as far as Wardhouse without finding any trace of the lost ships, and then turned round and sailed east again as far as Kegor on the Ribachi Peninsula (not far from modern Murmansk). It was there, at Kegor, where he met some people from Dronton (Trondheim) that Stephen Borough heard news of two of the ships he had been looking for. His informants told him that the *Philip and Mary* had sailed on from Trondheim towards London, and that the *Bona Confidentia* had been wrecked.[63]

Stephen incidentally noticed that the Dutch had also reached Kegor and were trading with the Lapps when he arrived there in 1557.[64] This was ominous, and in fact the Dutch were to become fierce competitors with the English, eventually overtaking them in the Russian trade, but this was not yet a matter of great concern.

The voyage of the *Serchthrift* in 1557 was an early masterpiece in the art of exploration and surveying. Stephen Borough measured and surveyed the whole coast from St Nicholas to Wardhouse with great accuracy, a feat that not only established the sea route to Muscovy but also showed how navigation and surveying could be done. His work, probably with a good deal of help from his younger brother, set a standard and a role model for others to follow. It was a first for the English; the methods that he used are discussed in Chapter 10.

The shape of the coast now is very much as he described it then, though other changes have overtaken the area, not all of them beneficial.[65]

CHAPTER 9

Stephen Borough's Navigation

The art of navigation demonstrateth how by the shortest good way,
by the aptest direction, and in the shortest time a sufficient
ship . . . may be conducted.[1]

Stephen Borough's first lessons in navigation must have been from his uncle, John Aborough, and he must have learned a good deal more from Richard Chancellor during the 1553 expedition to the north-east, particularly about the measurement of latitude. The accounts of the 1553 expedition give us only a very few clues as to how the ships actually navigated, but Stephen wrote his own accounts of the 1556 and 1557 voyages, and these include a lot of fascinating information. They are the first detailed accounts in English of any voyage, and they read almost like a log book.

Chancellor and Borough were English pioneers in the new methods of navigation, methods that involved actual measurements of distance and latitude. The purpose of this chapter is to look at the state of the art at this exciting time, and it is largely drawn from Stephen's own accounts of the 1556 and 1557 voyages.

The time was ripe for English navigation to flower. Sebastian Cabot had come back to England in 1548, bringing with him a wealth of geographical knowledge, which he had acquired as Pilot Major in Spain. John Dee, the mathematical genius and polymath, had recently returned from Louvain, the centre of cosmographical studies, in 1551, bringing with him armfuls of manuscripts and navigational instruments. Likewise Thomas Gemini, the first expert instrument maker in England, had moved from the Continent to set up in business in Blackfriars, and another factor was the first small awakening of an interest in mathematics in England, with the appearance in 1542 of the first textbook on the subject in English. Thus the ideas, the knowledge, the experience, the tools and also the money from the merchants all came opportunely together. It was not long until two very capable men, Richard Chancellor and Stephen Borough, were selected to put it all into practice.

COASTING

The methods of finding one's way at sea can be considered as having three levels of sophistication or complexity, the simplest of which is following the coastline, or coasting. This largely consists in sailing from one cape or headland to the next in as direct a line as is practicable, and it is sometimes referred to as 'caping'. Every shipmaster had to learn to recognise the various landmarks along his routes, just as Chaucer's famous shipman had done:

> He knew wel alle the havenes as they were,
> From Gootland to the cape of Finistere,
> And every cryke in Britayne and in Spayne.[2]

The basic requirements for 'caping' were knowledge of the coast, a lead line to check the depths, and a good lookout.

Finding a new route

The early English explorers spent some of their time coasting, but, of course, they were in unknown territory. They very much had to feel their way. One example of the many problems that they encountered when attempting to follow the line of the coast occurred in Willoughby's 1553 voyage, and was described as follows: 'The 21 day we sounded, and found 10 fadome, after that we sounded againe, and found but 7 fadome, so shoalder and shoalder water, and yet we could see no land, where we marveiled greatly: to avoid this danger, we bare roomer[3] into the sea all that night.'[4]

In fact there were numerous problems in trying to follow the coastline in what is now known as the Barents Sea. Natural landmarks were few and far between, the shorelines were often low-lying, there were extensive offshore shoals as described above, and mists and fog were, and still are, very frequent in the Arctic summer.[5] As Hugh Smith wrote, on one occasion with the Pet and Jackman expedition in these same waters, some twenty-five years later, 'whether it were land or no, I cannot tell well, but it was very like land, but the fogges have many times deceived us'.[6] Mirages and sea smoke also occur and can add to the difficulties.

Soundings

Stephen was meticulous in taking frequent soundings. He recorded the depths found by the lead line, together with a note of whatever was found sticking to the tallow in the bottom of the lead weight. For instance, 'five and twenty fadomes water and soft black ooze', at the Islands of Vaigats on 9 August;[7] and '20. fathoms and broken Wilkeshels', 24 leagues south-south-west of Kanin Nos on 1 September.[8]

Sounding leads of the kind that Stephen used were found in the wreck of the *Mary Rose*.[9]

Rutters

John Aborough had compiled a rutter or notebook, a sort of *aide-mémoire* for coasting, containing details of the distances between headlands, tide times related to the position of the moon and so on.[10] Stephen Borough almost certainly made similar rutters, for the route from London to St Nicholas, for the benefit of later Muscovy Company pilots, but none of them have survived.

Tide times

The times of high tide at a particular place were described by noting the direction of the moon at the time of the highest tides, at the first day of the new moon. High tides occur 48 minutes later each day, so the shipmaster had to look up in his almanac to find out how many days had passed since the moon was new to find the time of high water at a particular port on a particular day.

Stephen Borough made numerous observations of the times of high water. For instance, at the bar at the mouth of the Pechora river on 17 July 1556 he observed that 'It higheth on the barre of Pechora foure foote water, and it floweth there at a south west moone a full sea'; and at Point Lookout on 8 June he noted 'a south moon maketh a full sea'.[11]

Stephen Borough also occasionally noted the tidal streams, as for instance on 6 July when he noted that 'all alongst the coast it floweth little'. There is in fact a modest current that flows in a west-to-east direction along this coast.[12]

PLANE SAILING

Navigation ignoring the curvature of the Earth

The second level of sophistication in navigation is used on the open sea, where all that one can see is water. There may be a few clues as to where you are on the open sea, such as the direction of the flight of fulmars and guillemots in the morning and evening, a technique used by the Norsemen, but in general such clues are very few and far between, and the basic requirements for navigating on the open sea are a knowledge of distance travelled and direction.

Distance

What was new about the new navigation was the increasing use of measurement rather than estimation. For instance, the introduction of the log and line made it possible actually to measure the ship's progress through the water. The first description of the use of a log and log line, and also of a half-minute glass to measure the ship's way, is in Bourne's *A Regiment for the Sea* in 1574.[13] According to Waters, 'it can be deduced from the context (of Bourne's description) that the "English log" (as it came to be known) had been devised recently – probably for surveying by Muscovy Company pilots – for Bourne describes its use when making a running survey of the coast'.[14]

As Stephen Borough was Chief Pilot to the Muscovy Company at the time, and as it was he who had made a running survey of the coast of Lappia, it seems very probable that it was also he who had introduced the use of the 'English log' (he may even have invented it). The device consisted of a wooden board attached to a log line which had knots in it at intervals of 7 fathoms (42 feet). The board was hove out from the stern and the line allowed to run out freely while the half-minute glass ran.[15] The length of line that had run out, as indicated by the number of knots, gave the speed of the ship through the water.[16]

Willoughby's account includes a few records of distances sailed, probably from measurements made by Richard Chancellor or Stephen Borough, such as 'between Orfordnesse and Aegeland 250 leagues'.[17]

This distance had taken them from 23 June to 14 July, i.e. twenty-two days, a long time, owing to contrary winds for part of the way. The actual landfall seems to have been somewhere a little south of modern-day Bodø on the Norwegian coast, in which case the distance they covered was more like 310 leagues than 250, which would indicate an average speed of 14.1 leagues a day or 1¾ nautical miles an hour.

Stephen includes many more instances of distances travelled in his account of the 1556 voyage, such as, on 16 May, 'from this sayd South sunne, unto a North sunne twenty leagues Northwest', that is 60 miles in 12 hours, i.e. 5 knots, and on 19 May he recorded 'from a South sunne untill eight of the clocke, fifteene leagues North east', i.e. 45 nautical miles in 8 hours, which must have been an exhilarating 5½ knots.[18]

During his 1557 voyage he made more measurements of distance travelled, and these enabled him to compile his description of the north coast of Lappia.

Time

It was not until more than 200 years later that the problem of keeping accurate time on a ship was eventually solved, by John Harrison, when he finally succeeded with his chronometer at his fourth attempt in 1760.[19]

Stephen Borough had to rely on the use of sandglasses to tell the time at sea. They usually ran for half an hour at a time, but were not entirely accurate, partly because they had to be turned over at exactly the moment when they ran through, a job which was usually performed by the grommet, or ship's page.[20]

At night, but only when it was dark enough to see the stars in the Arctic twilight, seamen could use a 'nocturnal' to tell the time. The nocturnal was a dial, with a measuring arm revolving about the centre of the dial, by means of which one entered the date of the year. It was possible to tell the time at night by comparing the position of the measuring arm with the position of 'the Guards', two prominent stars in the body of the Little Bear, as they revolved around the Pole Star.[21] It was accurate to within half an hour or so.

Stephen Borough often indicated the time of day by noting the direction of the sun in relation to the compass. For example, on 4 July he indicated the time by using the expression 'at a Northnorthwest sunne', i.e. the sun's bearing was 337½° magnetic (about 327° true), which is just before 10 p.m.

Direction

The direction of travel was found from a magnetic compass, or by observing the position of the sun by day or that of the Pole Star at night, when they were visible.[22]

The position of the Pole Star has changed

Because the earth rotates each day and night, the Pole Star (or Stella Maris) appears to us to remain almost stationary in the sky (hence its being called the 'pommel' of the sky), while all the other stars revolve around it. However, the earth's axis has not always pointed to the Pole Star.

In Tudor times, it was 3° away. This was far enough away from true north to matter, so the early navigators used a method to find where the true north was in relation to the Pole Star based on the direction of 'the Guards' from the Pole Star. They had a set of 'rules' for the Pole Star, or a 'Regiment of the Pole Star' as it was called.[23] For example, one rule was 'When the Guards are in the west, the North Star stands above the Pole one degree and a half.'

The compass

By the sixteenth century the compass needle was permanently magnetised and fastened onto a card or 'windrose', with the thirty-two cardinal points marked on it.[24] The earliest English compass to have survived, complete with gimbals, was found on the *Mary Rose*, which sank in 1545.[25] Incidentally, it was John Dee who first produced 'my new Sea Compass', which had a scale of degrees around the edge of the card, such as we have now, instead of the cardinal points.[26] The constancy of the compass was much admired, but the problems of its variation were still only poorly understood.

Compass variation

This problem is largely due to the fact that the magnetic poles are not in the same positions as the geographical poles: at present, they are some 800 miles away from them.[27] The magnetic compass aligns itself along the lines of the earth's magnetic flux which run between the two magnetic poles, i.e. the compass points to the magnetic north pole. The angular difference, or 'variation', between geographical or true north and magnetic north is different in different parts of the world.

In Tudor times, the angle of compass variation was small in the Mediterranean but larger in the Atlantic, and the phenomenon of variation went unnoticed until Atlantic voyaging started. Columbus is reputed to have been the first person to have noticed that his compasses did not point to true north when he crossed the Atlantic in 1492, and John Cabot noticed a similar two-point (22½°) westerly variation of the compass on his voyage in 1497.

The debate about compass variation raged particularly fiercely in the first half of the sixteenth century. Some, such as Pedro de Medina, derided the existence of variation and declared that 'the northwesting and northeasting of the needle' was of little consequence.[28]

Others took it more seriously, and during the sixteenth and later centuries great efforts were made to measure the angle of variation in different places and to produce theories to explain the phenomenon. Jean Rotz, a pilot from Dieppe, who came to England for a while to work for Henry VIII, produced in 1542 an early instrument for measuring variation. It was basically a horizontal disc on which the sun's meridian (i.e. due south) and the direction of the compass needle (magnetic north and south) could be plotted together and compared.[29]

Stephen Borough used such an instrument and made several measurements of the variation of the compass on his 1556 voyage. For instance, on 17 July, at the mouth of the Pechora river, he records that he 'went on shoare and observed the variation of the Compasse, which was three degrees and a halfe from the North to the west'.[30]

During the 1557 voyage he made two more observations of the variation: at the mouth of the Dvina river, where it was 5° 10' from north to east, and at Dog's Nose (Mys Keretz), where it was 4° from north to east. [31]

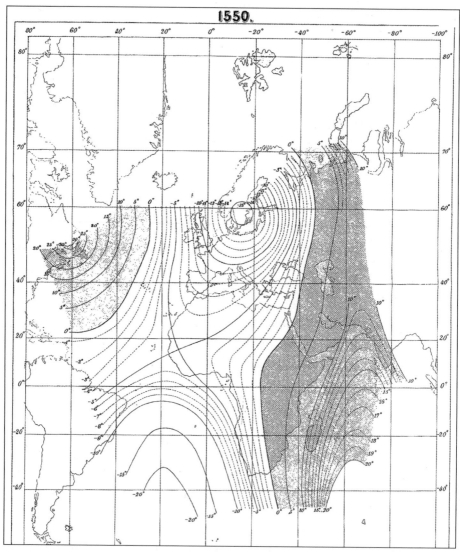

Van Bemmelen's Isogonic Chart, showing the lines of equal compass variation as they were in the 1550s. The shaded areas (which he notes as positive variation) show where the north end of the compass points to the west of true north, and the unshaded areas are where the north end of the compass points to the east of true north.

The Spaniards and the Portuguese had made observations of the variation of the compass some years earlier,[32] and a number of people had made such observations on land, but Stephen Borough's observations appear to be the first to have been made by an English shipmaster.

William Borough, Stephen's younger brother, wrote a *Discourse of the variation of the cumpas* in 1581,[33] based on his experiences of voyages in Arctic waters. It contained descriptions of a number of different methods for finding the variation of the compass, including, for instance, 'How to finde the Variation by Arithmetical Calculation upon any one observation in the forenoone or afternoone, the Latitude of the place and declination of the Sunne being given'.

Stephen Borough's readings of compass variation, and those of his son Christopher in 1579–81 from parts of Asia, together with similar observations from other explorers, were used many years later to compile an isogonic chart for the 1550s.[34]

Compass deviation

Compass deviation is a different problem from compass variation. It can be caused by any iron on board a ship producing a local distortion of the earth's magnetic flux. The problem must have existed in Stephen's time, even on ships built almost entirely of wood. It could, for instance, have occurred owing to putting an iron candle-holder near to the compass to illuminate it at night. The problem does not appear to have been appreciated in Stephen's time, but it must have bedevilled the study of magnetic variation.

The ship's log book

Stephen Borough's original journal no longer exists, but the account in Hakluyt is so detailed that it can only have been taken almost word-for-word from that journal.

It was not set out in tabular form, in columns, as a ship's log book is today. The columnar layout was not introduced until some thirty years later, by John Davis.[35]

Dead reckoning

The 'plot' consists of a straight line drawn on the chart in the direction that the ship has sailed during the previous twenty-four hours from its last known position, and the length of the line represents how far the ship has sailed. This method of plotting the progress, to provide an up-to-date picture of the ship's position (without any information derived from celestial or any other observations), is called 'dead reckoning'. The origin of the practice is obscure,[36] but Waters, the great authority on Tudor navigation, attributes the invention of the term 'dead reckoning' to William Borough.[37]

LATITUDE AND LONGITUDE

The third level of complexity in navigation at sea deals with the position of the ship on the surface of the earth, not as if it was a flat plane, but as a sphere. As Martin Cortes in his book *Arte de Navegar* had pointed out in 1545, plane charts 'because they are not globous, sphericall or rounde are imperfecte, and fayle to show the true distances'.[38]

Global or spherical navigation involves finding the latitude of the ship (how far north or south of the equator it is) and the longitude (the measurement of how far east or west it is round the sphere from Greenwich). The Tudors could measure latitude, but they could not measure longitude at sea, as they did not have any time-pieces sufficiently accurate for the purpose. Longitude they could only *calculate*.

Latitude

Stephen Borough had two different instruments, an astrolabe and a cross staff, with which he could measure the elevation of the sun or the Pole Star and hence determine the latitude. It is, however, far from easy to measure the elevation of a heavenly body from the deck of a small ship with either of these instruments, especially from a ship as small as the *Serchthrift*, only about 44 feet long. Even in calm seas, the ship is seldom still, and in heavy seas the navigator has to wedge his body into a hatchway to steady himself while trying to make the observation. For this reason, Borough, like Vasco da Gama and others before him, preferred to go ashore whenever he could in order to measure the latitude.[39]

The astrolabe

The astrolabe is basically a heavy metal dial, with a ring at the top to hang it up by. It has an arm that turns on a pivot at the centre of the dial, with a small sighting hole at each end of the arm. The observer holds up the dial or, better, hangs it from something steady so that it is at eye level. He then rotates the arm around on the dial until he can view the Pole Star (or the

Two methods of taking the altitude of the sun using astrolabes.

sun) through the two small sighting holes, and reads the angle from a scale engraved around the rim of the dial.

It was not an easy instrument to use. Eugenio de Salazar in the sixteenth century wrote, derisively, that 'It is something to see the pilot . . . take the astrolabe in his hand, raise his eyes to the sun, try to get the sun to shine through the openings in the astrolabe, and then give up without being able to complete his measurements properly. . . . At times his estimate rises so high that it is 1,000 degrees over the mark. And at other times it falls so low, that one would not arrive there in a thousand years.'[40]

When Admiral Samuel Morison tried using the astrolabe in about 1970, he found that he got the best results by steadying the instrument between his knees.[41]

The cross staff

The cross staff consists of a square-sectioned shaft of wood, some 3 feet or so long, with a cross-piece with a hole in its centre, which fits the shaft and allows the cross-piece to slide up and down the length of the shaft. The observer holds the base of the shaft to his cheek and lines up the Pole Star (or the sun) with the top of the cross-piece; he then slides the cross-piece up or down the shaft until the horizon is in line with the bottom of the cross-piece, and measures the angle from a scale of degrees on the shaft. (There were usually three different cross-pieces – transverses or transoms – of different lengths, and the most appropriate one was used, according to the size of the angle to be measured.)

The cross staff was probably more accurate than the astrolabe, but in the Arctic Seas the astrolabe was preferred for taking the altitude of the Pole Star. As William Bourne, a very practical man, pointed out in 1574, 'if it [the altitude] doe exceed 50 degrees then by the means of casting your eye upwardes and downwardes so muche, you may soone commit error . . . you must leave the cross staffe and use the Mariner's ring, called by them the Astrolaby'.[42]

However, George Best took a contrary view when he sailed in Arctic waters. He wrote in 1578 (after the three Frobisher expeditions) that 'Here [at 61°N] the north starre is so much elevated above the horizon, that with the staff it is hardly to be wel observed, and the degrees in the Astrolabe are too small to observe minutes. Therefore we alwaies use the staff and the sunne, as fittest instruments for this use.'[43]

Stephen Borough probably could not see the Pole Star for much of the time during his two voyages owing to the brightness of the Arctic twilight (except perhaps in late August and September), and he would have had to rely on the midday elevation of the sun for his latitudes most of the time. To do this he must have run a serious risk of going blind, as it involved staring directly at the sun for some considerable time.

He used sun tables, which gave the height of the sun above or below the equator for each day of the year. Such tables had originally been devised by the Portuguese, who needed them when they were sailing down the coast of Africa, south of the equator, where it is not possible to see the Pole Star at all, and so 'shooting the sun' was the only method that they had of finding their latitude.[44]

The sun tables that Stephen used had been compiled specially for use on the expedition by John Dee and Richard Chancellor. They had worked together making a series of observations to produce 'ephemerides', i.e. tables of the positions of the sun and of some of the stars each day or night, as predicted for a year or two in advance.[45] They made their observations in London on Richard Chancellor's large quadrant with a 5-foot radius, supported on a stand, and graduated along the edge to read to the nearest

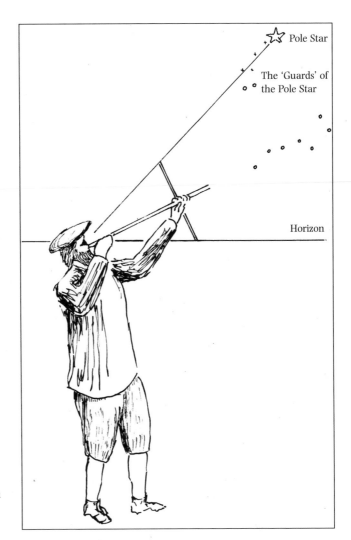

Pole Star

The 'Guards' of
the Pole Star

Horizon

Measuring the elevation
or altitude of the Pole
Star using a cross staff.

minute of arc.[46] Dee must have been impressed by Chancellor's skills, as he referred to him not only as 'an excellent mechanician' but also as 'the incomparable Richard Chancellor' and 'my dearly beloved Richard Chancellor'.[47]

Latitude measurements

Willoughby's account includes some measurements of latitude, the first two of which were probably made by Chancellor. For instance, on 15 June 1553 at Orwell the latitude was found to be 52°, which agrees exactly with the modern map. At the Isles of Røst off the coast of Norway the latitude was found to be 66° 30' N, whereas the modern chart makes it 67° 30' N.

Stephen took thirty readings of latitude on his 1556 and 1557 voyages in the *Serchthrift*, and these are shown in Appendix 8. He achieved a remarkable degree of accuracy with most of them. His only serious discrepancy was on 10 June 1556, at the mouth of the Kola river, where his latitude put him nearly 4° too far south (unless this is the result of a later mistake in the transcription of Stephen's account, when 9 was read as 5), but in general he seems to have been both diligent and accurate. He also seems to have improved his accuracy considerably with increasing experience.

Longitude derived from distance and direction run

The only way in which Stephen could have found his longitude was by calculation. He knew reasonably accurately how far and in which direction he had sailed, and he knew the latitude and longitude of his starting-point, London, and it would, at least in theory, have been possible to work out what his subsequent latitudes and longitudes were, using traverse tables.

John Dee had in fact calculated a 'traverse table' or 'departure table'.[48] It is a table of the easting or westing made good (i.e. the longitude) for each degree of latitude from 0° to 80°, and for each of the seven rhumbs or compass courses (11° 15', 22° 30' etc), thus allowing the resolution of a traverse.[49]

The longitude of London and other places had been established by astronomical observations, using the method of the eclipses or the method of linear distances. The Greeks had used the lunar eclipse method to establish longitudes, and so had the Chinese, according to Gavin Menzies, on their voyages round the world in 1421.[50] Robert Cuningham, in 1559, described how he had used both the lunar eclipse and the lunar distance methods to establish the longitude of Norwich.[51] However, neither of these methods would have been of any practical use to Stephen, as eclipses of the moon only happen two or three times a year and are of no use on a daily basis. The method of lunar distances is complicated, and lunar tables of sufficient accuracy were not produced until 1767.[52]

IMAGINE THE SCENE

It may be fanciful, but it is not impossible, to imagine Stephen Borough on the morning of 1 August 1556 being rowed ashore in the longboat to one of the Islands of Vaigats. On board the *Serchthrift* a man has been given the job of keeping a close eye on the shore party. Stephen, well wrapped up in a woollen cloak and with baggy woollen breeches, holds a wooden box on his lap containing his precious instruments, including a compass, a compass of variation, a planimetrum or theodolite-type of instrument, his cross staff (demounted into its two pieces), his astrolabe and a couple of quill pens and an inkhorn, and some paper or parchment on which to record his findings. The crew, while rowing, are looking about for any change in the weather that might indicate a hasty return to the ship, or any recurrence of the great amount of ice that they had seen the day before. A man in the bow of the longboat, with his crossbow ready, is on lookout for any dangers ahead, such as bears or whales, or even for any of the wild Samoyeds that they had heard about, who were said to shoot at strangers.

It takes a long time for Stephen, helped by his young brother William, to set up his instruments on shore and to take his observations to find the latitude, the variation of the compass and the bearings of the nearby islands, and all the time the crew are keeping lookout in this desolate place for any signs of movement or danger. There are no trees, but there is plenty of driftwood, brought down by the great rivers, and they light a fire in an effort to repel the mosquitoes. When Stephen has finished, they row back to the ship. He waits until he gets back on board before doing the calculations to turn his observations of the sun into a latitude reading.

CIRCUMPOLAR CHART

John Dee had drawn up what he called his *Paradoxal Compass in playne* in 1552 or 1553 especially for the 1553 expedition. It was an entirely novel concept, but a very useful one: it was basically a circumpolar chart, the forerunner of the circumpolar charts we use today. It was centred on the North Pole, with the meridians radiating out from it and the parallels of latitude shown as concentric circles, and it extended as far south as 50° N.[53] Such a chart required a completely different method for plotting a course. Dee's circumpolar chart has not survived, and there is no evidence as to whether Stephen Borough ever used it.

THE PROBLEMS OF POLAR NAVIGATION

There are special problems of navigation in the Arctic, as no doubt Stephen was well aware. Direction-finding depends largely on the compass, which may not be reliable owing to increasing and variable variation, and due to increasing compass dip. None of the stars are visible during the long, continuous days of summer, or in the Arctic twilight, and so direction can only be found from the sun, which goes round and round in a near circle. Time itself has little meaning in the absence of night and day, and can only be determined by noting the compass direction of the sun; and even the sun may not be visible for days at a time because of frequent fog.

The compass problems in the polar regions were partly overcome by the invention of accurate chronometers, which could be used with sun compasses, but they were not completely overcome until the invention of the gyroscopic compass for ships and inertial navigation systems for aircraft in the twentieth century. More recently the satellite Global Positioning System (GPS) has made life a lot easier for navigators in the polar regions.

INFORMATION FROM THE NATIVES

Almost all the most successful explorers have benefited greatly from establishing cordial relations with the local people and getting geographical information from them. Richard Chancellor and Stephen Borough were no exception. The friendly demeanour of Chancellor at the first meeting with the frightened Russian fishermen on the voyage of the *Edward Bonaventura* in 1553 has already been described in Chapter 7. It served to establish good relations from the beginning.

On the 1556 expedition Stephen Borough made contact with the locals on numerous occasions, some of which have already been mentioned. His contacts with Gabriel and Loshak were particularly helpful as far as navigation was concerned. For instance, he notes that 'according to [his] promise, this Gabriel and his friend did often strike his sayles, and taried for us forsaking their owne company'. This was in order to show Borough the way from Cape St John to Mezen, where 'it is all sunke land, and full of shoales and dangers, you shall have scant two fadome water and see no land'. Borough rewarded Gabriel later, giving him 'two small ivory combes, and a steele glasse, with two or three trifles more'.[54]

The incident in which Gabriel came out to them and lent them two of his anchors to save them from being carried onto a lee shore has also been mentioned previously, but this was not the end of Gabriel's kindness to them. On another occasion:

we saw the similitude of a storme rising at Northnorthwest, & could not tell where to get rode nor succor for that winde, and harborough we knew none: & that land which we rode under with that winde was a lee shore. And as I was musing what was best to be done, I saw a saile come out of the creeke under the foresayd Caninoz, which was my friend Gabriel, who forsooke his harborough and company, and came as neere us as he might, and pointed us to the Eastwards, and then we weyed and followed him, and went East and by South . . . and he brought us [the next day] into an harborough called Morgoviets.[55]

Later on in the 1556 voyage they met up with another Russian, called Loshak, on the coast of Novaya Zemlya. He gave them a good deal of advice and information about the place and also about the Samoyed people, and, Borough records, 'he made me also certaine demonstrations of the route to the (River) Ob'.[56]

Stephen Borough certainly seems to have made a point of treating the local people with respect and courtesy, and as a result they gave him a good deal of help and information. This shows a considerable contrast with the early Portuguese explorers, such as Albuquerque, who used his superior cannon to attack defenceless ports almost everywhere he went in the Indian Ocean, or the conquistadors of Spain, Hernando Cortes and Francisco Pizarro, who trashed Mexico and Peru respectively.

Frobisher, on his voyages, twenty years after Stephen Borough's, found that it was not always easy to set up good relations with the local people. He did make some attempts to communicate with them, but then he kidnapped an Eskimo man and brought him back to England, where he died. His relations with the Eskimos deteriorated after that and the following year, 1577, five sailors in a boat were taken and killed by the Eskimos. Frobisher himself was shot in the buttock with an Eskimo arrow in another incident. Later there was a small battle in which five or more Eskimos died, and after that Frobisher's men had to set up an armed guard whenever they went ashore.[57]

THE EARLY DAYS OF MATHEMATICS IN ENGLAND

It is remarkable that Stephen, and Chancellor before him, managed to navigate as well as they did, because at that time mathematics in England was in its very early infancy. There were, for instance, no conventions as to how sums should be written out, the equals sign (=) had only just been introduced, and the plus and minus symbols were not widely used until the seventeenth century.[58] There were no decimals or logarithms, algebraic symbols had not been devised and there was no elementary textbook of trigonometry.[59]

At the time of the first voyage to the north-east in 1553, there were scarcely more than a dozen people in the whole of England who could be described as having the slightest interest in, or enthusiasm for, mathematics or the new methods of navigation.[60] Many simply did not know anything about the subject. Frobisher himself, twenty years later, claimed that he lacked the wit to understand mathematics or celestial navigation.[61] Others were simply not interested, including the pilot of the Elizabethan galleon *Leicester*, who professed 'to give not a fart for cosmography'.[62] There were others who considered that all such knowledge was magical or supernatural. There is, for instance, a dialogue between a master and his pupil in Cunningham's *Cosmographicall Glasse* in which the master says, 'I will shewe unto you how much the circuit of the Earth is', to which the pupil replies, 'Sir, never take it in hand, for the common people will judge you mad.'[63]

Even as late as the seventeenth century, mathematics was rarely taught and was still viewed with suspicion. A certain Dr John Newton (1622–78) wrote that 'I never yet heard of any Grammar School in England in which [mathematics] is taught', and the antiquarian John Aubrey (1626–97) reported that, following the first foundation of a Chair of Mathematics at Oxford, some parents kept their sons away from the university for fear that they would be 'smutted by the Black Art'.[64]

There is indeed a form of magic in numbers, quite apart from magic squares, pentagrams and similar structures.[65] The magic lies in the understanding and control of numerical phenomena, but in the 1550s this was only just beginning to be appreciated.

Despite the fear of accusations of witchcraft, a few books on mathematics written in English did appear, the first of which was, *The Grounde of Arts teachyng the worke and practise of Arithmetike* in 1542, by Dr Robert Recorde. He followed it with a textbook on geometry and the use of the quadrant called *The Pathway to Knowledge containing the first principles of Geometrie* in 1551, and in 1556 he published *The Castle of Knowledge*, a treatise on the earth as a sphere, which was written and printed specifically for the Muscovy Company navigators. In 1557 he produced yet another mathematical textbook, also written specifically for the Muscovy Company and dedicated to its Governors, called *The Whetstone of Witte*.[66]

TEACHING NAVIGATION

A small amount of teaching of navigation did, however, take place. The Borough brothers are said to have had some instruction in the art from John Dee, at the request of the Muscovy Company, though it is not clear at what date this happened.[67] In 1557 the Muscovy Company included in its instructions for the voyage to Russia under Anthony Jenkinson the stipulation that 'Notes and entries be daily made of their navigations put in writing and memory, and that the yong Mariners and apprentices may be taught and caused to learne the same'.[68] By 1566 the Muscovy Company claimed that it was paying a man learned in cosmography £20 a year to teach its mariners.[69] No one knows if Stephen Borough ever passed on any of his knowledge of mathematical navigation, but his brother William certainly did.[70]

These few early indications of education in navigation show the beginnings of a certain openness about the dissemination of knowledge. Navigation had previously been looked upon as something of a 'mystery', as secret knowledge that could and should only be possessed by a few.

The first organised teaching of navigation in England started in 1575, when Gresham College was opened in London, but Hakluyt still felt it necessary in 1598 to make a powerful plea for lectures to be given in the subject. In fact, more than half of the *Epistle Dedicatorie* of the second edition of his *Principal Navigations* to Lord Howard of Effingham, Lord High Admiral, is an attempt to persuade the Lord Admiral of the need for regular lectures in the art of navigation, along the lines of those already established 'in the Contractation House in Sivil'.[71]

INSTRUMENTS AND INSTRUMENT MAKERS

The 1553 expedition stimulated and was accompanied by a burst of new technology, a bit like space exploration today. The construction of navigational instruments was a part of the new technology, and its leader was known as Thomas Gemini. He had come over from Flanders sometime before 1545, settling in Blackfriars as a printer, expert engraver and maker of instruments. He made, for instance, a beautiful astrolabe for Queen Elizabeth in 1559. It was lost for centuries but was rediscovered in a cupboard at the University Observatory at Oxford in 1936, and it is now in the Oxford Museum of the History of Science. It is, as Dr R.T. Gunther described it, a 'superb example of the astrolabist's art'.[72]

Thomas Gemini's monogram, from his 1559 astrolabe made for Queen Elizabeth. His real name was Thomas Lambrit, but for his monogram he used Thomas followed by the astronomical sign for Gemini, the Twins.

Without such instruments, the expeditions of 1553 and later could never have been undertaken.

SURVEYING AND CHART-MAKING

William Borough later described the methods used for surveying and chart-making on three different occasions; to do this he must have drawn on the methods that Stephen and he had used in the Arctic. The first description originated when he was asked to write some instructions to Thomas Bassendine for a proposed expedition in 1568.[73] For this expedition William Borough recommended an instrument with a pivoted sight rule, and a circle of degrees, orientated by a little compass needle. This instrument sounds very similar to the *instrumentum planimetrum* described by Gemma Frisius, which consisted of a horizontal graduated circular plate with an alidade or sighting vane pivoted about its centre. A compass was attached to the alidade and horizontal angles could then be measured as the difference of two magnetic bearings.[74] For charting at sea, according to William Borough's instructions at that time, a single compass bearing on a landmark with an estimate of its distance was considered sufficient.[75]

In the event, the Bassendine expedition was cancelled, but William Borough later amplified these instructions when he was asked to give advice to the Pet and Jackman expedition of 1580, an expedition that did take place. For them he recommended charting the position of a landmark by taking two intersecting bearings of it from two different positions of the ship, using the distance run and the compass course between the two positions as the base line.[76]

In 1582 an expedition to the east coast of America was planned, and once again William Borough was asked to draw up a set of 'Instructions', this time for the benefit of one Thomas Bavin, who had been given the task of charting the coast from Florida to Cape Breton. William's instructions include a large number of very practical suggestions about chart-making, again using the plane table as one of the principal instruments. It is interesting to note that these instructions included a suggestion about determining the longitude, 'if there might be had a portable Clock which would continue true the space of 40 or 50 houres together'. In the event the expedition was deferred until 1583, and then only a brief reconnaissance was made; Thomas Bavin and any charts that he may have drawn perished in the wreck of the *Admiral*.[77]

Both the Borough brothers contributed greatly to a map of Russia constructed by Anthony Jenkinson in 1562. S.H. Baron examined this map and commented on the contribution of the brothers. 'Stephen Borough', he wrote, proved to be not only a courageous and resourceful captain but a zealous and careful recorder of data. The log of his [1556] voyage is crammed with dates, place names (some coined by himself), calculations of latitude made with the aid of an astrolabe, distances between points, descriptions of the lay of the coastline, information on wind direction, water depths and currents. . . . The log [of his 1557 voyage] is even more detailed than the earlier one. Taken together the two logs could have provided an excellent basis for a chart of the waters of north-northeastern Russia.

William Borough is known to have drawn up six charts altogether, two of which have long been lost. One of his surviving charts is of northern Scandinavia and north Russia, extending from Trondheim to Novaya Zemlya, which Baron concludes was made in 1567–8.[78] This is the one that, in its delineation of the topography, stands up remarkably well to the modern Admiralty chart.[79]

AN ASSESSMENT OF STEPHEN BOROUGH'S METHODS AND FINDINGS

Longitude is not mentioned anywhere in Stephen Borough's accounts of the 1556 or 1557 voyages. It seems, therefore, that he did not use Dee's traverse table at all.

He recorded his distances run and his directions meticulously, and he observed his latitudes on a regular basis, but there is no evidence at all that he attempted to calculate his longitudes. One may imagine that, in the very difficult circumstances under which he was working, any attempt to sit down and tackle the problems of establishing longitude would have been too much.

There were very few people alive at the time who could have done more – only one or two geniuses, such as John Dee, who could understand the calculations for, or the importance of, global position-fixing.[80]

CONCLUSION

As Andrews commented, 'The great Elizabethan navigators tend to stand out like shining lights against a dim background: Chancellor, the Boroughs, Davis, Drake and a few more.'[81] Unfortunately, Chancellor was drowned, and so it fell to the Boroughs to lead the way and set the standard of navigation and of surveying for others to follow.

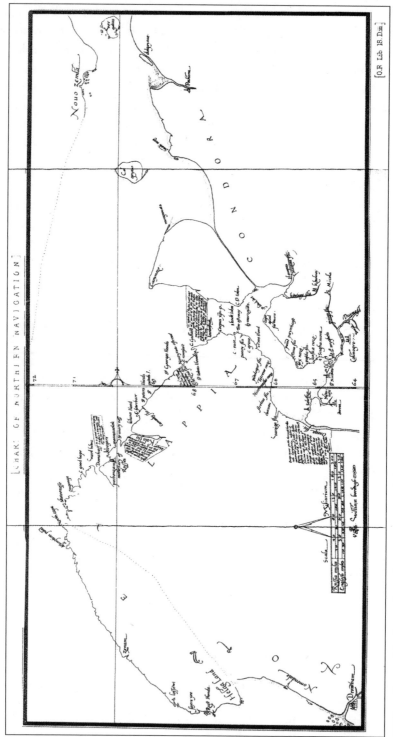

William Borough's chart of northern waters, probably drawn in 1567–8.

What Stephen and his brother were doing was basically plane sailing. They recorded and plotted their distances and directions, and they supplemented these basic observations with a series of latitude readings. They had been equipped with traverse tables by John Dee, by means of which they could have calculated their longitudes, but they did not do so. They stuck to what they had learned and knew, and they did it well. It was the Borough brothers who opened the gates of English exploration and showed what a great deal could be done by careful observation and plane-sailing navigation.

CHAPTER 10

The Muscovy Company

The establishment of the Muscovy Company was one of the major consequences of the first voyage of exploration in 1553. The Muscovy Company was founded in 1555, which was before Stephen Borough made his voyages in the *Serchthrift*, so we must now step back a couple of years to look at its beginnings.

THE EARLY DAYS OF THE MUSCOVY COMPANY

Richard Chancellor and Stephen Borough had a lot to report when they returned to England in the summer of 1554. The expedition that they began the previous year could have been seen as a disaster. The original investors had had high hopes of starting a rich trade with the Orient. Each one of them had invested £25 (equivalent to perhaps £15,000 in today's money), but now the merchants learned that the expedition had not discovered a route to Cathay and that only one of the three ships that they had sent out had returned.

On the other hand, they did hear the surprising news that the expedition had found a route to Russia, and that Chancellor had brought back a general permission to trade there, free of any customs or other dues. At that time Russia was almost completely unknown in the West, and the discovery of a route thither was utterly unexpected. While he had been in Russia, Chancellor had done his best to find out as much as he could about the country, its people and their ways, and he wrote a lengthy report of his travels for the benefit of the merchants.[1] He made another report of his experiences to Clement Adams (who took it down in Latin),[2] and John Hasse wrote a detailed report on the coins and weights and measures that were used in Russia.[3] Hasse had even gone so far as to suggest the town that he thought would be most suitable as a base for the Muscovy Company – Vologda. He gave a number of reasons for recommending Vologda, the main one being that he thought 'all things will there be had the better cheape by the one half'.[4]

PREVIOUS CONTACTS WITH RUSSIA

The London merchants had had no idea that their expedition was going to go anywhere near Russia, and they cannot have had the slightest idea of what Russia, or Muscovy, could possibly be like.

Until about 1235, most of what is now western Russia had been governed from Kiev. From then onwards, until 1478, the whole of what is now Russia, as well as most of what is now Poland, had been under the Tartars, and during that time it had been virtually cut off from any contact with Europe. There had been a few European travellers in Asia, the most famous of whom was Marco Polo, but they had almost without exception headed east to Mongolia and China and had bypassed Russia. It was not until 1478, when Ivan III (1462–1505, 'the Great') finally managed to throw off the yoke of the Tartars and make Moscow an independent Grand Duchy, that any contacts developed, but even then she still remained largely isolated from the rest of Europe, and particularly isolated from England, France and Spain.

There had been a few contacts.[5] German and Polish merchants had come every year along 'the German Road', which went by sea from Lübeck to Riga, then overland to Novgorod, to buy Russian furs. Maxim the Greek (Michael Trivolis) arrived in Moscow in 1506. He was a monk who had spent ten years in Vatopedi Monastery on Mount Athos translating religious texts before he went to Moscow to translate various Byzantine Greek texts into Russian, but he soon fell foul of the Orthodox Church authorities there, and he had to do his translations from prison for the next thirty years.[6] Marco Foscarini, an Italian, had been in Moscow in 1537, and a few other Italians were still there, as well as a few Germans, Greeks and Jews who had reached Moscow before the English arrived there in 1555.[7] The contacts were very limited.

There had been a small amount of diplomatic activity. Moscow had sent several embassies to visit the Holy Roman Emperor Charles V in Spain, and one of these had travelled via England in 1524. Moscow had also sent embassies to Rome, to try to set up a marriage between Ivan III and Sophia Fominischna Palaiologa, the daughter of the last Roman Emperor of Byzantium, who had fled to Rome to get away from the Turks.[8]

Nicholas Poppel from Breslau had visited Moscow in 1486 as a representative of the Hanseatic League, and the Hapsburgs had also sent embassies to Russia (including von Herberstein, who went there in 1512 and again in 1526) to sue for Russian assistance against the Turks. Other embassies to Moscow had been sent from Venice (also concerned about the Turks), from the Vatican and from Denmark and Sweden.[9] However, none of these fleeting contacts had done much to lift the veil of mystery that surrounded Russia. Chaucer may have written of knightly adventures in Lithuania and the borders of Russia, but in the minds of the merchants of London, Russia must have seemed like a very distant and almost unimaginable prospect.

THE DIFFICULT DECISION:
WHETHER TO SET UP A COMPANY TO TRADE WITH RUSSIA

There must have been many serious discussions among the merchants in the summer and autumn of 1554, as they tried to judge the advisability or otherwise of setting up a trading enterprise with a country which they knew so little about and which was some 2,000 miles away, across seas that had apparently already swallowed two of the three ships that they had sent out. The anxious merchants undoubtedly questioned Chancellor and Stephen Borough very closely to learn everything they could.

Sebastian Cabot would also have been involved in many of the discussions. He may have been 80 years old but he was still lively, the grand old man of the enterprise. It was he who had masterminded the expedition from which Chancellor and Stephen had just returned. Sir George Barne and William Garrard, the two 'principall doers' of the 1553 expedition, must have been much involved in the debate too.

The London merchants would also have borne down heavily on their colleagues who had actually been to Russia on board the *Edward Bonaventura*. They were George Burton, the Cape merchant (or captain of the merchants), who was also one of the twelve counsellors of the expedition,[10] and Arthur Edwards, who was a grocer and who in later years was employed by the company as an agent (he eventually died in the service of the company at Astrakhan in 1580).[11] There was also James Delabere, who was a counsellor on the 1553 voyage, Thomas Francis and John Hasse, and the four other men who had sailed in the *Edward Bonaventura* but who were not crew members and may have been either merchants or gentlemen. They were William Kempe, Richard Johnson, Nicholas Newborrow and John Segswike.[12]

All of these would have been questioned by the subscribers to the expedition, and they no doubt discussed and debated among themselves whether to continue with this hazardous undertaking. One can but admire the speed and boldness with which the 200-odd subscribers did eventually change their plans. They were forced to abandon the hope of reaching the riches of the Orient, at least for the time being, and they had to decide whether to try to start trading with Russia, the great unknown.

The *Serchthrift* in 1556, sheltering in the lee of a low and desolate island. (*Drawing by Mark Myers, 2004*)

Borough, the manor house and farm where Stephen Borough was born in 1525. The picture shows the house after Thomas Leigh had enlarged it, in about 1580.

The village square in Northam, c. 1890. Church House is the building to the right of the cart, with the outside stone stairs, which lead up to the schoolroom on the first floor.

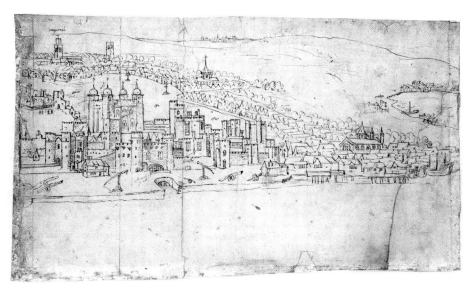

The Thames and the Tower of London in 1543, with Ratcliffe in the distance on the right, on the outside of the first bend in the river below the Tower. Ratcliffe is where the ships of the 1553 expedition were launched and where Stephen Borough lived between 1562 and 1572. (*Drawing by Anthony van den Wyngaerde, c. 1543, Ashmolean Museum, Oxford*)

Small merchant ship by Hans Holbein the Younger, *c.* 1532. The activities on board suggest a 'ship of fools', but the ship is real enough.

The *Dragon*, one of the smaller ships of Henry VIII's navy, of 140 tons, built in 1542.

Ships at Antwerp in 1468. Even as early as this, two of the ships are three-masted.

English ship off Dover in 1538.
The hull appears awkwardly high,
the forecastle is prominent and the
sterncastle even more so. (*Drawing
by John Thompson, 1538*)

The *Teager* (or *Tyger*), a detail
from the 'Smerwick Map', in
1580. She does not have the high
fore- and sterncastles of previous
decades.

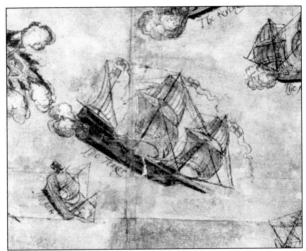

Placentia Palace and the Thames.
(*Drawing by Anthony van den
Wynegaerde*, c. 1550, *Ashmolean
Museum, Oxford*)

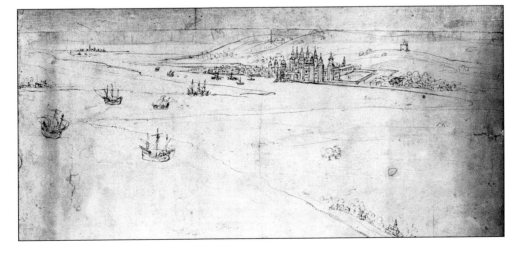

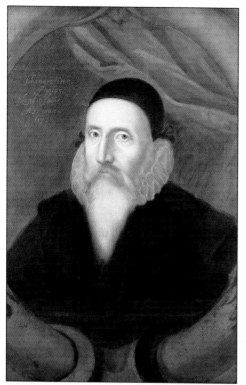

Above, left: Dr John Dee (1527–1608), polymath and cosmographer. He was principal adviser on geography to the 1553 expedition. (*Ashmolean Museum, Oxford*)

Above: Sebastian Cabot (*c.* 1474–1557), the principal organiser of the 1553 expedition. He was the son of John Cabot (*c.* 1450–98), who set foot on mainland America in 1497.

Left: Sir Hugh Willoughby, the 'Captaine Generall of the fleete', a full-length portrait, painted posthumously. Lord Middleton informed me in a letter that one of his forebears in the seventeenth century had portraits painted of some of his illustrious ancestors to hang on his walls, and Sir Hugh Willoughby's is one of them. The gentleman does appear tall, but apart from that, nobody knows how good or bad a likeness the portrait may be.

Olaus Magnus's *Carta Marina* of 1539, one of the very few maps that showed a possible sea route round the north of Scandinavia.

The Old English Court in Moscow, exterior. (*Photo courtesy Mr John Power*)

The three ships of the 1553 expedition sailing up the coast of Norway. They are, from left to right, the *Bona Confidentia* (90 tons), the *Bona Esperanza* (Sir Hugh Willoughby's flagship, 120 tons) and the *Edward Bonaventura* (Richard Chancellor and Stephen Borough, 160 tons). (*Drawing by Mark Myers, 2004*)

In the event, the merchants of London went for the bold option: they seized the opportunity and set about obtaining a Royal Charter, quickly forming a company to take advantage of this new trade.

THE MUSCOVY COMPANY CHARTER

The charter was granted on 26 February 1555. It was 'the Charter of the Marchaunts of Russia, graunted upon the disoverie of the said Country by King Philipe and Quenne Marie'.[13] It gave the merchants 'licence freely to traffique' in 'landes, territories, Iles, Dominions and Seigniories unknowen, and by our subjects before this not commonly by sea frequented, which by the sufferance and grace of Almightie God, it shall chaunce them sailing Northwards, Northeastwards, and Northwestwards'.

The consortium of London merchants to whom this charter was granted was basically the same group who had financed the first voyage. There were 213 men and 2 women, most of them merchants of London. They included seven peers of the realm and numerous high officers of state, and just one person from outside the capital – a merchant from Bristol. Sebastian Cabot was named as the first Governor of the company (perhaps roughly analagous to a chairman today), and the first four consuls (to some extent similar to managing directors) included the two 'principall doers' of the original voyage, Sir George Barnes and William Garret (or Garrard); there were twenty-four assistants to the Governor and consuls (acting somewhat as board members do today).

THE FIRST VOYAGE UNDER THE MUSCOVY COMPANY
AUSPICES IN 1555 (THE SECOND VOYAGE TO RUSSIA)

The first voyage of the newly formed company began in May 1555. It consisted of two ships, the *Edward Bonaventura* and the tactfully named *Philip and Mary*. The *Edward Bonaventura*, the same ship as had survived the 1553 expedition, had already been loaded with trade goods when, on 1 May 1555, 'the whole [Muscovy] Company assembled in open court' to approve the instructions to be given to the fleet and to appoint Richard Chancellor to be 'the Grand Pilote of the fleete'.

The instructions given by the company were very explicit. John Buckland, who had been Stephen Borough's mate on the 1553 expedition, was appointed master of the *Edward Bonaventura*. The company sent out Richard Gray and George Killingworth as their first two agents in Russia, and sent

John Brooke, a merchant, in the *Philip and Mary*, to be their agent at Wardhouse. He was to enquire into the possibility of trading English 'cloth, meale, salt or beere' for 'a large quantity of fish, drie or wet' or 'traine oyle' (usually whale oil, particularly oil from the Northern Right whale).

The company gave instructions that the *Edward Bonaventura* was to proceed to St Nicholas and return to England in the same year, i.e. not to overwinter in Russia; Chancellor was to travel to Moscow with Gray and Killingworth and to present letters from Philip and Mary (written in Greek, Polish and Italian) to the Emperor, asking him 'to confirme and graunt such other liberties and privileges to the Company as the Agents requested'; trading houses were to be set up where practicable; and detailed instructions were given about when and how discipline was to be kept, how the accounts were to be kept and such like. They were enjoined to learn as much as possible about the goods, the merchandise and the coins, weights and measures used in Russia, and to trade as best they could.[14]

The company had not by any means given up hope of reaching China and the Orient, and they ordered the agents to 'use all wayes and meanes possible to learne howe men may passe from Russia, either by land or by sea to Cathaia'.[15]

They were also to enquire about Sir Hugh Willoughby, and to give him and his crews any assistance that might be required. (The company in London did not yet know that he and his crews were already dead.)

The company's instructions gave little detail about the wares that the English took out with them to trade with, but George Killingworth tells us more in a letter that he wrote home a little later (see below).

RUSSIAN PELTRIES

The Muscovy Company certainly catered for the demand for furs, or 'Russian peltries' as they were called. The demand had existed since before the Muscovy Company was created, and the evidence for this is in several famous portraits, as Hamel has pointed out.[16] For instance, three of Hans Holbein's portraits show the sitters proudly displaying their furs: Warnham, Bishop of Winchester, who died in 1532; Chancellor Sir Thomas More, who was executed in 1535; and Anne Boleyn, who was also executed, in 1536. All three show off their valuable furs in their portraits, demonstrating that demand already existed, and such conspicuous consumption can only have excited a desire for more. (It is possible that the advent of the 'Little Ice Age', which is now considered to have started about 1550, may also have had something to do with the trend.) Elizabeth later prohibited the wearing of any fur that had not been produced in England, but this proscription does not seem to have been very effective.

GEORGE KILLINGWORTH'S LETTER REPORTING
ON THE 1555 VOYAGE

The early results of the 1555 voyage were reported back from Moscow to the company in London in a letter written by George Killingworth, dated 27 November 1555, and carried for him by a 'merchant of Terwill' in Polonia (Poland).[17] In those days letters could be sent home from Moscow overland via Poland and Smolensk.[18] He gives no information about the storms and other perils that they faced on the outward voyage. He mentions only that on arrival at Colmogro, William the cook fell into the River Dwina and was drowned.[19]

In his letter Killingworth reports that they had brought all their wares as far south as Vologda, where, to begin with, they rented a warehouse to store them (from September to Easter, for 10 roubles).[20, 21] Vologda was where John Hasse had recommended that the company should make its trading headquarters, and anyway they could not take the goods any further south because the roads were impassable to goods traffic until the winter. Killingworth mentions that they had broadcloths and sugar for sale, and he specifically mentions 'the Emperor's sugar', which was probably a special consignment sent as a gift to His Majesty. He describes in some detail the splendid reception and banquet they were given when at last they reached Moscow. The Tsar was particularly impressed by the great length of George Killingworth's beard, as well he might be, as it measured 5 feet and 2 inches long.[22] Killingworth also mentions that they were warned by some Italians 'to take heed whom we did trust', and he also mentions that the Emperor was 'troubled with preparations to warres'.[23] The Tsar's preoccupation with war was a topic that was to recur several times over the years in his contacts with the Muscovy Company.

Killingworth mentions that he bought wax at 6*d* a Russian pound, the Russian pound being somewhat less than the English one, and that he had bought 5cwt of yarn at 8¼*d* per Russian pound. He also mentions that a 'butte of Hollocke' destined for the Emperor was lost when a sled overturned. (Hollock was a kind of sweet red Spanish wine.)[24]

THE PRIVILEGES THAT THE TSAR GRANTED TO THE
MUSCOVY COMPANY IN 1555

The requests in the letters from Philip and Mary were discussed between Killingworth and the Tsar's Secretary and his 'under Chancelor', as Killingworth calls him. Eventually the Tsar granted them everything that they requested: the right to travel and to trade anywhere in his kingdom, without paying any tolls or customs duties; to have the monopoly of English trade; to set up trading stations or 'factories' in various places; the right to employ local people as boatmen, storekeepers, wagoners or whatever; and the right to govern their own people by English law.[25] The Tsar did not ask for anything in return, at this time.

THE FIRST COMPANY PROPERTIES IN RUSSIA

These 'factories' and storehouses were the first footholds outside western Europe of what would eventually become England's commercial empire. The two earliest were at Rose Island, opposite St Nicholas, and the premises that Killingworth rented at Vologda for the storage of the company's goods in 1555.

ST NICHOLAS, COLMOGRO AND VOLOGDA

The most northerly house of the English was the warehouse on Rose Island (now called Yagry Island) at the mouth of the great Dvina river. 'Rose Island is full of Roses, damask and red, of violets and wild Rosemarie: This island is neere 7 or 8 miles about, and good pasture . . . the Island hath Firre and Birch, and a faire fresh spring neere the house built there by the English.'[26] For the first year or so, the English may have used an existing building on Rose Island to store their wares, as it was not until the winter of 1555–6 that discussions were held in Moscow about obtaining permission from the Tsar to erect any buildings at Rose Island, Colmogro, Vologda or in Moscow.[27]

Opposite Rose Island, on the mainland shore, stood St Nicholas, variously described as a convent or abbey. Some thirteen years later Thomas Randolfe wrote of St Nicholas that 'There standeth an abbey of Monkes to the number of twenty, built all of wood. Their church is faire. Their own houses are low and small roomes. . . . They are much given to drunkenesse, unlearned, write they can, preach they doe never. . . . Towne or habitation at St. Nicholas there is none more than about four houses neere the abbey, and another built by the English Company for their owne use.'[28]

From Rose Island heavy, flat-bottomed barges (doshnikes and nassadas) were rowed, towed, poled or sailed slowly up the Dvina river some 100 miles to Colmogro.[29] The company set up a rope factory there in 1557 and within a few years had built a house, with the Tsar's permission, and this was confirmed in a later grant.[30] By 1568 an English visitor could report that at

Colmogro 'The English have lands of their own given by the Emperor and many fair houses with offices for their company, built all of wood',[31] and in 1605 another visitor found 'surely the largest, tytest and fairest . . . of wharehouses, ambarres and workhouses'.[32] Colmogro was then a great mart for many of the northern districts of Russia, to which came Lapps, Samoyeds, Karelians, Russians and Tartars to trade in fish, fur, feathers and oil.

From Colmogro water transport continued for 1,000 versts (about 600 miles) up the Dvina, and then up its tributary, the Sukhona, to Vologda.[33] Anthony Jenkinson made this river journey in 1557. It took him thirty-six days, and he describes how 'All the way I never came in house, but lodged in the wilderness, by the rivers side, and caried provision for the way. And he that will travell those wayes, must carie with him an hatchet, a tinder boxe, and a kettle, to make fire and seethe meate, when he hath it: for there is small succour in those parts, unlesse it be in townes'.[34]

At Vologda the company built a large warehouse and 'factory' on land given to them by the Tsar.[35] They also, a little later, in 1566–7, obtained permission to construct iron foundries at Wichida (or Vutschegda), to work the iron ore north-east of Vologda.[36]

The best time to travel from Vologda to Moscow was in winter, when it was described as 'an easy and pleasant passage in sleds . . . in which a man, though he go at a Hackney pace, may as easily reade as slepe'.[37]

At other times of year, it was still possible to travel to Moscow by circuitous waterways for some of the route, but part of the journey inevitably involved overland travel with carts (telugas), which was incredibly slow and laborious owing to the prodigious mud.

By late 1555 the company had two trading posts, at Vologda and Colmogro, and by 1561 it had a chain of trading stations extending south from St Nicholas some 100 miles by water to Colmogro, and from there another 600 by river to Vologda, and from there about 250 miles overland to Moscow, where the company had another house by 1561.[38] (By 1566, only five years later, they also had trading stations at Jaroslav, Kostroma, Nijni Kazan, Astrakhan, Novgorod, Pskov, Narva and Dorpat.)[39]

THE MUSCOVY COMPANY HOUSE IN MOSCOW

The first company house in Moscow was almost certainly made of wood. Originally nearly all the houses in Moscow were of wood, which was at least warm and cheap. They were described as being 'rude' (i.e. low-status), low and roofed with shingle, and most of them were surrounded by spacious courtyards and gardens. In theory, the streets were about 40 feet wide, to

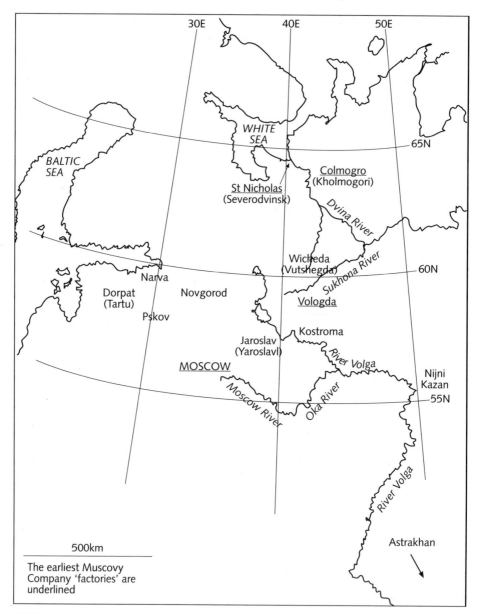

Within about twenty years from 1553, the trading stations or 'factories' of the Muscovy Company extended from the north to the south of Russia.

reduce the risk of fire, and paved with logs to counteract the mud, but in practice they were narrower and very treacherous with mud, especially when the snow melted in the spring.[40]

This first Muscovy Company trading post and headquarters in Moscow was in the then merchants' or 'foreign' (or 'German') quarter, in the Kitai-Gorod district, near the Yoniga river, which was then navigable and flowed into the Moscow river. It was more or less where the Nikolskaya Ulitsa is today.[41] I believe that all traces of it have long since disappeared, and indeed this may have happened as early as 1571, when the Tartars succeeded in setting fire to Moscow, at which time the company sustained heavy losses of life and property.[42]

In view of Moscow's turbulent history, it seems quite amazing that any houses from that time still stand. However, one of the buildings that has survived is 'The English House'. It was granted to the company, rent free, by Ivan the Terrible, in a grant of 1567.[43] It was very extensively restored in the 1990s. It is now the 'Museum of the History of Moscow' and is referred to as the 'Old English Court' or the 'English Ambassadorial Court'. The two titles for the building reflect its dual function, as it was both the Russian headquarters of the Muscovy Company and the base of the English ambassador to Russia. (For the first thirty years or so of the company's existence, the company's chief agent in Russia was also, *de facto*, the English ambassador.) There is an Official Hall, with an entrance and a wide staircase, and vast storerooms on the lower and upper floors.[44] Queen Elizabeth II and Prince Philip were shown round the 'Old English Court' during their visit to Moscow in October 1994.

THE MUSCOVY COMPANY HEADQUARTERS IN LONDON

The first headquarters of the company in London were in a house 'in the parish of St Dunstan in the East', at Ratcliffe, until 1564,[45] and after that in a house in Seething Lane, until 1580.[46] The first agent in London from 1560 to 1563, and maybe for longer, was a certain William Mericke.[47] The company had its own wharf, St Botolph's Wharf, which it leased, with a crane, from the City of London, at least as early as 1573. This was on the north bank of the Thames, just west of where Watermans Hall and the Custom House now stand, just below London Bridge. St Botolph's Lane now runs towards where the wharf was.[48]

THE VOYAGES IN 1556

The *Edward Bonaventura* and the *Philip and Mary* returned to London later in 1555. The 1556 voyage was the one in which Stephen Borough sailed in the *Edward Bonaventura* as far as Wardhouse. There he transferred into the *Serchthrift*, which parted from the other ships and set off to explore further to the east.

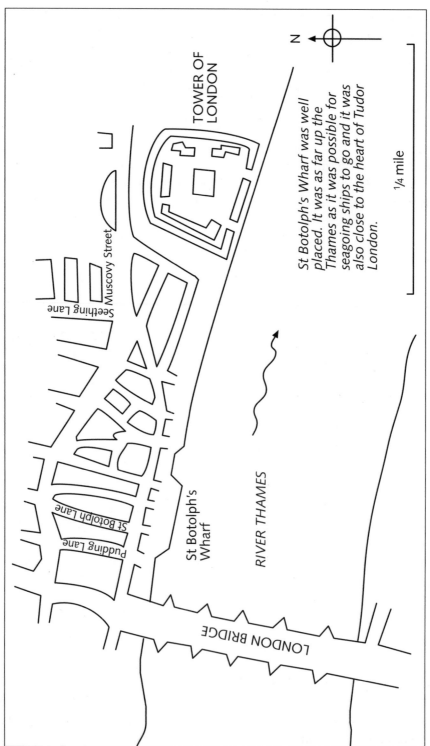

TOWER OF LONDON

Muscovy Street

Seething Lane

St Botolph Lane

Pudding Lane

St Botolph's Wharf

RIVER THAMES

LONDON BRIDGE

N

¼ mile

St Botolph's Wharf was well placed. It was as far up the Thames as it was possible for seagoing ships to go and it was also close to the heart of Tudor London.

The Muscovy Company used St Botolph's Wharf, which was in the centre of London and just downstream from London Bridge, the only bridge in London over the Thames. The first company office was in Ratcliffe but it was moved to a house in Seething Lane in 1564.

The *Edward Bonaventura*, with Chancellor as Pilot and Buckland as master, and the *Philip and Mary* sailed on to St Nicholas in Russia. The ships carried 'extraordinarie masters and saylers to bring home the two ships which were frozen in Lappia, in the river of Arzina aforesaid',[49] i.e. supernumerary crews to man the *Bona Esperanza* and the *Bona Confidentia* and sail them back to England.

On the return voyage, the *Edward Bonaventura* had seventeen Russian passengers on board, including the first Russian ambassador to England. He was Ossip Grigorjevitsch Nepeja, the Boyar of Vologda, and he embarked with a suite of sixteen fellow Russians and a cargo of goods worth £20,000.[50]

THE TRIPLE DISASTER

Disaster struck on this return voyage in 1556. The four ships, the *Edward Bonaventura*, the *Bona Esperanza*, the *Bona Confidentia* and the *Philip and Mary* set off together from St Nicholas on 20 July 1556 and sailed round the North Cape as far as 'Drenton Water' (Trondheim), 'where the saide *Confidentia* was seene to perish on a Rocke'.

The *Bona Esperanza* was thought to have wintered somewhere on the Norwegian coast, but it later transpired that she had vanished without any trace ever being found. The *Philip and Mary* eventually reached London, but not until April the following year, 1557.

The *Edward Bonaventura*, having been at sea for four months, managed to reach the coast of Scotland, off Pitsligo in Aberdeenshire, in November 1556, 'where by outrageous tempests, and extreme stormes, the said ship being beaten from her ground tackles, was driven upon the rockes on shore, where she brake and split in pieces'.[51]

Richard Chancellor was drowned, but not before he had managed to save the life of his Russian passenger, Ossip Nepeja. Richard Chancellor's brave death befitted him. He had been brought up alongside Philip Sidney in the Sidney household, and Philip Sidney was known as the epitome of the Elizabethan gentleman, whose guiding principle was 'virtue in action'.

THE FIRST RUSSIAN AMBASSADOR IN ENGLAND

After the shipwreck of the *Edward Bonaventura* it was three months before Ossip Nepeja reached London from Scotland. When he did at last arrive, he was given a magnificent reception at the Muscovy Company's expense, but he was soon to embroil them in international politics. His activities in London included 'divers secret talks and conferences' with Thomas Thirlby, the Bishop of Ely, and Sir William Petrie, one of the Principal Secretaries of State (who also happened to be a subscribing member of the Muscovy Company). The gist of these talks became apparent over the next few years.[52]

THE CONTRAST BETWEEN THE MUSCOVY COMPANY'S NEEDS AND THE TSAR'S

The Muscovy Company simply wanted to trade profitably with Russia and, if possible, find a practicable route to China and the riches of the Orient.

The Tsar, however, had very different needs – political ones. He had recently, in 1552, conquered the Tartars of the Khanate of Kazan, to his east.[53] He now had warlike ambitions against several more of his neighbours: Sweden, the Holy Roman Empire and the Grand Duchy of Poland and Lithuania to his west, and against the Khanate of Astrakhan near the Caspian Sea to his south-east. In an attempt to further these aims, the Russian ambassador, Ossip Nepeja, made a number of demands to Queen Elizabeth for England's help. The Queen deliberately dragged out the negotiations, but Nepeja and his successors persisted over fifteen years or more. The Tsar wanted an offensive and defensive alliance between England and Russia against his enemies; he wanted the Queen to promise the Tsar a safe haven in England for him, his family and his retinue if ever he should need one; and he wanted skilled men, such as ship-builders, doctors, and apothecaries to be sent to Russia.[54]

The Queen did eventually respond to some of his requests: she sent him some skilled men, and she offered him and his entourage sanctuary in England. She thought that her subjects might be very upset about this, especially if they found out that the Tsar had also offered her refuge in his country, so her offer was made in 'This our secrit lettre whereunto none are privie besides our selfe, but our most secreite councels'; she got the members of the Privy Council all to sign it,[55] which certainly suggests something surreptitious.

THE MARRIAGE NEGOTIATIONS

The Tsar had married his first wife, Anastasia, in 1547; he seemed to have been happy with her, but after she died in 1560 he had five more wives in rapid succession, most of whom died in dubious circumstances or were dispatched to convents. Then, according to Hamel, there were negotiations, in the greatest of secrecy, about an offer of marriage between the Tsar and Elizabeth.[56] Morgan and Coote put it more strongly when they state that 'It is generally known that Ivan solicited the hand of Queen Elizabeth'.[57] The Tsar's first overtures were made in an oral message and then a secret letter entrusted to Anthonie Jenkinson in 1567.

A certain Dr Bomel, or Bomelius, seems to have stirred things up. He had been born at Wesel, in Westphalia, studied medicine at Cambridge and passed as a skilful astrologer. Archbishop Parker had him put in prison in 1570, but he was released on condition that he quit England, which he did, going to Moscow in company with the Russian ambassador Savin. There he developed something of a Rasputin-like relationship with the Tsar. 'He deluded the Emperor, makinge him believe that the Queen of England was younge, and that yt was very favourable for him to marry her.'[58]

The Tsar was very angry when he eventually received a letter from Elizabeth declining his offer.[59] At the end of 1570 he wrote back a very irate letter, complaining bitterly that his concerns had not been properly addressed, that the Queen was apparently ruled by her ministers, and even rudely referring to her maidenly menstrual periods. He also suspended all the Muscovy Company charters and privileges. Bomel's fate is related here in a footnote, so that the squeamish can avoid reading it if they want to.[60]

Ivan continued to complain that none of the various ambassadors from England had done anything to address his personal concerns. For instance, he complained of Thomas Randolfe that 'all his talke with us was about merchants affaires and nothing touching ours'.[61] It should be pointed out that although a number of historians have been convinced that the Tsar made a proposal of marriage to Queen Elizabeth, there is no remaining direct evidence, and Tolstoy in fact categorically denies it. He states that 'The tradition as to [the tsar's] intended marriage with Queen Elizabeth is proved to be entirely without foundation.'[62]

However, eleven years later, in 1581 (when the Tsar was actually married to his seventh wife, though he claimed that the union had no legal status) he sent an ambassador to England to treat for a marriage to Lady Jane Hastings, a niece of Queen Elizabeth's. As a result Lady Jane was mockingly nicknamed 'the Empress of Muscovia' in the English Court and also referred to as 'Lady Mary Huntingdonska'.[63] The fact that she, poor lady, was scarred by smallpox was not the reason that the suit dragged on and on. The negotiations did continue, into 1583, but they got nowhere. All these diplomatic transactions were conducted by the agents of the Muscovy Company, and at the expense of the Muscovy Company.

STEPHEN BOROUGH BECOMES CHIEF PILOT OF
THE MUSCOVY COMPANY

The previous section, concerning the various diplomatic negotiations, has jumped ahead a little. Let us now return to 1556, when Chancellor's death led to Stephen Borough's being appointed as chief pilot to the infant Muscovy Company. Richard Chancellor had been a gentleman, intelligent and practical, who had been trained to the job of chief pilot on the training voyage of the *Bark Aucher* organised by Cabot,[64] and he had doubtless learned a great deal in the sessions he spent creating a table of ephemerides under the guidance of John Dee.[65]

His replacement, Stephen Borough, was effectively a promotion from the ranks, a 'tarpaulin captain'. As Scammell points out, there were other examples of such upward social mobility in English maritime circles during Tudor times, including Frobisher, Cross, and Drake.[66] Such mobility was possible in England, and it has been said that it was one feature that distinguished English society from that of the rest of Europe: it afforded relatively easy access for self-made men to power and status, i.e. England had an 'open elite'.[67]

Stephen Borough's promotion to chief pilot meant that he now had the reponsibility to see that the company's ships managed to sail the 2,000 miles or more from London to St Nicholas each year, and that they returned in safety. He had become a member of the Muscovy Company by paying in a subscription of £25 on or before 26 February 1555.[68]

THE VOYAGE OF 1557

What makes this voyage particularly interesting is that by this date the company's agents in London and in Russia had more understanding of the commodities to be traded and the prices that were likely to prevail, and some of these are described in more detail.

This time the company's instructions, dated 3 May 1557, were issued in the name of the lieutenant (not the governor) of the company, together with the consuls and assistants. This was very probably due to the fact that the Governor, Sebastian Cabot, was dying or already dead when the instructions were being drawn up.

Four ships were sent in 1557: the *Primrose* with Anthonie Jenkinson as captain general of the fleet; the *John Evangelist*; the *Anne*; and the *Trinitie*. The names of the owners of the ships are listed in the instructions.[69] The company was not using its own ships for this voyage, as it had done on previous ones, but was chartering them. It was probably forced to charter ships because it could not afford to buy new ones after the loss of three of their ships the previous year.

The ships were instructed to keep within sight of each other as far as possible, presumably owing to the constant fear of pirates. The detailed instructions include several interesting passages, one of which refers to problems at Wardhouse, the Danish outpost and fortress at the northern tip of Norway: 'Special foresight is to be had, that at the Wardhouse no treacherie, invasion, or other peril of molestation be done or procured to be attempted to our ships by any kings, princes, or companies, that do mislike this new found trade by seas to Russia, or would let & hinder the same: whereof no small boast hath bene made.'[70]

The instructions go on to advise against putting in at Wardhouse at all if it could be avoided.

It is not clear from these instructions what exactly the threats against the company were, but an event in Poland in April of the following year, 1558, throws some light on the matter. Thomas Alcocke, an employee of the Muscovy Company, was travelling overland from Moscow to England on horseback, via Poland and the kingdom of Denmark, when he was arrested near Terwill in Poland. Most of his money and possessions were taken, and after five weeks in fetters he was interrogated by 'one of the Lordes of Danske (Denmark)': 'Then they burdened mee, that wee brought thither thousandes of ordinance, as also of harneis, swordes, with other munitions of warre.' Alcocke told his interrogators that the only things they had carried were 'about one hundred shirts of mayle, such olde thinges newe scowred as no man in England woulde weare'. Perhaps they believed him. After his release Alcocke discovered that various 'Ambassadours from the townes of Danske, Lubeck, and Hamburgh, as also out of Liefland' were determined 'to stoppe all such shippes as shoulde goe out of England for Moscovia'.[71] Alcocke had been fortunate to be released alive, and the threats against the company at Wardhouse had almost certainly been due to the fear of gun-running.

GUN-RUNNING?

The Tsar wanted guns and ammunition. There survives, for instance, a letter of his from 1567 in which he asks 'that the Q.ma-tie [Queen's Majestie] would suffer him to have out of England all kynde of Artillerie and things necessarie for warre'.[72] Elizabeth and her advisers were faced with a difficult choice. They could not afford to antagonise Sweden, the Holy Roman Empire or the Grand Duchy of Poland and Lithuania by assisting the Tsar to make war against them, but neither did they wish to jeopardise the prospects of the new-found trade with Russia by denying the Tsar's requests. Elizabeth responded in the only way she could: she procrastinated for year after year. Whether she ever did send the Tsar any of the guns he wanted remains unresolved, though there are strong suspicions that she did.

In Europe there were rumours that she had in fact sent guns to Russia, and that these had enabled the Tsar to attack Livonia in 1558 and to capture Narva, the port that gave him access to the Baltic. Sigismund, King of Poland, was convinced that Elizabeth had been shipping guns to Russia. He wrote her several letters complaining bitterly about it. One of them contains the sentence 'The muscovite . . . made more perfect in warlike affaires with engines of warre and shippes will make assaulte this way on Christendom.'[73] Similar complaints came from King Frederick of Denmark in 1565 and King Eirik of Sweden.[74] In 1561 the Senates of Hamburg and Cologne informed Elizabeth of complaints from certain princes of the Holy Roman Empire that the arms she was buying in Germany were being sent to Russia. The Senate of Hamburg stopped the shipment of arms until it was assured that they were intended only for the Queen's service.[75] The Queen found it necessary to write to the Senate of Hamburg denying these allegations, and similar letters were also sent to Sigismund, Frederick and Eirik, but still the rumours persisted, becoming so rife that in July 1561 she sent William Hertle to Antwerp, Amsterdam and Bremen specifically to try to refute them.[76] Some of the Muscovy Company ships are known to have carried cargoes of sulphur and lead to Russia, presumably for making gunpowder and bullets.[77] It is more than possible that they also carried guns, in the greatest possible secrecy, in order not to outrage the Swedes. It is thus possible that Stephen Borough was, among other things, a gun-runner.

There is another secret letter, from 1572, in which Queen Elizabeth almost admitted to supplying guns when she wrote to the Tsar that the Muscovy Company had already supplied him with such commodities 'as her Majestie doth not suffer to be transplanted forth of her realme to no other prince of the world', which certainly suggests something surreptitious, very probably guns.

Commodities and prices of the 1557 voyage

The list of goods that the company sent out to Russia included:

25 fardels [bundles] containing 207 sorting [assorted] clothes, one fine violet in graine and one skarlet, and 40 cottons for wrappers, begining with number 1 and ending with number 52 [sic].

The sorting clothes may cost the first peny [meaning unclear] 5.li. 9.s. the cloth, one with the other.

The fine violet 18.li. 6.s. 6.d.

The skarlet 17.li 13.s. 6.d.

The cottons at 9.li. 10.s. the packe, accompting 7. cottons for a packe.

More 500 pieces of Hampshire kersies, that is 400. watchets [sky-blue cloth], 43 blewes, 53. reds, 15. greenes, 5 ginger colours and 2. yelowes which cost the first penny 4.li. 6.s. the piece and 3. Packes containing 21 cottons at 9.li. 10.s. the packe: . . .

More 9. Barrels of Pewter of Thomas Hasels making, &c.

Also the wares bee packed and laden as is aforesayde, as by an Invoyce in every Shippe more plainly may appeare.[78]

The invoices mentioned above for each of the ships have long since disappeared. The ships must have carried more than is catalogued here, as this list does not include anything like four shiploads of goods.

The company's instructions to the crew for the 1557 voyage

Some of the company's instructions refer to what sort of goods should be purchased for the return voyage:

Lette the chiefest lading of these four shippes be principally in wexe, flaxe, tallow and trayne oil . . . of furres we desire no great plentie . . . as for Felts, we will in no wise you send any . . . in no wise you send any of them [hemp] unwrought, because our fraight is 4.li. a tunne or little less. . . . As for Masts, Tarre, Hempe, Feathers or any such otherlike, they would not beare the charges to have any, considering our deere fraight.[79]

In the event, the return goods were mostly natural raw products: wax, tallow, flax, train oil and furs of various kinds. Wax for candles, for instance, sold at £4 per cwt. Train oil, some of which came from seals rather than whales, sold at £9 per ton. Hemp for cordage and tar both fetched 15s per cwt.[80]

The company had already established that the freight rate for the route was £4 per ton, or a little less, i.e. they calculated that the total cost of transporting a ton of freight from London to St Nicholas (or vice versa) was £4. It is of course vital for any transport business to establish the freight rate for a particular route, because without it, it is impossible to tell what goods can profitably be carried.

The instructions then ask for samples of Russian steel, copper and dyes to be sent to England. The company sent out a skinner to inspect any skins they bought, and they sent two coopers to make barrels to put the train oil and tallow in. They also sent out a young man named Leonard Brian, whose job it was to inspect any yew wood and 'to shewe you in what sorte it must be cut and cloven'.[81]

Another interesting item sent out to the agents in Russia was a book of ciphers. The agents were requested to write back to the company each year before Christmas or Candlemas and to send their letters overland via Moscow, which was the quickest route. The company was already much concerned about rivalry from other enterprises and so the agents were asked to use ciphers when they wrote in their letters anything that might require commercial secrecy. They may have used books of codes or 'cardan grills', which were a favourite method of making ciphers in Tudor times. These were basically pieces of leather with various rectangular holes cut out in them, each hole having a number beside it. The message had to be written in such a way that the secret part could be seen in bits, through each of the numbered holes in order.[82]

Embarkation

This must have been a scene of great activity. While the crew worked on the ship and brought on board ships' stores of various kinds, the company's men carried bales of cloths up the gangplank to two of the pursers, who carefully checked the contents of each load. There were three copies of the bill of lading: one for the ship; one for the agent or factor at the ship's destination; and one for the company's office in St Dunstan's in the East.[83] The lighter loads were dropped down through the hatch to be stowed below. The heavier loads, such as the barrels of pewter, were lowered into the hold, using one of the ship's spars as a crane. (There was a crane at St Botolph's Wharf, but it was probably only used for heavier items, such as cannon.) The hold smelled of tar and of wool. On deck, you could smell wood smoke from the pipe of the cooking stove in the hold, where the cook took advantage of the stationary ship to make a hot meal for the crew before departure.

(All the voyages made by ships of the Muscovy Company in the first thirty years of its existence are listed in Appendix 6.)

ANTHONIE JENKINSON AND OTHER ENGLISHMEN WHO JOURNEYED OVERLAND TO THE EAST

The Muscovy Company had, for the time being, abandoned its efforts to find a sea route to the Orient, instead determining to try to find a land route there. It therefore employed Anthonie Jenkinson, and later Christopher Borough and others, to try to find that route. As William Hertle described it, the company still hoped 'to attain Cathayia by a nearer route than the world yet knew'.[84]

Anthonie Jenkinson has already been mentioned as the captain general of the company's fleet in 1557. He was a truly remarkable man, who had already visited most of the countries in the Middle East before he was employed by the Muscovy Company. In 1557 he was appointed for three years, at £40 per annum, to be the captain general of the Muscovy Company fleet, and he made a number of expeditions on the company's behalf.[85]

His two major explorations were overland, via St Nicholas. In 1557–9 he travelled to Boghar (Bukhara, now in Uzbekistan) via Nijny Novgorod and Kazan, down the Volga in boats (called 'stroogs') to Astrakhan, where he bought a boat and sailed across the Caspian Sea, where he joined a caravan of 1,000 camels and crossed the Oxus river to Bokhara (on 'the silk road' and about 100 miles west of Samarkand), surviving attacks by robbers, storms and other hazards, both on the outward and on the return journeys.[86] He reported that he was unable to go further east owing to the 'uncessant and continuall warres, which are in all these brutal and wilde countreys, that it is at this present impossible to passe, neither went there any Caravan from Boghar that way these three years'.[87]

Jenkinson travelled again, in 1561, with the intention of setting up trade with the Grand Sophie of Persia. This time he travelled via Moscow and Astrakhan, south over the Caspian Sea to Derbent and on to Kasvin (Qasvin, about 100 miles north-west of Tehran), where he met the Grand Sophie.[88] The company continued to trade with Persia by this extremely tenuous route for the next twenty years, and it was only abandoned when the Mediterranean reopened and the Levant Company took over the eastern trade.

Jenkinson was also sent, on two occasions, as a trusted ambassador to manage some particularly difficult negotiations with the Tsar in Moscow, in 1566–7[89] and again in 1571–2.[90]

Other agents of the company who were sent on expeditions to Persia included Thomas Alcock et al. in 1563,[91] Richard Johnson et al. in 1565,[92] Arthur Edwards et al. in 1568,[93] Thomas Banister in 1569–74,[94] and Morgan Hubblethorne in 1579[95] (though in Hubblethorne's case there is no evidence that he ever actually made the journey).[96]

Christopher Borough, Stephen's son, was also sent to Persia, and he wrote the chronicle of his journey there in 1579–81. He travelled from St Nicholas to Vologda and Yaroslav (north of Moscow), and thence to Astrakhan, and by ship to Derbend and Baku, two ports on the shores of the Caspian Sea. At Derbend he traded for silks, and at Baku he encountered the religion of fire-worshippers. He survived numerous tribulations on his journey, and he noted

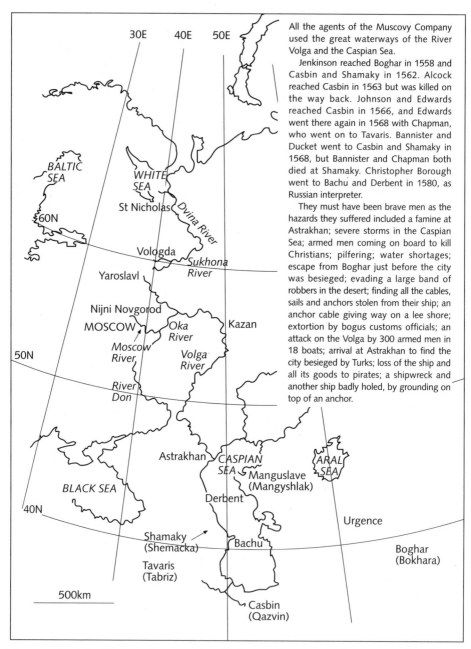

All the agents of the Muscovy Company used the great waterways of the River Volga and the Caspian Sea.

Jenkinson reached Boghar in 1558 and Casbin and Shamaky in 1562. Alcock reached Casbin in 1563 but was killed on the way back. Johnson and Edwards reached Casbin in 1566, and Edwards went there again in 1568 with Chapman, who went on to Tavaris. Bannister and Ducket went to Casbin and Shamaky in 1568, but Bannister and Chapman both died at Shamaky. Christopher Borough went to Bachu and Derbent in 1580, as Russian interpreter.

They must have been brave men as the hazards they suffered included a famine at Astrakhan; severe storms in the Caspian Sea; armed men coming on board to kill Christians; pilfering; water shortages; escape from Boghar just before the city was besieged; evading a large band of robbers in the desert; finding all the cables, sails and anchors stolen from their ship; an anchor cable giving way on a lee shore; extortion by bogus customs officials; an attack on the Volga by 300 armed men in 18 boats; arrival at Astrakhan to find the city besieged by Turks; loss of the ship and all its goods to pirates; a shipwreck and another ship badly holed, by grounding on top of an anchor.

The agents of the Muscovy Company travelled great distances in the pursuit of trade and to try and find a land route to Cathay and the riches of the Orient.

the decay of Persia and the growth of Turkish power.[97] His account also includes his measurements of the latitudes and compass variations of the places he visited.[98] His account was 'sent to his uncle, M. William Burrough' (which is another small confirmation that he was Stephen Borough's son).[99]

THE FINANCIAL PROGRESS OF THE MUSCOVY COMPANY

The company continued in business for many years, but it could hardly have been described as flourishing at any time. There must presumably have been some 'dividends' paid out, but there is little evidence of them, and in fact the subscribers were called upon for more money on a number of occasions. These further calls for cash are shown, for instance, in Sir William Cecil's memorandum book:

£25 on 5 April 1555 [the initial subscription]
£5 on 26 July 1555
£15 in 1556
£30 on 11 March 1557
£40 more by 1564
£60 in 1564 [specifically to develop the trade with Persia]
£50 in 1570
£200 on 21 March 1572.[100]

In retrospect, it is difficult to understand why any of the subscribers should have continued to pay out these vast sums of money when they were apparently getting little or nothing in return. Of course, not all of them could or did stump up, but many of them did, including worldly-wise characters like William Cecil.

RÉSUMÉ OF THE LATER HISTORY OF THE MUSCOVY COMPANY

The Muscovy Company was not finally wound up until 1917, although it went through a number of changes and even complete reformations before then. Throughout its existence the company suffered from the long sea journey to its trading stations, or 'factories', in Russia. Its ships could only ever hope to make one delivery a year, and each entailed a long and hazardous voyage. Another on-going problem that the company complained bitterly about on occasion was the tolls it had to pay to the kingdom of Denmark at the entrance to the Baltic. In 1568 one company agent wrote,

'This trade [by the northern route] . . . will furnish the Queen's navy with cables, cordage, masts, sails, pitch and tar whereby her Grace is delivered out of the bondage of the King of Denmark and the town of Dantzig.'[101]

One potential problem that the company does not seem to have had too much trouble with was piracy. Piracy was rife in those times: it was a quick way to get rich and there was virtually no law of the seas, and very few attempts were made to suppress pirates. Perhaps the company's ships were sufficiently well armed to deter any potential attacks, and they also sailed, as far as they could, in small convoys. (William Borough was in charge of one of the very few attempts that were made to suppress pirates. He sailed to the Gulf of Bothnia in 1570 with thirteen armed merchantmen and attacked a nest of pirates there. He was highly successful, capturing four of the six pirate ships, burning another and taking eighty-three men prisoner).[102]

Another potential problem for the company might have been competition from the Hanseatic League. The League had at one time been the controlling power in trade over a huge area extending from Iceland to Bergen and Novgorod, south through the Baltic, and across to Hull, Norwich, London, Bruges and many ports on the western seaboard of Europe. The League still traded in Russian goods between Novgorod and their 'Steelyard' in London, but by 1555 it had lost much of its power and many of its trading privileges. There do not appear to have been any serious clashes between the infant Muscovy Company and the waning Hanseatic League.[103]

The Russians gained a port on the Baltic when they captured Narva in 1558; the Muscovy Company sent ships to trade there, but so did many other English merchants. The Muscovy Company considered them as interlopers, or 'outleapers', and there was a protracted legal battle about whether the Muscovy Company's monopoly rights to trade with Russia included the port of Narva. Eventually, in 1566, the company won when an Act of Parliament not only confirmed its earlier privileges but also gave it a monopoly of the Narva trade. The main imports from Narva were nautical supplies: masts, spars and other timber for ships; pitch and tar; hemp for ropes; poldavies (a coarse canvas); and flax.[104]

Until 1581, when the Russians lost the port again, the company also used Narva as the base for its trade with Persia. This was profitable, despite the enormous length and uncertainty of the route, which stretched some 600 miles from Narva across country to the Volga, about 1,000 miles down the Volga, and a further 600 miles across the Caspian Sea to Persia.[105]

The Muscovy Company traded large quantities of naval supplies from Russia. It has been said that 'the fleet that defeated the Spanish Armada was largely rigged with Russian cordage and cables', and nearly all of this was supplied by the Muscovy Company.[106] The problem with these commodities, particularly in the early years of Queen Elizabeth's reign (which began in 1558) was that the company had to wait a very long time, years sometimes, before they received any payment for these supplies, due to Elizabeth's strained finances.[107]

Another problem for the company was the troubles in Flanders that were a major blow to all branches of English trade. Philip II of Spain had insisted that his subjects in the Netherlands should rejoice in the Catholic faith – and he sent his general, the Duke of Alva, with a large army to enforce his will. The resulting conflict effectively closed Antwerp, the hub of England's export trade, which led to a financial crisis that lasted from 1569 to 1574.

Another problem that surfaced from time to time, at least to some extent, was private trading by the company's employees and agents, that is trading in their own goods without paying the freight charges. Even Stephen Borough was involved. On one voyage in 1571 he had private trade of 72 short cloths, and Anthonie Jenkinson had 135 kerseys.[108] These goods must have occupied space in the ship's hold but brought no profit to the company.

Problem followed problem. The Tsar, for a time, rescinded all the Muscovy Company's privileges in 1570. The company had to be reorganised, and a new joint stock company was formed.

Another setback occurred in 1571 when the Tartars succeeded in entering and setting fire to Moscow. The destruction was so complete that it was said that 'not a post was left to which a horse could be fastened'.[109] The company sustained the loss of twenty-five men, women and children who died 'stifeled in our beer-cellar', as well as the loss of some 10,000 roubles' worth of merchandise.[110]

From 1581 onwards competition also came from the Levant Company. The Mediterranean had previously been blocked to English ships by the pirate Barbarossa (or 'Redbeard', Khair-ed-din) and his Ottoman Turkish fleet, but in 1571, against the odds, the Turkish fleet had been defeated at the Battle of Lepanto. English ships could once more sail to Aleppo and other ports in the Levant to buy spices, and in 1581 the Levant Company was formed with a monopoly on trade in the region. As a direct result the Muscovy Company stopped trading to Persia. From 1600 onwards the Muscovy Company also had competition from the East India Company, which brought spices directly from the Moluccas round the Cape of Good Hope.

The French were also active in the Baltic trade. The customs records from the Sound at the entrance to the Baltic, controlled by Denmark, show for instance that between 1578 and 1581 more than 200 French ships passed through each year. The French were also potential competitors in the Russian trade, but it was not until 1586 that the first French vessel got as far as St Nicholas, with a merchant called Jehan Sauvage of Dieppe on board. In the same year the first French ambassador, François de Carle, arrived in Moscow: he managed to get permission for the French to use the port of Colmogro, with a 50 per cent reduction of the customs dues there. However, for a number of reasons discussed by Kirchner, the French were never willing or able to mount much of a challenge to the English in the trade to St Nicholas.[111]

The Dutch were very different: they did provide intense competition. Hamel and Unwin both state that the Dutch did not start trading with the Lapps until 1565, and that it was 1577 before they reached the Dvina Estuary.[112] However, it seems that the Dutch had started earlier than that, as Stephen Borough had found Dutchmen already busily trading with the Lapps at Kegor when he arrived there in 1557.[113] Whatever date it was that the Dutch started trading in north Russia, by the beginning of the seventeenth century they had overtaken the English in the trade to the Dvina Estuary.[114] In 1600, for instance, thirteen Dutch ships docked at Archangel'sk against twelve English ones; by 1604 there were seventeen Dutch ships and only nine English; from then onwards the Dutch dominated the trade there.

The Dutch did have some advantages. One was that they used their famous 'fluyt' ships – simple, lightly manned and unarmed merchantmen, which gave them the great advantage of low freight rates. (They could afford to go unarmed as they dealt mostly in bulk goods, which were of little interest to pirates.) The Dutch also had some commercial advantage from their access to the products of Germany, Italy, Spain and Portugal, which meant that they could offer the Russians a variety of goods, such as silk, pepper, spices, sugar and paper, as well as cloth. In 1583 Sir Jerome Bowes claimed that the Dutch merchants used underhand methods to obtain trading privileges from the Tsar. The Dutchmen were accused of having borrowed a small amount of money from three of the Tsar's chief advisers and then paid them 'interest at five and twenty upon the hundred [in other words a continuous bribe, which amounted to 500 marks a year] and the English merchants at that time had not one friend in Court'.[115]

The Muscovy Company turned to other ventures. Some of its members were involved in setting up the Frobisher expeditions of 1576, 1577 and 1578, under the auspices of 'the Company of Cathaia', but this was something of a financial disaster.[116] Morison puts it more succinctly when he says 'all three voyages, which cost the stockholders about £20,160, were complete failures'.[117]

The Muscovy Company still had losses of its own ships and crews to cope with. In 1582, for instance, the entire crew of the *George Bonaventure* were lost. They 'all perished with frost in unseasonable time of year'.[118] Another ship, the *Susan Ann Parnell*, was lost when she burnt down to the waterline in the Port of London in 1590. Apparently what happened was that 'the carpenters boy going down with a candell, which chanced to fall into the oakum, did incontinent take fire and so burned up the ship with her lading down to the water'. This loss cost the company £3,000.[119]

The company's trade did badly during Russia's 'time of troubles' (1598–1613), during which there was a series of crises: civil war, famines, Cossack and peasant revolts, invasion by the Poles and dynastic struggles.

The company developed an interest in whaling and walrus-hunting. The first evidence of this comes in 1575, when William Borough was asked to make a list of how many men and what equipment a 200-ton whaling ship would need. The detailed list that he produced was printed by Hakluyt. It included fifty-five men, their food supplies and many other items, such as five pinnaces, and fifteen 'great javelins'.[120] However, as it happened, the first such expedition was a walrus-hunt on Cherry Island (now Bear Island), organised for the Muscovy Company by Sir Francis Cherry,[121] and it was not until 1604 that the Muscovy Company started whale-fishing.[122] The whaling turned out to be highly successful, especially between 1608 and 1615, when the company paid out an average of 42 per cent per annum to its subscribers.[123] About 1618 the Muscovy Company set up a joint whaling venture with the East India Company, but this failed after only two or three years.

Still hoping to find a usable route to the Orient, the company sent Henry Hudson on two expeditions to investigate. He tried to find such a route via the North Pole in 1607 and via the North-East Passage in 1608, but without success. He tried again, under different sponsors, via the North-East and North-West Passages in 1609 but died on his fourth expedition, trying to find a north-west passage.

In 1630, the company ceased to function on a joint stock basis but continued as a regulated company, in which each merchant traded his own goods on his own acount within a framework of rules for cooperation.

In 1649 the Tsar ended the company's special trading privileges in Russia, and in 1698 it lost its monopoly of the Russian trade in England, but somehow it still survived as an influential institution in the City of London, and in fact it shared in the general revival in Anglo-Russian trade that occurred in the eighteenth century.[124]

It is remarkable that despite its many setbacks and upheavals the Muscovy Company should somehow have survived, in one form or another, for 350 years. It was not wound up until 1917. The Muscovy Company, and the much smaller and very short-lived Africa Company, were the first joint stock companies (and the only ones from 1553 to 1560). Their financial influence on the nation should not be overestimated: it has been calculated that, in those early years, the two companies together only controlled 0.013 per cent of the nation's capital, clearly a very small percentage.[125]

However, it was not the size of the Muscovy Company's operation that was significant so much as the fact that it was the very first of England's big overseas trading companies, and that it survived to become the role model for all the others that came later.

CHAPTER 11

Other Consequences of the First Voyages and Subsequent Attempts on the North-East Passage

G.B. Parkes is one of several authors who have commented on the tremendous consequences of the early voyages of discovery, observing that this was 'the new commercial expansion of England overseas, which we may date from 1553, an expansion which roused the national interest and inspired Hakluyt'.[1] Hakluyt himself had referred to the 1553 expedition as 'that first worthy enterprise'.[2] Nordenskiold, the first man who successfully navigated the whole of the North-East Passage in 1878–9, said of these early expeditions that they were 'the very first germ of the seagoing merchant fleet of England'.[3] Loades put it more poetically when he said that 'the genie of English maritime enterprise, having first escaped from the bottle with official encouragement, could not now be forced back'.[4]

THE JOINT STOCK COMPANIES AND COMMERCIAL EXPANSION

The impetus for the early voyages came from the London merchants who set up the Muscovy Company, which was the first of the English joint stock companies. The Muscovy Company itself had a relatively small effect on Britain's import and export trade, but it was the beginning and it was how it all started. Where it did have an enormous effect was on the commercial organisation of the nation, because it became the model for nearly all the other overseas ventures, some of them small and short-lived, but others as big and powerful as the great East India Company, which eventually brought India, the 'Jewel in the Crown', into the British Empire. As Sir C.P. Lucas put it, 'in the construction of the Empire, joint stock played a part which can hardly be overestimated'.[5] (The English joint stock companies are listed in Appendix 10.)

The Muscovy Company's first trading stations at Vologda and Colmogro were the places where the expansion of the British commercial empire began.

THE EMERGENCE OF THE SEA DOGS

The early voyages by Richard Chancellor and Stephen Borough led to a great surge of interest and of confidence in maritime adventure, to such an extent that the Venetian ambassador in Paris could write in 1588 that 'the English are men of another mettle from the Spaniards and enjoy the reputation of being, above all Western Nations, expert and active in all naval operations, and great sea dogs [*grandissimi guerrieri*]'[6] – and that was written before the Spanish Armada had set sail.

THE SOCIAL EFFECTS OF THE VOYAGES

The social effects of the voyages – the effects they had on the habits, thoughts, attitudes and practices of the English and Russian peoples respectively – are harder to define or evaluate.[7]

The effects on Russia

Madame Lubimenko points out that, in the early days, Anglo-Russian relations were of more importance to the Russians than they were to the English, because, for the Russians, England was the first western European country to open up regular trade and diplomatic contact with them, whereas for England, Russia was just another country to trade with, even if it was exotic and remote.[8] The English who visited or stayed in Moscow for a time – the merchants, the company agents, the doctors and apothecaries – can have had little effect outside the court of Tsar Ivan the Terrible, and they seem also to have had little influence on the Tsar himself, though they did have considerable influence on his famous successor, Peter the Great (1672–1725). He was the first in Russia to take much interest in the achievements of the West; one of his many initiatives was the setting-up of the first Russian ship-building yards, at Archangel'sk.

The other Englishmen in Russia – the architects, ropemakers, coopers and shipwrights – must, by reason of their skills, manners, clothes and customs have had some effect on a limited number of the people of Russia, but it is impossible to point to any hard evidence for this.

The effects on the English

As for the effect of the Russians upon the visiting English, some at least of the visitors found the Russians coarse and savage. Thomas Randolfe, for instance, described the people of Colmogro as 'rude in maners, and in apparell homely' and 'given much to drunkennesse, and all other kinde of abominable vices'.[9] Randolfe had also visited the monks at St Nicholas and found them 'more in drink than in virtue'.[10] George Turbevile gained a similar impression: he wrote of 'A people passing rude, to vices vile inclinde. . . . Drinke is their whole desire, the pot is all their pride.'[11] Richard Chancellor thought Moscow was as big as London, 'but it is very rude and standeth without all order'; of the buildings he thought that 'we have better in all points in England'. He was, however, tremendously impressed by the trappings of the Tsar's palace, and by the power of the Tsar and his attention to the English. He noted the severity of some of the Russian laws, and he also noticed the 'innumerable poore'. He described the Greek Church and how superstitious the Russians were.[12]

Some impressions of Russia seem to have become embedded in English minds. For instance, John Milton (1608–74) had the ice in the Kara Sea in mind in his *Paradise Lost* when he wrote:

> Mountains of ice, that stop th'imagined way
> Beyond Petsora eastward, to the rich
> Cathaian coast. . . .[13]

THE NEW TRADES

The opening of trade with Russia demonstrated a new, dynamic spirit in England's commerce, a surge in the nation's confidence.[14] The main body of English overseas trade in the second half of the sixteenth century was with western Europe, and it was largely cloth that was exported, and wine and manufactured goods that were imported.

The new trades with Russia and Africa, and later with America, the East Indies and the Levant, were all relatively small in volume at this time, but they were different in character. They brought in a great variety of goods, some of them exotic, from far-away countries, including cordage, tallow and wax from Russia, currants and silks from the Levant, sugar from Barbary and spices from the East Indies. In return, the English at first exported cloth, but before long they began to respond to the demands for manufactured goods, and the rest of that story is, as they say, history.

England changed from being a small offshore island exporting wool and cloth. She changed to become a manufacturing country, in response to the demands of her new trading partners further afield, starting with Russia, who wanted manufactured goods as well as cloth (and later they also wanted sugar and tobacco, which England imported from her American Colonies, and then re-exported).

SUBSEQUENT ATTEMPTS TO FIND A NORTH-EAST PASSAGE

There follows a brief summary of the later voyages, but perhaps, to put these heroic efforts into some kind of perspective, it may be worth mentioning a few fragments of the previous history of these northern parts.

Until recently the oldest-known prehistoric site in Siberia was at a place called Berelekh, at 70° N, which dated to 14,000 years ago. But a report in 2004 described the finding of a much earlier Paleolithic site, on the banks of the Yana river in Siberia, at 71° N, only about 60 miles south of the Laptev Sea. This site revealed evidence of human existence from about 30,000 years ago, well before the last Ice Age.[15]

In historical times the earliest recorded voyage in these waters, according to Russian sources, was in 1032, when a certain Uleb from Novgorod sailed through the Yugorskiy Shar Strait (between Vaygach Island and the mainland) and into the Kara Sea.[16] Russian sources also have evidence of regular voyages in the second half of the sixteenth century from the White Sea, through the Kara Strait and the Kara Sea to the mouths of the Rivers Ob and Yenesei, along what was called the 'Great Mangazea Route'.[17]

However, none of this previous history was known when the first western European voyages of discovery were made in search of a north-east passage to the Orient. Their voyages were into entirely unknown territory and seas, and they were full of heroism, death and disappointment.[18]

After Stephen Borough's voyage in 1556 and 1557, the next attempt was made in 1564 or 1565 by a Flemish sailor and explorer called Olivier Brunel. He reached the mouth of the Dvina river, near where the city of Archangel'sk now stands, and where he set up a trading post, but he was denounced as a spy by the Muscovy Company's agent and was arrested by the Russians, who put him in prison at Yaroslavl. He was eventually released in 1570, through the intervention of the Stroganov family; he then worked for them as their agent, travelling widely in north Russia and trading Russian furs and skins in Antwerp and Paris.[19]

The next attempt, in 1580, was made by two Englishmen, Arthur Pet (who had sailed with Stephen Borough in 1556) in the *George*, of 40 tons, and Charles Jackman, who sailed in the *William*, of 20 tons. Before they sailed, they had the benefit of a great deal of advice and instruction: from William Borough (on how they should survey the coast);[20] from Richard Hakluyt (the Elder, of Eyton, on the commodities they should trade in);[21] from Dr John Dee (on the supposed geography of the route);[22] and even a letter from Mercator, saying that 'The voyage to Cathaio by the East, is doubtlesse very easy and short.'[23] Their commission instructed them to sail through the Kara Sea to

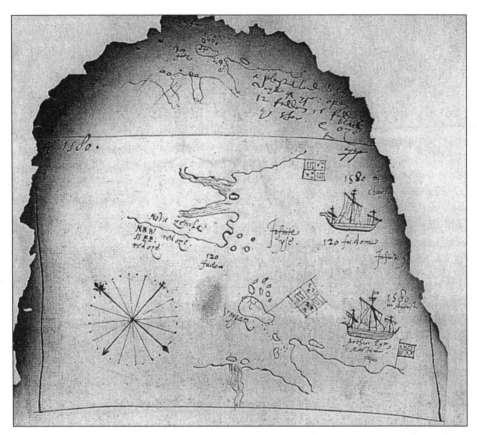

Hugh Smyth's sketch map of Pet and Jackman's ships in the Kara Sea in 1580, showing two areas of 'infinite yse' (and English standards planted on Novaya Zemlya and the Islands of Vaigats).

the River Ob, and then: 'Doe you in Gods name proceed . . . thence Eastwards, keeping the same [land] alwayes on your starboordside in sight . . . until you come to the countrey of Cathay'.[24]

Like Stephen Borough before them, they reached the entrance to the Kara Sea (at what was then called 'Borough Strait'), but there the way was blocked by a wall of 'infinite yse'. They were trapped in the ice for weeks but eventually worked their way free and were forced to retreat. Pet returned to England, but Jackman and his ship were lost the following year, having last been seen overwintering in Norway.[25] There is in the British Library a sketch map drawn by Hugh Smyth, one of the members of the Pet and Jackman expedition, which shows the two ships in the Kara Strait blocked by that 'infinite yse'.[26]

Olivier Brunel made another attempt either in 1581 or (more probably) 1584. He seems to have sailed from Enkhuizen in a ship laden with merchandise bound for the River Ob. He called in at Kola and at New Colmogro (the site of present-day Archangel'sk) and sailed on to the Kara Strait, which he found blocked with ice. He overwintered at or near the mouth of the Dvina river and the following year sailed east again, but was again blocked by ice. He retreated to the mouth of the Pechora river, where he went ashore in the ship's boat to negotiate, but the boat was wrecked on the return journey and Brunel was drowned. His ship eventually returned to Holland.[27]

Then, in 1584, there was a story passed on to an Englishman, Anthony Marsh, by a Russian, to the effect that 'Heretofore your people have bin at the said river of Obs mouth with a Ship, and there was made shipwracke, and your people were slaine by the Samoeds which thought that they came to rob and subdue them.'[28] But what that ship was, or who the unfortunate crew were, is not known.

In 1594 Balthazar de Boucheron of Middleburg and others set up an expedition of three Dutch ships, the *Swan*, the *Mercury* and one other under the command of Wilhelm Barents. Sailing in the *Mercury* Barents reached the northernmost tip of Novaya Zemlya; the other two ships managed to get through the Kara Strait and proceeded some 150 miles further east before they both turned back for home.[29]

The following year a larger fleet was sent to try again. It consisted of seven ships and was again commanded by Barents, with Jacob van Heemskerck and Gerrit de Veer in the complement. However, they were frustrated by large amounts of ice and could get no further east than the Kara Strait, which they called 'the Strait of Nassau'.[30]

In 1596–7 the Netherlanders made their third and most famous attempt, again under the command of Barents. They sailed round the northernmost point of Novaya Zemlya, which is at 77° north, but eventually were forced ashore on the north-east coast of the island, where they became the first Europeans to overwinter in the high Arctic. The story of how they endured scurvy, the intense and persistent cold, the attacks of polar bears and a near-disaster (from what was almost certainly carbon monoxide poisoning), and their eventual return voyage of 1,500 miles in open boats is an epic, though Barents himself did not survive.[31]

The Dutch continued to trade to Archangel'sk, but they did not make any more attempts to discover a north-east passage. They saw no further need of it, because in 1597 Cornelis de Houtman had just returned from the 'Eerste Scheepvaart', the first Dutch voyage to the Malay Archipelago, via the Cape of Good Hope, with cargoes of pepper and spices.[32]

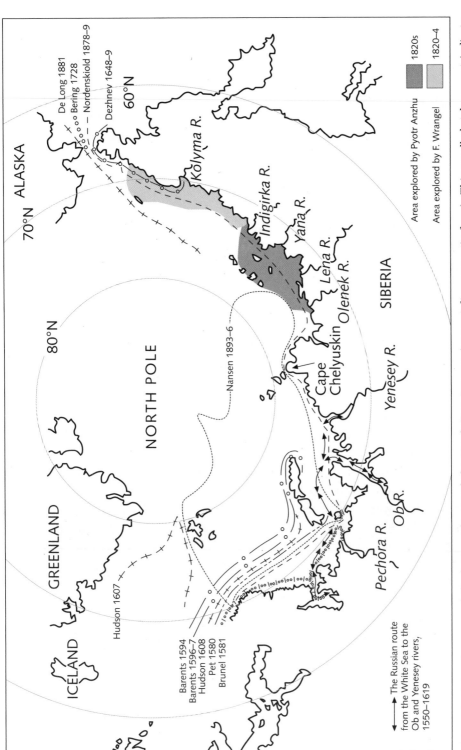

The routes taken by some of the later explorers of the North-East Passage (in semi-diagrammatic form). This small sketch cannot indicate anything of the enormity of the distances or of the hazards they faced.

De Long 1881
Bering 1728
Nordenskiold 1878–9
Dezhnev 1648–9

ALASKA
70°N
60°N
80°N

Kolyma R.
Indigirka R.
Yana R.
Lena R.
Olenek R.
Cape Chelyuskin
Yenesey R.
Ob R.
Pechora R.

SIBERIA

NORTH POLE

Nansen 1893–6

GREENLAND
ICELAND

Hudson 1607

Barents 1594
Barents 1596–7
Hudson 1608
Pet 1580
Brunel 1581

The Russian route from the White Sea to the Ob and Yenesey rivers, 1550–1619

Area explored by Pyotr Anzhu   1820s
Area explored by F. Wrangel   1820–4

However, the Muscovy Company persisted, and in 1607 they sent out Henry Hudson in a small ship with a crew of ten to try to find a route to the east by sailing northward. He sailed as far north as he could up the east coast of Greenland, until his way was blocked by ice and 'our sayle and shroudes did freeze'. He followed the edge of the ice east to Spitzbergen, where he saw many whales, and on the return voyage he discovered the island now known as Jan Mayen Land.[33] His report of the whales at Spitzbergen was the spur that started the English whaling industry.

In 1608 he was sent again by the Muscovy Company. This time he attempted the North-East Passage but failed to find any way through the ice on the west coast of Novaya Zemlya. He planned then to try for a north-west passage, but his crew forced him to return to London.

The following year Hudson tried again, this time at the behest of the Dutch East India Company. He was repeatedly foiled by headwinds, fog and ice near the North Cape, and so he crossed the Atlantic to try the North-West Passage. He tried first at 40° N, where he explored the river that now bears his name, and he founded the site of what was later to become New York.

His last, and fatal, expedition does not directly concern us here, as it was from the start a search for the North-West Passage, not the North-East. In brief, however: in 1610 he sailed via Iceland, the southern tip of Greenland and up the coast of Labrador and into Hudson Bay, where he and his crew were forced to spend a harsh winter, plagued with hunger and scurvy. Hudson was a driven man, and when the spring came he wanted to continue the search for a north-west passage, but his crew had had enough and desperately wanted to head for home. The crew mutinied and put Hudson, his young son and a few others into a small shallop (a light open boat) and set it adrift. They were never seen again. Hudson had been very successful in charting large parts of the Arctic, but his successes were overshadowed by his inability to carry his crew with him, which led to the mutiny and his death.[34]

In 1611 there was a voyage as far as the Islands of Vaigats by Josias Logan and William Gordon of the Muscovy Company. They wintered at the Pechora river and returned to England.[35]

Russian hunters explored the vast tracts of their northern lands in search of furs, but they had little interest in mapping the region. There were a few more sporadic (and inept) attempts at the North-East Passage. In 1625, for instance, one Cornelis Bosman managed to reach the Kara Sea before he was forced to turn back by the ice. In 1648–9 Alekseyev-Popov and Semyon Dezhnev discovered the strait that we now call the Bering Strait, between Asia and North America, by sailing from the Kolyma river east and south into the Pacific Ocean, but their records did not come to light until a hundred years later. Another Dutch ship made an unsuccessful attempt in 1653. The English, under a certain Captain Wood, made an attempt in 1698. One of his two ships, the *Speedwell*, broke up on a rock off Novaya Zemlya; all who survived this calamity were brought home in the other ship, the *Prosperous*. After this experience Captain Wood wrote, apparently with feeling, that 'It is the most miserable Country that lyeth on the Foundation of the Earth.'[36]

In 1725 Peter the Great sent Captain Vitus Bering, a Dane in the service of the Imperial Navy, to determine whether or not Russia and America were joined together. Bering and his crew travelled overland to Kamchatka, where they constructed several ships, and in 1728 Bering (in effect) rediscovered the strait that bears his name and showed that the two continents were quite separate. However, ice prevented him from exploring the eastern end of the North-East Passage any further.[37]

Between 1733 and 1740 the Russians mounted 'The Great Northern Expedition' to explore the entire northern coast from Archangel'sk to the Bering Strait. It consisted of four sections, separated by the Rivers Ob, Yenesey and Lena, with a fifth section, under Bering, to explore the north Pacific. In spite of many setbacks, the expedition collected a great deal of information, including the fact that Cape Chelyuskin was the most northerly point of mainland Russia.[38]

Other explorers included Commodore Phipps and Captain Lutwidge in the *Racehorse* and the *Carcase* (what a terrible name for a ship) in 1773.[39]

In 1785 Joseph Billings from London joined the Russian Navy and was commissioned to explore the coasts of Alaska and eastern Siberia. His two ships spent nine years making accurate maps of the area.[40]

Otto von Kotzebue explored the eastern end of the North-East Passage in 1815–18.[41]

In the 1820s Lieutenant Pyotr Anzhu, travelling by dog-sled in winter and by kayak and horseback in the Arctic summer, succeeded brilliantly in mapping a huge extent of the coast between the Olenyok and Indigirka rivers, and offshore to the New Siberian Islands (Novosibirskye Ostrova), and at the same time (1820–4) Lieutenant Wrangel and Fyodor Matyushkin charted another large area along the coast of the East Siberian Sea, eastwards from the Indigirka river as far as Wrangel Island (Ostrov Vrangelya).[42]

By about the 1860s the development of reliable boilers made it possible for steamships to attempt the passage. They were much more manoeuvrable in the edges of the ice than sailing ships had been. Using steam in the 1870s, Joseph Wiggins and Nils Nordenskiold both succeeded in crossing the Kara Sea and reaching the mouth of the Yenesei river.[43]

However, it was not until 1878–9 that the passage originally sought by Willoughby, Chancellor and Borough in 1553 was at last achieved – by Nils

Adolf Erik Nordenskiold (1832–1901). He set out in the *Vega*, a barque built largely of oak, with a 60-horsepower steam engine and a crew of thirty. They sailed across the Kara Sea, around the Yamal Peninsula, past the Ob and the Yenesei, and around Cape Chelyuskin at the tip of the Taymyr Peninsula, and slowly, because of ice, journeyed across the Laptev and East Siberian Seas to Kolyuchin Bay, which was almost at the end of their journey. There they remained trapped in the ice for nine months. They completed the passage the following year.[44]

An American explorer, George Washington De Long, was less fortunate. In 1879 he sailed from California in the *Jeanette*, hoping to find a quick route to the North Pole via the Laptev Sea. His ship was crushed in the ice and sank. The crew took to their boats, but nineteen of them, including De Long himself, perished before they could reach civilisation.[45] An island called Ostrova DeLong preserves his name.

Fridtjof Nansen made his famous voyage in the *Fram* from 1893 to 1896, starting from the Bering Strait and drifting, with his ship locked in the ice, all the way across the Arctic to Europe.[46]

Baron Eduard von Toll was already famous for his investigations of frozen woolly mammoths and rhinoceroses in the Siberian Arctic before he led a Russian coastal expedition in the *Zarya* in 1903, in which he perished. The bravery and determination of all of these men, and many others too numerous to mention here, shine on long after their exploits.

The ice-breakers *Vaigach* and *Taimyr* made the complete traverse from east to west in 1914–15, and numerous other voyages have followed, though it was not until 1932 that the Soviet ice-breaker ship *Sibirakov* succeeded in traversing the whole passage in a single season. Since the Second World War, with the advent of powerful ice-breakers, the use of helicopters as scouts, and with the benefit of meteorological and satellite ice reports, radar and echo depth-sounding devices, convoys of ships have used the route to bring in stores and to take out cargoes of timber, furs, grain and minerals. During the 1950s and 1960s probably 200 or 300 ships operated in these waters each year. The biggest trade is to and from the Yenesei river, where there are nickel mines at Norilsk and timber at Igarka.[47]

But despite all the benefits of modern technology, it is still the ice that rules in these regions. There have been many losses and disasters, one of the biggest of which occurred in 1937, when twenty-six ships, including seven of the eight available ice-breakers, were trapped by ice and had to spend the entire winter out at sea.

It is no more possible to 'conquer' the ice than it is to 'conquer' Mount Everest. In the Arctic, man has to bow to nature. In this respect, we are considerably more fortunate than our forefathers, who had to cope with the Little Ice Age. The main phase of the Little Ice Age lasted from about 1550 to 1700.[48] It is the relative scarcity of ice now, compared with the 'Little Ice Age', as much as modern technology, that has made the passage somewhat easier. The ice has receded so much that, in 2002, it was possible for two boats separately to sail the full length of the passage from west to east in a single season: Eric Brossier and his crew in the 13.7m steel cutter *Vagabond*, and Arved Fuchs in an ex-Baltic fishing boat, the *Dagmar Aaen*.[49]

The tendency of the area of ice in the Arctic to shrink has been especially noticeable since the late 1970s, and if it continues at the present rate, the Arctic could be almost ice-free in the summer months by 2050.[50] However, sea ice is never entirely predictable, and it is worth mentioning that in 2004 the ice in the Laptev Sea never thawed and ships could not get through.[51] But if the general trend does continue, as seems very probable, then the North-East Passage will at last become a practical sea route because, for a number of destinations, it is far shorter. For instance, the distance from London to Tokyo is some 16,500 sea miles via the Cape of Good Hope, or about 11,500 miles using the Suez Canal, but it is only 7,500 miles via the North-East Passage. This could shorten a sea journey from the UK to Japan by twelve days.[52] Perhaps, at last, the Tudor dream of a waterway to the riches of the Orient will be realised, in the form of supertankers pushing their way round Cape Chelyuskin.

CHAPTER 12

A Summary and Assessment of Stephen Borough's Nautical Career

Stephen Borough first came to notice in 1553, at the age of 27, when he was appointed as master of one of the three ships in the expedition to seek a north-east passage to the Orient.[1] (His home and his family life have been described in Chapter 2.) His ship, the *Edward Bonaventura*, was the biggest of the expedition and had Richard Chancellor on board as chief pilot, and, as it happened, she was the only ship to survive.

Nobody knows how or where Stephen learned his trade, how he earned the reputation that warranted his appointment on the *Edward*, or where he gained the judgement and experience that enabled him to survive his years of sailing to the Arctic. He may have learned a lot of this as an apprentice to his uncle, John Aborough (as discussed in Chapter 2), but there is no hard evidence that this was in fact how he did it.

The incident on the expedition in 1553 was a test and a demonstration of his skill. The other two ships were blown away over the horizon by a sudden storm off the coast of Norway, and eventually lost. Stephen was much quicker than the other two masters. He noticed the signs of the rapidly approaching storm and got most of his sails shortened before it struck.[2]

The next crucial event was the selection of Stephen as the leader of the second attempt at finding a north-east passage. Chancellor was not chosen; neither was John Buckland, Stephen's mate on the 1553 expedition. In 1556 Stephen sailed in the pinnace *Serchthrift*, with a crew of ten.[3] He managed to sail about 500 miles further east than any western European had ever been before and found the strait into the Kara Sea, between Novaya Zemlya and the Islands of Vaigats. He survived numerous storms, fog and ice, as well as the hazards of the unknown geography, until eventually he was forced back by a wall of ice. Not only did he survive, but he also managed to keep careful observations on his positions and on the coasts and currents and much else besides, a tremendous achievement considering how small the boat was (44 feet long), and how primitive the conditions must have been, as well as the cold and wet.

In 1557 the *Serchthrift* sailed back westwards along the north coast of Russia, searching for three Muscovy Company ships that had been lost, and making a careful survey of the coast as they proceeded. This was the first time that such a survey had been made by any English seaman, and the observations that resulted were so accurate that Stephen's younger brother, William, was later able to draw up a chart of the area, the shape of which shows a remarkable resemblance to the maps of today.[4]

After the premature death of Chancellor in 1556, Stephen was appointed chief pilot to the Muscovy Company. He continued to sail regularly to Russia; the records of the Port of London show that he sailed there in 1560, 1564, 1565, 1567, 1568 and 1571, and there could have been more voyages.[5] His voyages on the long and hazardous route to Russia spanned a period of eighteen years: they started in 1553 and the last one that we know about was in 1571.

The Spaniards, the acknowledged experts at world exploration and navigation, recognised his achievements and invited him to visit the Casa de Contratación at Seville in 1558, probably at the instigation of Queen Mary's consort, Prince Philip. All of Spain's overseas trade was by law channelled through Seville, and the Casa was its administrative control centre. The Casa was also the centre for information about overseas discoveries and navigation, and it was a school and examination centre for ships' captains and pilots. Hakluyt reported that:

> Master Steuen Borrows tolde me that newely after his returne from the discoverie of Moscovie by the North in Queen Maries daies, the Spaniards, having intelligence that he was master in that discoverie took him into the cotractation house at their admitting of masters and pilots, giving him great honour and presented him with a payre of perfumed gloves worth five or six Ducates.[6]

Borough brought back to England with him a copy of the *Breve compendio de la sphera y de la arte de navegar* of 1551 by Martin Cortes. He persuaded the Muscovy Company to pay for it to be translated into English by his friend Richard Eden, whose work is entitled *The Arte of Navigation*.[7] This book has been described by Waters as 'One of the most decisive books ever printed in the English language. . . . It held the key to the mastery of the sea.'[8] Eden wrote in the preface to his work:

> As touching Stephen A. Borough, the chiefe Pilote of your viaages of discovery . . . he is neither malicious nor envious of his arte and science . . . he desireth ye same for the comon profite to be comen to al men: And for the same intent was the first that moved certen worshypfull of your company . . . to have this worke translated into the Englyshe tongue.

Eden recognised that Stephen was a pioneer in wanting knowledge to be made freely available and not kept restricted as a 'mystery'. The book soon went into several editions.

Stephen came back from Spain with the firm conviction that England would benefit greatly if there was a body similar to that in Spain to examine and certify the fitness of English sea captains. He wrote a lengthy proposal to this effect, addressed to Queen Elizabeth, under the title 'Three especiall causes and consideracions amongst others wherfore the office of Pilott major ys allowed and esteemed in Spayne, Portugale, and other places where navigation flourisheth'.[9] This proposal was considered, and Stephen Borough himself was judged to be the right man for the post. A draft Royal Commission for his appointment as 'Cheyffe Pilote of this owr realme of Englande' was drawn up.[10] However, it was never proceeded with, probably because it involved financial outlay that Queen Elizabeth could ill afford and possibly also because it might have detracted from the traditional rights of the Trinity Houses to oversee the activities of pilots.[11]

Borough was, however, appointed as one of the four masters of the Queen's ships in the Medway in 1563, a position he held until his death.[12] His duties included the 'kepyng and over syght of owr shipps', 'to direct and oversee the Boatswains and Shipkeepers', 'to carry in and out of the River [Medway] such ships as happened to be prepared for the seas', and to select suitable men to be masters of the Queen's ships from names submitted to him by the Trinity House, a position of great responsibility.[13]

He became a member of the Brethren of Trinity House of Deptford (D.W. Waters has described him as 'the most sagacious' of that brotherhood)[14] and he was elected master of that body in 1573–4.[15] He was also, incidentally, a 'shipkeeper' of the *Victory* in 1562.[16]

The last record we have of him as master of a ship was in 1572, when he was listed as master of the *Black Greyhound*, 200 tons, of the Port of London, but there are no records of any of his voyages in that year.[17]

In 1574 Stephen Borough and his brother were both advisers to the Frobisher expedition, which went in search of a north-west passage in 1576, and again in 1577 and 1578.[18] Borough even sold 'a small pynasse [pinnace] boat' to Frobisher[19] and William drew up a chart of the North Atlantic for Frobisher to plot his discoveries on.[20]

There is a conundrum concerning the events of December 1585, when Robert Dudley, the Earl of Leicester, set sail for the Netherlands with a force of 1,000 cavalry and 6,000 foot soldiers to help the Dutch in their struggle against the Spanish. Stephen Borough was recorded as the chief pilot for this armada.[21] But he had died in 1584, and we have both a death certificate and a burial record as proof. It has been assumed, probably correctly, that it was his brother William, and not Stephen, who was the chief pilot of this fleet.[22]

There is no doubt that both the Borough brothers were held in high esteem by their contemporaries. For instance, Thomas Randolph, ambassador to Muscovy, on his arrival at St Nicholas on 12 August 1568 wrote in a letter to Sir William Cecil apropos of the Borough brothers, saying 'I thynke that I maye boldilye saye that these are two soche as the Queene's Maiestie hath not the lyke'.[23]

Stephen Borough seems to have had a remarkably successful career as a shipmaster. He sailed the hazardous route to St Nicholas for the Muscovy Company at least eight times and maybe more, a remarkable record. Without such a competent and reliable chief pilot, the Muscovy Company would have had great difficulty in getting established and would not have been able to maintain its trade along its long and dangerous line of communication.

Stephen pioneered the exploration of the North-East Passage and returned with an accurate description of the geography of those parts. By contrast, Frobisher, who sailed twenty years later in 1576–8, had the misfortune to come back with an incorrect description of the geography (Frobisher Strait turned out to be a landlocked bay), with no prospects of trade and with thousands of tons of what turned out to be fool's gold.[24]

It has been stated that 'the fleet that defeated the Spanish Armada was largely rigged with Russian cordage and cables' supplied by the Muscovy Company. It has also been said that it was the great leap forward in English maritime enterprise and navigational ability, inspired by Stephen Borough and a few other like-minded Englishmen, that made it possible to get the English fleet together at the right place and time to resist the Armada.

Stephen Borough can be seen to have had an important position not only in the history of exploration, but also in the history of navigation, as one of the earliest English practitioners of the new scientific methods, as well as being a pioneer in disseminating information about it. Furthermore, he played a pivotal role in the infancy of the first of Britain's great overseas trading companies. And he was one of the few Tudor sea captains, possibly the only one, who never fired a shot in anger.

There is no available information about his appearance. There are no portraits and very little by way of biographical detail. In the absence of such definitive data, perhaps it is permissible to create a mental image of the man – pure conjecture, you understand. In my imagination, he was fairly small, wiry and physically like a bearded Eric Tabarly, the world-famous French yachtsman, but by inclination less of a loner and more down to earth. Mentally, he was hard-working, shrewd and definitely courageous, but always very practical, more like a Nordenskiold. For instance, I can imagine it being said of Stephen Borough, as it was of Nordenskiold, that 'His confidence, his composure, his indomitable energy inspired all who were with him with a sense of security.'[25]

His exploits are almost all that we know about him, though we do have his will, written in his own hand. This shows his devout belief and trust in God, which he shared with many Elizabethans, and which may have given him some of the boldness and confidence that he showed, for instance, in the face of storms, fog and ice on the *Serchthrift* voyage of 1556. And yet his boldness must have been tempered by an adequate measure of caution, without which he would never have survived all his voyages. He must also have had great stamina and determination: there is nowhere in any of his accounts of the voyages any mention of hold-ups or delays due to fatigue, injury or sickness. He was an achiever.

His confidence appears to have been transmitted to his crews, as he seems to have had none of the problems of disobedience or mutiny that other skippers of the time experienced, such as Sebastian Cabot, Hudson or even the great Sir Francis Drake. There is no doubt that he also had a considerable amount of good luck, but then many adventurous men have had that, or they would have perished in their attempts.

Stephen deserved and received the respect of his peers, as was shown when he was elected to be master of the body of senior shipmasters, the Trinity Brethren. He appears to have been the ideal man to have been selected to do the difficult and demanding job of searching for the North-East Passage and then sailing repeatedly on the route to north Russia.

APPENDIX 1

Stephen Borough's Dates

1525   25 September, born at Borough, Northam, North Devon. (Memorial plaque, St Mary's Church, Chatham, now Medway Heritage Trust)

1536   Brother William born, also at Borough. (He later became Comptroller of the Queen's Navy) [DNB]

c. 1545 Married Eleanora, née Smithe, daughter of John Smithe of Cleve (Clive in Shropshire). (Administration document at her death)

c. 1550 Son Christopher born, who later explored Astrakhan and Persia as an agent of the Muscovy Company, c. 1580. (Hakluyt, *Principal Navigations*, Everyman, vol. II, pp. 172–201)

1553   Appointed Master of the *Edward Bonaventura*, 160 tons, and also one of the twelve 'Counsellors' for the voyage to find a north-east passage. (Hakluyt, *Principal Navigations*, Everyman, vol. I, pp. 241 and 245)

 10 May, departure of the three ships of the expedition from Ratcliffe, towed down the Thames, under the command of Sir Hugh Willoughby. [Hakluyt, *Principal Navigations*, Everyman, vol. I, p. 248)

1553–4 The *Edward Bonaventura* wintered at St Nicholas, near Archangel'sk. Richard Chancellor travelled overland to Moscow and obtained trading rights from the Tsar, Ivan IV (the Terrible). The crews of the other two ships perished in the Arctic winter. (Hakluyt, *Principal Navigations*, Everyman, vol. I, pp. 253–4, 277–99)

1554   The *Edward Bonaventura* returned to London (Hakluyt, *Principal Navigations*, Everyman, vol. II, p. 265)

1555   A company is founded to explore 'unknowne landes'. Charter issued 26 February (*Cal. Pat. Rolls* 1554–5, pp. 55–9)

 Chancellor's second voyage to Russia and back, the Muscovy Company's first trading voyage. He took out the first Muscovy Company agents, Gray and Killingworth. (Hakluyt, *Principal Navigations*, Everyman, vol. I, pp. 299–307 and vol. II, pp. 265–7)

1556   Sailed in the *Serchthrift*, exploring eastwards along the north coast of Russia 'towards the River Ob'; reached Kara Strait and Novaya Zemlya, wintered at Colmogro. (Hakluyt, *Principal Navigations*, Everyman, vol. I, pp. 333–52)

 Chancellor's ship sailed to Russia and brought the first Russian ambassador to Britain. Chancellor is drowned (Hakluyt, *Principal Navigations*, Everyman, vol. I, p. 358; vol. II, p. 267)

1557   Stephen, in the *Serchthrift*, sailed west along coast to Wardhouse and made a survey of the coast. (Hakluyt, *Principal Navigations*, Everyman, vol. I, pp. 367–77) Returned to London. Appointed Chief Pilot of Muscovy Company.

?1558 Visited Casa de la Contratación (Contratación House) at Seville (headquarters of all overseas maritime enterprises in Spain). Brought back a copy of Martin Cortes's *Arte de Navegar*. (Hakluyt, 'Epistle Dedicatorie' in *Divers Voyages Touching America* [1582] Hakluyt Society, series 1, vol. VII, 1850)

1560   Sailed to Russia and back in the *Swallow*, in charge of three Muscovy Company ships (the seventh company voyage, the first without loss). (Hakluyt, *Principal Navigations*, Everyman, vol. I, pp. 399, 404–5)

1561   *The Arte of Navigation* published, at Stephen's behest, translated by Richard Eden and paid for by the Muscovy Company. Sold widely. (M. Cortes, *The Arte of Navigation*, trans. R. Eden, London, 1561)

1562   Wife Eleanora dies, in February. Stephen then living at Ratcliffe. (Family Record Centre, Myddleton Street, London, PRO PROB 6/1, folio 58, *Administration of Eleanor Borough*)

       His Petition to the Crown to appoint a pilot-major to teach and examine English sea captains in navigation. (British Library, Lansdowne MS 116, folios 6 and 7)

       Named as the 'shipkeeper' of the *Victory* (T. Glasgow, 'Vice Admiral Woodhouse and Shipkeeping in the Tudor Navy', *Mariner's Mirror*, 63 (1977) 253–63, at 260)

1563   20 March, married second wife, Joanna Overye of Stepney, by whom he had five girls. (J.L. Chester and G.J.A. Armitage, *Allegations for Marriage Licences issued by the Bishop of London, 1521–1610* (2 vols, London, Harleian Society, 1887, no. 25), p. 26; Centre for Kentish Studies, Maidstone, *Will of Stephen Borough, 1 July 1584*)

1563 or Royal Commission drawn up, appointing Stephen as 'Cheyffe Pylott of
1564   this our Realm' (British Library, Lansdowne MS 116, folios 4 and 5), but this commission was never implemented.

1564   Sailed to Russia and back in the *Swallow*, with three ships (Exch. K.R. Customs 90/11)

       Appointed one of the four Masters of the Queen's Ships in the Medway (to examine and supervise ships and their masters). He seems to have continued in this post until he died. (Stephen Borough, Memorial Plaque, St Mary's Church, Chatham, now Medway Heritage Trust)

1565   Sailed to Russia and back, with two ships. (Exch. K.R. Port Books 2/1) Became member of the Brethren of Trinity House, Deptford. (G.G. Harris, *The Trinity House of Deptford, 1514–1660* (London, University of London, 1969), p. 273)

1567   Sailed to Russia and back in the *Swallow* (Exch. K.R. Port Books 4/2)

1568   Sailed to Russia and back in the *Harry* (Hakluyt, *Principal Navigations*, Everyman, vol. II, pp. 80–5)

1569   Sailed to Russia and back (J. Hamel, *England and Russia* (London, F. Cass, 1968), p. 150)

1571   Sailed to Russia and back (Exch. K.R. Port Books 5/1)

1572   Still living at Ratcliffe, acquired lease of John Rabelo's house in Barking (Family Record Centre, PROB 2, folio 216, *Administration of John Rabelo (1572)*, John Rabelo)

    Named as master of *The Black Greyhound* (National Archives, PRO, State Papers, Domestic, Addenda (1547–1625) 15/22/folio 10 (microfilm), *Register of the Merchant Ships of England compiled by Thomas Colshill*)

1574   Adviser to Frobisher expeditions (1576, 1577 and 1578) (R. Collinson, *The Three Voyages of Martin Frobisher* (London, Hakluyt Society, 1867), p. 89)

1575?   Elected Master of Trinity House. (G.G. Harris, *The Trinity House of Deptford, 1514–1660* (London, University of London, 1969), p. 273)

1578   Sold a small 'pynasse bote' to Michael Lok for the Third Frobisher expedition, for £7. (I. Friel, 'Frobisher's Ships: the Ships of the North-Western Atlantic Voyages, 1576–1578', in T.H.B. Symons (ed.), *Meta Incognita: a Discourse of Discovery: Martin Frobisher's Arctic Expeditions, 1576–1578* (Quebec, Canadian Museum of Civilisation, 1999), pp. 299–352, at 301)

1584   Died 12 July at his house 'Goodsight' in Chatham; buried at St Mary's Church, Chatham. (City of Rochester upon Medway, Archives, *Burial Record of Stephen Borough*; Memorial plaque, St Mary's Church, Chatham, now Medway Heritage Trust)

Stephen Borough's Famous Relatives and Other Members of his Family

WILLIAM BOROUGH (YOUNGER BROTHER OF STEPHEN)

William became a shipmaster and a pilot for the Muscovy Company. Later he became an Admiral in the Royal Navy and achieved fame by rounding up a gang of pirates in the Baltic in 1570.[1] In 1581 his *Discourse on the Variation of the Compas* was published. In 1583, in charge of two naval barques, he captured ten privateers. He served under Drake in the attack on Cadiz in 1587, where he was nearly executed for urging caution, and he became Comptroller of Queen Elizabeth's Navy. He was a churchwarden at Stepney and died in 1598 and was buried there.[2] William mentions two properties in his will, namely a farm in Stepney and a house in Tower Street, London, together with various items of silver and gold and a coach with two horses.[3]

CHRISTOPHER BOROUGH (STEPHEN'S SON)

Christopher achieved fame as an agent of the Muscovy Company. He travelled overland to Persia and Bokhara, with twenty-five wagonloads of goods, trying to find a land route to Cathay. He made some notable journeys between about 1579 and 1581, and he also took careful measurements of the latitudes of the places he reached.[4]

JOHN VASSALL (STEPHEN'S SON-IN-LAW)

Stephen's daughter Judith married a Thomas Skott of Colchester as her first husband in 1586, two years after her father had died.[5] She married for the second time (and he for the third time) a John Vassall (or Versall) of Ratcliffe, on 23 March 1593 (or 1594).[6] He was a wealthy shipowner and ship-builder and a Merchant Adventurer who had a house on Ratcliffe Wall (now Broad Street) at Ratcliffe, Stepney. He also had a substantial property at Eastwood, near Leigh in Essex, near to Samuel Purchas, the maritime historian. In his voluminous works, Purchas refers to John Vassall as having travelled in Barbary and brought back a lion skin from there.[7] John Vassall was one of the founders of the colony of

Virginia. There is a strong local tradition in Leigh that the *Mayflower*, of the Pilgrim Fathers, was built at Leigh. It is also thought that John Vassall may have been one of her owners, or even her builder.[8] He certainly fitted out and was captain of two ships in the fight against the Spanish Armada: the *Samuel*, of 140 tons, and after her the *Little Tobey*, also of 140 tons. He died of the plague at Stepney in 1625.[9]

STEPHEN BOROUGH'S OTHER DAUGHTERS

Elizabeth Burroughe, another of Stephen Borough's daughters, married George Bartlett, a merchant, at Stepney on 5 March 1603 or 1604.[10] (Elizabeth was said to have been about 23 at the time of her marriage in 1603, which, if true, means she could only have been 4 years old when her father died in 1584.) Two other daughters also married: Anne became Mrs Wright, and Susan became Mrs King.[11] It is not known whether Mary married.

OTHER MEMBERS OF THE FAMILY

The members of the Borough family are shown in the family tree (illustration on page 7). One of John Aborough's children was David, of Northam, who was a ship-owner.[12] The youngest of John Aborough's children was Agnes; she was less than 16 years old in 1556 when John Aborough made his will, but when he died in 1570 she inherited the house, Borough.[13] She married a Thomas Leigh,[14] a wealthy man who owned properties in Northam, Abbotsham, Frithelstock, Barnstaple, Witheridge and Delbridge, as well as a windmill, ships and boats, and he made several improvements to Borough.[15]

Other members of the family who should be mentioned briefly include Peter Borowghe, a son of John Aborough and brother of David, Thomasine and Agnes. He died in 1586.[16] Ann Boroughe was the widow of David; she died in 1589, and she mentions in her will Thomasine and Agnes (her sisters, though she does not indicate her relationship to them).[17]

There were a number of other people called Borough in the parish of Northam at the time. They appear as baptisms or burials in the Northam Parish Records, though not as marriages.[18] (The record of baptisms starts in 1538, that of burials in 1541, but marriages were not recorded in the register until 1606.) There is, however, insufficient information to be able to fit them into the family tree (and anyway it is possible that a few of them may have died young).

ROBERT BUROUGH, POSSIBLY RELATED

There is one other Burough who may be connected to the family, but again there is not sufficient evidence at present to do so. This was a Robert Burough, described as a sea captain from Devonshire, who appears in a High Court of Admiralty Examination of 1543.[19] He was a privateer who captured a hoy as she was leaving St Malo harbour laden with canvas. He stated that he thought she was French, but the High Court decided that she belonged to the Low Countries and was thus not a lawful prize, and they ordered him to make restitution. This Robert may be the same shipmaster who appears in a Register of Ships in 1572,[20] where Stephen Borough and William Borough and Robert Burough all appear, each of them listed as the master of a ship in the Port of London: Stephen of *The Black Greyhound*, of cc (200) tons; William of *The Margaret*, of cxx (120) tons and Robert Burrow of *The Black Burre*, of c (100) tons.

OTHER EVIDENCE

Other supporting information for the family tree is to be found in the Devon Lay Subsidy Rolls of 1524–7.[21] It mentions various members of the family in Northam with the amount that they were assessed on for taxation. In this case they were all assessed on goods, rather than on land or wages. Those named were John at Buroughe, goods £8; Stephen at Buroughe, goods £20 (the highest assessment in the parish) – he may have been Walter's father, i.e. Stephen's grandfather; Walter at Buroughe (probably Stephen Borough's father), goods £7; and William at Buroughe, goods £4.

The Devon Lay Subsidy Rolls of 1543–5 were similar.[22] They listed John Borough as taxable on £20 (probably John Aborough); David Borowe, £4 (probably John Aborough's son); William Borow £10; and Walter Borowe £1 (probably the father of Stephen and William).

The Devon Muster Roll for 1569 was somewhat similar again, except that this time the assessment was for the provision of military equipment, rather than money, and it applied to all men aged over 16 and under 60.[23] On this roll, John Boroughe was assessed at between £10 and £20, and he had to equip himself with a corselet, a bow, a sheaf of twenty-four arrows, a steel cap and a ball (he must have been over the upper limit of 60 years of age by this time); Peter Boroughe (probably John Aborough's son) had a similar assessment but was listed as an harquebusier, and he had to equip himself with a harquebus as well, whereas Walter Borough jun., who was listed as an archer, had to have one longbow, one sheaf of arrows, one sword and one dagger.

The Devon Taxes List for the 1581 Subsidy reverts to the format of the Subsidy Rolls. It mentions only three members of the Burroughs family in the parish of Northam: Ann Burrough, widow; Peter Burrough (probably the same Peter, son of John Aborough); and Christina Burrough. (Ann may have been one of Stephen Borough's daughters but it is not possible to positively identify either her or Christina as yet.)

Further supporting evidence of John Aborough is in a grant dated 1544 of some premises, a messuage and tenement 'next the highway on the south' in the parish of Northam to 'Jn. Bourgh, Richd. Chappell and Wm. Valett' of Northam.[24]

John Aborough is listed in the Devon Subsidy Rolls of 1524 (as John At Buroughe)[25] and of 1543 (as John Borough).[26]

The Ordinances for the 1553 Expedition

Ordinances, instructions and advertisements of and for the intended voyage to Cathay, compiled made and delivered by the right worshipfull M. Sebastian Cabota squier. 9 May 1553[1]

Here follows a brief précis of Sebastian Cabot's orders for the 1553 expedition.

1. The company to be knit and accorded in unity.
2. Not to leave off the voyage until it be accomplished.
3. To obey the Captains; and that these ordinances be read out every week.
4. Every man shall do the duties assigned to him.
5. The Captains and the counsellors to meet and agree all the courses. (The Captain General to have a double voice.)
6. The fleet to keep together.
7. Keep a record of the navigation, the observations, the land and the tides.
8. All exploration of new lands to be done cautiously, and all contacts with Princes to be done by the Captain General.
9. The stewards to keep a close check on the provisions.
10. Any negligent or useless officer to be demoted and punished.
11. Any sailor found to be incapable to be put ashore anywhere in His Majesty's dominions and another taken on.
12. No blaspheming, ribaldry, dicing or card games.
13. Morning and evening prayers to be said in every ship.
14. Every officer to have an inventory of his charge, to be sparing in the use of powder and shot, and to take care of the instruments of navigation.
15. Maintain cleanliness in the ballast, the cookhouse and elsewhere. The 'gromals' to be trained in navigation.
16. The liveries are only to be worn on special occasions, by order of the Captain.
17. Keep account of clothes issued to sailors from the slop chest.
18. The sick are to be cared for and no one to refuse to do the sick man's duties.
19. If anyone dies, his goods are to be kept for his widow, and his wages to be paid until the date of his death.
20. All buying and selling of merchandise must be done under the control of the Captain and the head merchant.
21. No private trading.

22 Do not mention anything to do with religion.

23 Learn as much as you can about the people that you encounter. No violence.

24 Treat the natives well. You can make them drunk to learn their secrets.

25 Do not be lured too far from your boats when exploring.

26 Treat the natives with respect, not contempt.

27 Make a note of the names of the people and their commodities and metals.

28 If you see them on the shore, you may play the drums or other musical instruments to attract them.

29 Be wary of ambushes, and keep your weapons handy if you go to eat with them.

30 Do not be afraid of them if you see them wearing lion or bear skins.

31 Keep a close watch day and night for natives swimming out to climb on board the ship in some islands.

32 If at all possible, send one or two men home with news of progress of the expedition.

33 No conspiracies and no false rumours. Justify the trust put in you by the backers of the expedition. God be with you.

APPENDIX 4

The Dimensions of the Expedition Ships

THE CALCULATION OF THE DIMENSIONS OF THE
EDWARD BONAVENTURA

We know from William Borough's *Proportions* that the length of the keel was 2½ times the breadth of the ship, and that the height between the top of the keelson and the bottom of the deck beams was ⅖ of the breadth.[1]

We know also, from Mathew Baker's Old Rule, that the tonnage (cubic capacity) of a ship was given by the length times the breadth times the depth (height between the bottom of the deck and the top of the keelson), divided by 100.[2]

$$\text{i.e. tonnage} = \frac{\text{length} \times \text{breadth} \times \text{depth}}{100}$$

Let X be the number of feet in the breadth of the ship:

$$\text{then tonnage} = \frac{\frac{5}{2} \times X \times X \times \frac{2}{5}X}{100}$$

Thus, for the *Edward Bonaventura*, of 160 tons' burthen:

$$\text{tonnage } 160 = \frac{(\frac{5}{2}X \times X \times \frac{2}{5}X)}{100}$$
$$16,000 = X^3$$
$$X = 25 \text{ feet}$$

So, on this basis the *Edward Bonaventura* would have had a breadth or beam of 25 feet, and from this figure the length of the keel can be found. It would have been 62½ feet in length, and the depth below the main deck to the top of the keelson would have been 10 feet (all figures very approximate).

If her proportions resembled those of the *Mary Gonson*, then her overall length would have been 87½ feet. (The *Mary Gonson* was a somewhat earlier ship, launched in 1514, and she had a keel length of 80 feet, an overall length of 113 feet, a beam of 32 feet, and a depth below the main deck of 17 feet.)[3]

A CHECK ON THE RELIABILITY OF THIS METHOD OF
ESTIMATING THE DIMENSIONS OF THE SHIPS

There were two other ships of the time, of similar sizes to the expedition ships, the tonnages and the dimensions of which are both known. They can be used as a check on the reliability of the method that has been used here to estimate the sizes of the expedition ships. One is the *Aid* (or *Ayde*) built in 1562.[4] Her dimensions were 73 feet by 22 feet by 14 feet,[5] and if we calculate her tonnage from them, using the same formula, it works out at 224.8 tons, near enough to her actual tonnage, which was variously described as 200 or 225 tons. This goes some way to show that the method of relating the tonnage to the dimensions does indeed work.[6]

The other example, the *Cygnet*, of 29 tons, one of the smaller ships of Frobisher's expedition, gives a similar result. Her dimensions were 40 feet by 12 feet by 6 feet, and from these her tonnage, using the same formula, works out at 28.8 tons, which agrees well with her stated tonnage of 29 tons.[7]

APPENDIX 5

The Courses Taken by Sir Hugh Willoughby

The courses are those sailed by Sir Hugh Willoughby and his two ships in 1553 following the violent storm at Seynam (Senja Island). The information below is taken from Sir Hugh Willoughby's own account in Hakluyt, *Principal Navigations*, Everyman, vol. I, pp. 251–3. See also the chart of Sir Hugh Willoughby's courses (see page 65).

Date	Direction sailed	Distance run and comments	Compass course in °	True course °
31 Jul–3 Aug	N by E	Drifted before storm for 4 days, @ probably 1–2 knots = perhaps 150 sea miles	011	006
4–6 Aug	NE by N, and NE	Ran 'fiftie leagues' = 150 sea miles. 2 days at probably 3–4 knots = probably 200 sea miles Depth sounded 160 fathoms 'whereby we thought to be farre from land and perceived that the land lay not as the globe made mention'	034	029
6–8 Aug	SE by S	Probably reaching '48 leagues' = 144 sea miles 2 days at probably 3 knots = 133 sea miles	146	141
8 Aug	ESE	Drifted one day at perhaps 1–2 knots = about 36 sea miles; depth 160 fathoms	112	107
9 Aug	NE	Reaching, wind SSE, '25 leagues' = 75 sea miles; depth, no bottom found 1 day at probably 3 knots = 72 sea miles	145	140
10 Aug	SE	Reaching, wind NE, '48 leagues' = 144 sea miles	135	130

Date	Direction sailed	Distance run and comments	Compass course in °	True course °
10 Aug		1 day at probably 3 knots = 72 sea miles		
11 Aug	??	Wind S; depth 40 fathoms		
12 Aug	E and E	Reaching, wind S by E, '30 leagues' = 90 sea miles	090	085
	by N	1 day at probably 2 knots = 48 sea miles	079	074
13 Aug	??			
14 Aug	??	Saw land, but could not reach it due to the shallowness of the water and much ice; 72 degrees latitude.		
15–17 Aug	N	'Plyed northward', probably tacking 3 days at perhaps 1 or 2 knots = perhaps 40 sea miles	000	355
18–20 Aug	SSE	Reaching, wind NE, '70 leagues' = 210 sea miles; 3 days at perhaps 3 knots = 216 sea miles	157	152
21 Aug	?NW and W	10 and later 7 fathoms' depth but no land in sight: ?wind direction 1 day at perhaps 1 or 2 knots = 36 sea miles	? 304	? 299
22 Aug	WSW	Depth 20 fathoms, wind direction ? 1 day at perhaps 1 or 2 knots = 36 sea miles	247	242
23–8 Aug	W, then N by E, then WNW, then WSW, then NE, then NW, then W	Saw land, but shoal water and dry sand Landed on shore, found some crosses but no houses Sailed along the coast, generally W or WNW for 5 days = perhaps 150 sea miles	281	276
28 Aug– 4 Sept	NW	'16 leagues' = 48 sea miles	315	310
4–8 Sept	W	Contrary winds, tacking, lost sight of coast, maybe 15 sea miles	270	265
8–12 Sept	W by S	'30 leagues' = 90 sea miles; saw coast again	259	254
12–14 Sept	NW by W	Near shore, sailed along the coast, perhaps 30 sea miles	304	299

Date	Direction sailed	Distance run and comments	Compass course in °	True course °
14 Sept		Anchored 2 leagues from the shore in 60 fathoms, found a good harbour		
18 Sept		Returned to the harbour that they had found on the 14th, where they moored for the winter, and where they all later perished (subsequently found to be the Arzina river)		

NOTE

N by E = north and by east, that is to say 11¼° to the east of north, which is 011¼° on a 360-degree compass. In similar fashion, NE by N = north east and by north is 11¼° to the north of north-east, or 033¾°.

The compass courses, in degrees, have been converted to true courses by applying the magnetic variation that existed around 1550, as deduced and plotted by van Bemmelen in 1899.[1] His Isogonic Chart is shown on page 96. The depths found by Sir Hugh's ships at several positions during the voyage give useful confirmation of the courses that they sailed, when compared with the soundings shown on the modern Admiralty Chart 2962, *The North Cape to Uyedinyeniya Island.*

The bearings and distances in the table above have been used to find the (approximate) dead-reckoning positions of the ships at different dates. The overall effects of leeway, together with the easterly flow of the ocean current, would both have carried them further to the east than their dead-reckoning positions indicated, as the strong winds in the first eight or nine days would have produced more leeway to the east than the winds later in the outward voyage set them to the west.

The Voyages of the Muscovy Company Ships (1553–82)

Year	Ships' names	Voyages made	People and cargoes	References
1553	Edward Bonaventura (160 tons)	London to find NE Passage, arrived at St Nicholas	Chancellor (Pilot General) S. Borough (Master) J. Buckland (Mate)	Hak i, 244, 266–93 Hak ii 265
	Bona Esperanza (120 tons) Bona Confidentia (90 tons)	London to find NE Passage, wintered at Arzina, all crew perished	Sir Hugh Willoughby (Captain General)	Hak i, 244–54 Hak ii 265
1554	Edward Bonaventura (160 tons)	St Nicholas to London (homeward robbed by Flemings)	Chancellor (Pilot General) S. Borough (Master) J. Buckland (Mate)	Hak ii 265
1555	Edward Bonaventura (160 tons) Philip and Mary	London to St Nicholas and return	Chancellor (Pilot General), J. Buckland and J. Howlet (Masters), outward with George Killingworth and Richard Gray, Muscovy Co. agents	Hak i 299–303 Hak ii 265–7
1556	Edward Bonaventura (160 tons)	London to St Nicholas	Chancellor (Pilot General), J. Buckland (Master), with extra masters and crews to sail the Bona Esperanza and the Bona Confidentia home	Hak i 333–6 Hak ii 267

Year	Ships' names	Voyages made	People and cargoes	References
1556	*Philip and Mary*	London to Wardhouse		Hak ii 267–8
	Serchthrift (pinnace)	London to search farther east for NE Passage, reached Kara Strait and Novaya Zemlya, retreated to Colmogro	Stephen Borough (Master) with William Borough, Richard Johnson and eight others	Hak i 333–52
1556	*Edward Bonaventura* (160 tons)	St Nicholas to Pitsligo (Scotland), wrecked	Chancellor (drowned) Buckland and Ossip Napea survived	Hak i 357–8
	Bona Esperanza (120 tons) *Bona Confidentia* (90 tons)	St Nicholas to Norway, both lost	£6,000 goods of Ossip Napea's lost	Hak i 358 and 381
1556 –7	*Philip and Mary*	St Nicholas to London, reached London in 1557	With wax worth £4,256 K.R.	Hak i 358, 375 and 381; Exch. Customs A/CS 86/6
1557	*Serchthrift*	Colmogro to Wardhouse and back to Kegor, search for lost ships	Stephen and William Borough, and nine others	Hak i 367–77
	Primrose (240 tons) *John Evangelist* (170 tons) *Anne* (160 tons) *Trinitie* (140 tons)	London 12 May to St Nicholas 13 July, and returned to London	Buckland (Master of *Primrose*) outward with Anthonie Jenkinson (Captain General of Fleet); Ossip Napea returned to Russia. And 610 tons of cargo out	Hak i 377–91, 408–12; Hak ii 268; Hamel 155; Willan 1948, 309
1558	There must have been voyages in 1558 and 1559, as the voyage in	London to St Nicholas and return	?	Hak i 399, 'The seventh voyage', 404–5
1559	1560 was described as the 'seventh voyage'	London to St Nicholas and return	?	

Year	Ships' names	Voyages made	People and cargoes	References
1560	*Swallow* *Philip and Mary* *Jesus*	London to St Nicholas and return. 'First safe returne, without loss or shipwracke or dead fraight & burnings'	S. Borough, Thomas Wade and Arthur Pet (Masters respectively), cloth, sack etc. (Hakluyt has a detailed inventory)	Hak i 399, 'The seventh voyage', 404–5; Hak ii 268; Hamel 149
1561	*Swallow* and two other ships	Gravesend 14 May to St Nicholas 14 July and return	Outward with Anthonie Jenkinson, 'delayed by diversitie of windes'	Willan 1956, 48 Hak ii 4–5, 9
1562	?			
1563	?			
1564	*Swallow* and two other ships	London to St Nicholas and return (9 July– 28 September). Outward with lead, sulphur, wine, canvas etc.	S. Borough (Master) Anthonie Jenkinson made the return journey	Exch. K.R. Customs 90/11; Willan 1948 309–10; Hak ii 28
1565	Two ships	London to St Nicholas and return. Outward with cloths and kersies	S. Borough (Master)	Exch. K.R. Port Books 2/1; Willan 1948, 310
1566	*Harry* 'Our own shippe'	Gravesend 4 May to St Nicholas 11 June (or 10 July)	William Borough (Master), Anthonie Jenkinson. Jenkinson sent home a loysche (an elk)	Hak ii 73; Hamel 143; Willan 1956, 48–9; Morgan and Coote i, 8 and 9
1567	*Swallow* (120 tons)	London to St Nicholas, and return to London 16 October	Stephen Borough (Master), homeward with Anthonie Jenkinson; Twerdicoff and Pogorell, Russian merchants,	Exch. K.R. Port Books 4/2; Dietz 6; Hamel 181 and 197; Willan

Year	Ships' names	Voyages made	People and cargoes	References
			and 322cwt wax and 140cwt of tallow (cwt = 112lb/51kg)	1948, 311 (Johnson); Morgan and Coote II, 225
	Charity (130 tons)	London to St Nicholas, and return to London 16 October	189cwt wax and 119cwt tallow homeward, Richard Gybbes (Master)	
	Three other ships	London to St Nicholas and back	Outward with cloth and haberdashery	
1568	*Harry*	Harwich 22 June to St Nicholas 23 July, and return to London	S. Borough (Master), outward with Thomas Randolph and twenty gentlemen, and Twerdicoff and Pogorell	Hak ii 78, 80–5; Hamel, 143
	?	London to St Nicholas, and return on 12 August	William Borough	Morgan and Coote II, 256–7, 261; Landsdowne MS 11, No. 37; Hamel 199
	Charitie (100 tons)	Russia to London 8 September	Thomas Awdley (Master), 750cwt cordage, 170cwt wax, 80lb raw silk, 10 calf skins in the hair, various skins, 20lb rhubarb etc.	Exch. K.R. Port Books 4/2; Dietz 130
	Lyon (75 tons)	Russia to London 10 August (presumably from Wardhouse)	John Dunstan (Master), 74 tuns traine oil	Exch. K.R. Port Books 4/2; Dietz 116
1569	?	London to St Nicholas & return (end of July to September)	Stephen Borough (Master), homeward with Randolphe and Co.	Hak ii 85; Hamel 150

Year	Ships' names	Voyages made	People and cargoes	References
1570	?	?	?	?
1571	*Harry* *Swallow* *Magdalene*	London to St Nicholas 26 or 27 July and return	Stephen Borough (Master), outward with Anthonie Jenkinson, and corn for Russian famine, and 425 short and 2 long cloths	Hakluyt ii 135, 136; Exch. K.R. Port Books 5/1; Hamel 210 and 214; Willan 1948, 313
1572	Three ships	London to St Nicholas and 23 July return	Homeward with Anthonie Jenkinson	Hakluyt ii 136; Willan 1948, 313
1573	?	?	?	?
1574 –5	?	?	William Borough was Muscovy Company agent in Russia 1574–5	Hak ii 169; Hamel 143
1576	Six ships	London to St Nicholas and back	Cottons, paper, sack etc.	Willan 1948, 313
1579	*Harry* and other ships	London 19 June to St Nicholas 22 July	Outward with Christopher Borough and goods for trade with Persia	Hak ii 172; Willan 1956, 48
1580	*George* (40 tons)	London to explore NE Passage, reached Kara Strait, returned to London	Arthur Pet (Master)	Hak ii 227–44; Hak. photolitho 455 and 459
	William (20 tons)	London to explore NE Passage, reached Kara Strait, wintered in Norway, then lost	Charles Jackman (Master)	
1581	*Elizabeth*; *Thomas Allen*; *Mary Susan*; *William and John*; *Tomasin*	St Nicholas 25 and 26 July to London (Limehouse, Wapping) 25 September	One ship brought back goods from Persia	Hak ii 200; Willan 1948, 313
1582	Ten ships, the	London 1 June to		Hak ii 244

Year	Ships' names	Voyages made	People and cargoes	References
	largest fleet until now, including *Solomon* (Admirall), *Thomas Allen* (Vice Admirall) and *Prudence*	St Nicholas		
c. 1582	*George Bonaventura*	London to St Nicholas	'Crew all perished with frost in unseasonable time of year'	Camb.Univ. Lib. Ms Dd ix 2(c) f. 31; Willan 1956, 5

REFERENCES

Camb. Univ. Lib. = Cambridge University Library

Dietz = B. Dietz, *The Port and Trade of Early Elizabethan London Documents* (London, London Record Society, 1972)

Exch. K.R. Customs = National Archives, Kew, Exchequer King's Remembrancer, Customs Accounts

Hak i = Hakluyt, *Principal Navigations*, Everyman, vol. I

Hak ii = Hakluyt, *Principal Navigations*, Everyman, vol. II

Hak photolitho = Hakluyt, *Principal Navigations*, in photolithographic edition, D.B. Quinn and R. Skelton (eds) (Cambridge, Hakluyt Society, 1965)

Hamel = J. Hamel, *England and Russia* [1854], trans. J.S. Leigh (London, Frank Cass, 1968)

Johnson = A.H. Johnson, *The History of the Worshipful Company of Drapers of London* vol. II, pp. 456–7, quoted in Willan, 'Trade between England and Russia', pp. 307–21, at 310–11

Lansdowne MS at British Library

Morgan and Coote = E.D. Morgan and C.H. Coote, *Early Voyages and Travels to Russia by Anthonie Jenkinson and Other Englishmen* (2 vols, London, Hakluyt Society, 1886), vol. I, pp. lxxii and lxxiii

Willan 1948 = T.S. Willan, 'Trade between England and Russia in the Second Half of the Sixteenth Century', in *English Historical Review*, 63 (1948), pp. 307–21

Willan 1956 = T.S. Willan, *The Early History of the Russia Company, 1553–1603* (Manchester, Manchester University Press, 1956)

Note that the Russians captured Narva, a port in the Baltic, in 1558, but they lost it again to the Swedes in 1581. During the twenty-two years that the

Russians held the port, the Muscovy Company sent ships there, as well as to St Nicholas, and during this time they maintained a trade with Persia from Narva by a long and hazardous overland route. Variable numbers of ships were involved in the trade to Narva: in 1566, for instance, the company claimed to have sent as many as fourteen ships there.[1]

Stephen Borough was 56 years old in 1571, when he made what seems to have been his last voyage for the Muscovy Company. By way of comparison, Scammell mentions a certain James Covenant who was still both owner and master of the *Phoenix* at the age of 68.[2]

Stephen Borough's Survey of the North Russian Coast (Summary)

A list of the main headlands in Stephen Borough's survey of the coast from St Nicholas to Kegor
(Modern names are in brackets)

From Berozova Guba bar, near St Nicholas, it is 3½ leagues north and by west to
Coscaynos or Koska Nos (Kouiski Point), and from there it is 8 leagues north-north-west to
Dog's Nose (Keretz Point), and from there it is 3 leagues north and by west, to
Fox Nose [M. Verprevskiy], and from there it is 6 leagues to Zolatitsa (Zolotitsa).
[There follows a gap in the account of about 20 leagues]

From Crosse Island (Sosnovets Island), it is 7½ leagues north-east to
Cape Grace (Krasni Point), and from there it is 5 leagues Northnortheast to
2 Islands or Tri Ostrove (Trekh Islands), and from there it is 2 leagues north and by west to
Cape Race (Cape Orlov), and from there it is 6 leagues north and a half point east to
Corpus Christi Point (Mys Bol. Gorodetskiy).
[There follows a gap in the account of about 14 leagues]

From Cape Gallant or Sotinoz (Svyatoi Nos), it is 7 leagues west-north-west and a half point north to
Juana Creos (Cape Cherni and Nokuev Island), and from there it is 14½ leagues north-west and half a point north to
St George's Islands or the Seven Islands (Seni Islands), and from there 11 leagues north-west to
St Peter's Islands (Mogilni Island), and from there it is 6 leagues north-west and by west to
St Paul's Islands (Gavrilovskie Islands), and from there it is 5 leagues north-west and by west to
Cape Sowerbeer (Cape Teriberski), and from there it is 6 leagues west-north-west to
Kildina Island (Kildin Island).

[There follows a gap in the account of about 2 leagues, across the entrance to the Kola river, where Murmansk is now.]

From Cape Bonaventure (Pogan Point), it is 10 leagues north-west and a little to the west to
Chebe Navaloche (Tsip Navalok Ft.), and from there it is 9½ leagues north-west and half a point to the west to
Kegor (Ribachi Peninsula).
[And from Kegor it is about 15 leagues to Wardhouse.]

The modern names (in brackets) are from E.D. Morgan and C.H. Coote, *Early Voyages and Travels to Russia and Persia* (2 vols, London, Hakluyt Society, 1886, repr. B. Franklin, New York), vol. II, p. 253, and from the Admiralty Chart 2962, *The North Cape to Uyedinyeniya Island.*

The Latitudes Recorded by Stephen Borough in 1556 and 1557

Table of the latitude readings recorded by Stephen Borough on his 1556 and 1557 voyages in the *Serchthrift*, compared with latitudes taken from the Admiralty Chart 2962, *The North Cape to Uyedinyeniya Island*.

Date	Latitude found by Stephen	Modern latitude	Geographical position	Page in Hakluyt, vol. I*
			1556 VOYAGE	
15/5	58½°		7 leagues off coast of Norway	334
16/5	59° 42'		Off St Dunstan's Island	334
18/5	63½°			335
20/5	67° 39'		South of Lofoten Islands	335
21/5	69½°		72 leagues SW of Kedelwike Chapel	335
10/6	65° 48'	69½°	Mouth of Kola river	337
28/6	66° 50'		Cape St John	341
7/7	68½°		SE of Kanin Nos	342
9/7	68° 40'	68° 40'	Kanin Nos	343
13/7	68½°		Morgiovets, 30 leagues ESE of Kanin Nos	343
17/7	69° 10'	68° 20'	Mouth of Pechora river	344
23/7	70° 11'		At sea, ENE of Pechora river mouth	345
24/7	70° 15'		At sea, ENE of Pechora river mouth	345
25/7	70° 20'		Near St James's Island	345
27/7	70° 42'		At St James's Island	345
6/8	70° 25'	70° 25'	Vaigats Islands (latitude measurement taken on shore)	348
18/8	70° 10'		Vaigats Islands (Vaygach Island extends from 69° 40' to 70° 30' N)	349
21/8	70° 8'		15 leagues N of Pechora river mouth	350
22/8	70½°			350
23/8	70½°			
24/8	70½°		'There was a billow so that we could not . . . take the latitude exactly but by a reasonable guess'	351

Date	Latitude found by Stephen	Modern latitude	Geographical position	Page in Hakluyt, vol. I*
25/8	70° 10'			351
27/8	70° 10'	69° 40'	3 leagues N of Kolguyev Island	351
			1557 VOYAGE	
23/5	64° 25'	64° 45'	Colmogro (Kholmogory)	367
2/6	65° 47'	65° 18'	Dog's Nose	368
8/6	66° 24'	66° 35'	Crosse Island	369
10/6	67° 10'	67° 4'	Near Cape Race	369
?/6	66° 58½'	67° 5'	Tri Ostrove	370
?/6	67° 29'	67° 35'	2 leagues S of Corpus Christi Point	371
22/6	68° 1'	68° 2'	St John's Islands, near Sotinoz (Svyatoi Nos)	371

* The page references are from Hakluyt, *Principal Navigations*, Everyman, vol. I

Stephen Borough took thirty readings of latitude on his 1556 and 1557 voyages and achieved a remarkable degree of accuracy with most of them. His only serious discrepancy (if this is not a transcription error of 'five' for 'nine') was on 10 June 1556, at the mouth of the Kola river, where his latitude put him nearly 4° too far south, but in general he was both diligent and accurate. He improved his accuracy considerably with increasing experience.

APPENDIX 9

Navigational Instruments

This is a list of the instruments that would have been available and were very probably taken on the 1553 and subsequent voyages.

Compass, several, mounted on gimbals, in a box (binnacle), with a lantern attached.

Azimuth compass or compass of variation, a compass with which the bearing of a star can be measured against the bearing of magnetic north, most commonly so that the magnetic variation at that point can be determined.

Lodestone, to remagnetise the compass needle, the magnetic properties of which wore off after some weeks, as the needle was made of soft iron.

Half-hour glasses, several. (Also called 'running glasses'.)

Traverse board and pegs, to record the course steered every half-hour.

Astrolabe, a cast brass dial with a revolving sighting arm (alidade), with a sighting hole at each end.

Nocturnal, to find the time at night from the date and the relative positions of the the 'Guards' and the Pole Star.

Quadrant.

Cross staff (also referred to as a 'balestow'), with (usually) three different cross arms (also called transverses or transoms), e.g. 5°, 15°, 30°.

English log line and reel.

Lead lines for sounding, with tallow to insert into the bases to sample the sea bed for texture, colour, taste and smell. (The expression 'in soundings' means that the depth is no more than 100 fathoms, i.e. within the continental shelf and thus not far from land). For great depths, a heavy lead weighing 14lb was used (the deep sea or 'dipsie' lead), with up to 200 fathoms of line, marked at 10-fathom intervals by knots. For coastal work, a smaller lead was used, weighing 7lb and marked by knots at shorter intervals.

Mercator's 1541 terrestrial globe. (A copy is in the National Maritime Museum at Greenwich.)

Celestial globe.

Pairs of dividers.

Planimetrum or plane table.

Richard Caundish's (or Cavendish's) *Chart of the Thames Estuary, c.* 1535.

Sea cardes: small charts on leather showing the main headlands and ports in an area such as the east coast of England, with a compass rose showing radiating lines of rhumbs (e.g. *Booke of the Sea Carte*, British Museum, Add. 37,024).

The New Rutter for the Sea, printed by Robert Proude in 1541, which covered the coast of England.

The Arte of Navigation, translated by Richard Eden from Martin Cortes's *Arte de Navegar*, was available for voyages after about 1561.

One or more *Tables of Ephemerides*, including the one compiled by John Dee and Richard Chancellor.

John Dee's *Astronomicall and Logisticall Rules*, designed for use on the 1553 voyage.

John Dee's traverse tables, his *Canon Gubernauticus: an Arithmeticall Resolution of the Paradoxall Compas*.

John Dee's Circumpolar Chart, his *Paradoxal Cumpas in Playne* of 1552.

Robert Recorde's *Ground of Arts*, on arithmetic, and his *Pathway to Knowledge*, on geometry and the use of the quadrant. Robert Recorde's *Castle of Knowledge* (1556), was a treatise on the spheres which appeared in time for the later voyages and was specifically written for the use of the Muscovy Company navigators. Robert Recorde also wrote *The Whetstone of Wit* (1557), an elementary textbook on mathematics, which he dedicated to the Governors of the Muscovy Company.

An Almanac, probably that by Leonard Digges, *A Prognostication of Right Good Effect* (Blackfriars, T. Gemini, 1555), which included some astronomical and nautical tables and a discussion of the use of some simple astronomical instruments.

Tide tables – E.G. Brouscon's *Tide Tables* of *c.* 1545, which showed on a small chart of the coasts of Europe as far north as Holland the 'establishment' of every major port in relation to the time of high tide at full moon.

Possibly two books in English that were related to navigation: Roger Barlow, *A Brief Summe of Geographie* (1536) and J. Rotz, *The Booke of Hydrographie* (1542).

For contrast, the list of the instruments mentioned on the voyage of the *Barbara* to Brazil in 1540 included only 'A Pilotte's carde, a Master's carde, the pilotte's estrolaby, a balestely [cross staff], a nocturnal and a very excellent goodly carde . . .', which covered the Atlantic, including England and Guinea and the 'quoaste of Brasell, and Kennyballs [cannibals], all th' empirours Indians, so alonge Newe foundlande, with divers other places'. The *Barbara* probably also had a compass and a lead line or two, but these are not mentioned. R.G. Marsden (ed.), *The Voyage of the Barbara to Brazil, Anno 1540*, Naval Miscellany, no. 2 (London, Naval Records Society, 1912), vol. XL, pp. 3–66.

The English Joint Stock Companies

Name of company	Dates	Comments	References
Guinea (or Africa)	1553–c. 1566	Short-lived. Had five 'Chief Adventurers' and a number of 'Underadventurers' (and seven merchants among its thirty-seven shareholders.) Had no charter and no monopoly. Made big profits for a few years from African gold, ivory and spices. Ended about 1566.	Scott 18, 23; Loades 117
Muscovy (or Russia)	1553–1917	Charter granted 26/2/1555. The first joint stock company of importance traded to Russia via St Nicholas (and also for a time to Narva in the Baltic). Monopoly of Russia trade. Had 200 or so subscribers, each of £25 initially. Three-quarters of them were London merchants, and many of the rest were high officers of the Court, including seven peers of the realm.	Scott 17; Loades 146–8
Cathaia	1574–c. 1578	Provided the financial backing for Frobisher's voyages to find a north-west passage, 1576–8. A financial disaster.	McDermott, quoted in Symons (vol. I) 147–78
Spanish	1577	Ineffectual and short-lived.	Coleman 57–9
Eastland	1579–1689	English trade with Baltic, especially for masts and other naval supplies; exporting mostly cloth, its privileges were stopped in 1673, though it continued to exist until 1689.	Loades 146–8; Comp. Brit. Hist. 255–7
Levant	1605–1825	Formed from amalgamation of two groups of London merchants; 529	Loades 139;

Name of company	Dates	Comments	References
		members; had to sail in armed convoys because of North African corsairs. Exported cloth, tin and lead to Constantinople, Aleppo and Smyrna, and imported cotton, silk, spices, drugs, wine and currants.	Comp. Brit. Hist. 466
East India	1600–1858	Originally traded to Spice Islands, but by 1640 also to Madras; by 1667 to Bombay and by 1690 to Calcutta. Prospered as Portuguese (and later Spanish) control over the Indian Ocean waned. Became immensely powerful and eventually exercised imperial control over India. Had over 1,000 shareholders, of whom 20–25 per cent were gentlemen investors. Big rivals were the Dutch Verenigde Oostindische Compagnie (VOC). (The Dutch were the commercial giants of the early seventeenth century.) Imported spices, calicoes and silks from India, and tea from China. Exported bullion, metal goods and woollens to India, and opium from India to China. India became part of the British Empire ('The Jewel in the Crown') very largely owing to the East India Company and its private army.	Comp. Brit. Hist. 255–7; Loades 117, 140; Sutton 169–70; Wild 180 and 186
Baffin		Eight shareholders.	Loades 117
Virginia	1606	1,000 shareholders, of whom 20–25 per cent were gentlemen. Its main product was tobacco. The island of Bermuda was chartered to the company from 1612, after a Virginia Company ship had foundered there in 1609. (Bermuda or 'The Bermouthes' was the island where Shakespeare set *The Tempest*.)	Loades 117; Coleman 57–9; Comp. Brit. Hist. 76
New Plantation of Ulster	1609	To 'plant' or colonise the forfeited lands of north-east Ireland with Scots and other Protestants.	
French	1611	Ineffectual and short-lived.	Coleman 57–9

Name of company	Dates	Comments	References
Massachusetts Bay	1628–84	Founded to promote settlement and exploitation of the Colony but was the least well-funded of all the joint stock trading companies. Political power was in the hands of Congregationalist ministers.	Coleman 57–9; Comp. Brit. Hist. 506
Providence Island	1629–42	Formed by several Puritan aristocrats to make a base for privateering against the Spanish, but Providence Island (in the Caribbean Sea off the coast of modern Nicaragua) was captured by the Spanish in 1642.	Coleman 57–9; Comp. Brit. Hist. 624
Royal African	1662–1752	Monopoly right to trade with the coast of Africa from Sallee to the Cape of Good Hope. Most of the trading was to the Gulf of Guinea in slaves, gold, silver and redwood.	Loades 146–8; Comp. Brit. Hist 665; Hair and Law 255–8
Hudson Bay	1670–present	The author has some Eskimo sculptures purchased at the Hudson Bay Company Stores at Goose Bay on the Coast of Labrador in 1969.	Loades 146–8; Braddick 295
South Sea	1711–1854	To trade with South America and the Spanish Colonies there, and to take over part of the National Debt. (It survived the 'South Sea Bubble', a speculative boom that crashed in 1720.)	Comp. Brit. Hist. 707

There were many other early joint stock companies, including: Barbary; Bermuda; Cavendish; Drake; Gilbert; Gosnold (unsuccessful expedition to New England, 1602); Guiana; Irish Plantation; Mineral and Battery Works; Mines Royal; Newfoundland; New Merchant Adventurers; New River; Plymouth Plantation (New England); Senegal; Staple Merchants; Venice; Weymouth, and others. See T.K. Rabb, *Enterprise and Empire: Merchant and Gentry Investment in the Expansion of England, 1575–1630* (Cambridge, Massachusetts, Harvard University Press, 1967), p. 104; N. Canny (ed.), *Oxford History of the British Empire, Vol. I, the Origins of Empire* (Oxford, OUP, 1998), passim.

REFERENCES

Braddick = M.J. Braddick, 'The English Government, War, Trade and Settlement, 1625–1688', in Canny, *Oxford History*, vol. I, pp. 286–308, at 295

Coleman = D.C. Coleman, *The Economy of England, 1450–1750* (London, OUP, 1977)

Comp. Brit. Hist. = J. Gardiner and N. Wenborn, *The History Today Companion to British History* (London, Collins and Brown, 1995)

Hair and Law = P.E.H. Hair and R. Law, 'The English in Western Africa to 1700', in Canny, *Oxford History*, vol. I, pp. 255–8

Loades = D. Loades, *England's Maritime Empire: Seapower, Commerce and Policy 1490–1690* (Harlow, Pearson, 2000)

Scott = W.R. Scott, *The Constitution and Finance of English, Scottish and Irish Joint Stock Companies to 1720* (2 vols, Cambridge, Cambridge University Press, 1910–12, repr. 1993)

Sutton = J. Sutton, *Lords of the East: The East India Company and its Ships* (London, Conway Maritime, 1981)

Symons = T.H.B. Symons, *Meta Incognita: a Discourse of Discovery: Martin Frobisher's Arctic Expeditions 1576–1578* (Quebec, Canadian Museum of Civilisation, 1999)

Wild = A. Wild, *The East India Company: Trade and Conquest from 1600* (New York, Lyons Press, 2000)

APPENDIX 11

The Charts and Globes Available in 1553

The geography of the proposed North-East Passage, as depicted in the main maps and charts (and four globes) which were compiled in the hundred-odd years before the departure of the 1553 expedition.

Chartmaker	Year	Geographical features shown, relating to a possible north-east passage
C. Clavus	1427	*Hafs-botn*, an arm of the Atlantic, extending as far as the White Sea but no further.[1]
Germanus	1460	An enormous promontory blocks the North-East Passage route.[2]
Unknown	1482	A huge promontory extends north from north-east Asia.[3]
H. Martellus	1490	A land bridge connects Greenland to northern Scandinavia.[4]
M. Behaim (globe)	1492	Earliest European globe to have survived. A land bridge connects Greenland to northern Scandinavia.[5]
F. Roselli	1492	A land bridge connects Greenland to northern Scandinavia.[6]
Laon (globe)	1493	A land bridge connects Greenland to northern Scandinavia.[7]
G.M. Contarini	1506	A land bridge connects Greenland to northern Scandinavia.[8]
J. Ruysch	1507	A large promontory, labelled Hyperborean Europe, blocks the route.[9]
M. Waldesmuller	1507	A large promontory projects a long way north from northern Scandinavia.[10]
F. Roselli	c. 1508	A land bridge connects Greenland to northern Scandinavia.[11]
J. Stobnicza	1512	A large promontory projects a long way north from northern Scandinavia.[12]
M. Waldesmuller	1513	A land bridge connects Greenland to northern Scandinavia.[13]
Argentinae	1513	Route blocked by a huge promontory of Greenland.[14]
Balenger	1514	Route blocked.[15]
Leonardo da Vinci	1514	His 'mappe mande' in four segments to each hemisphere, shows a passage.[16]

Chartmaker	Year	Geographical features shown, relating to a possible north-east passage
Schoner (globe)	1515	A complete blockage extends to the North Pole and beyond.[17]
P. Apianus	1520	A large promontory projects a long way north from northern Scandinavia. [18]
G. Frisius	1522	A land bridge connects Greenland to northern Scandinavia. The 'mare congelatum' lies to the north of this land bridge. [19]
R. Thorne	1527	His map, from a Spanish source, does not extend far enough north to show whether there is a route or not.[20]
B. Bordone	1528	A large promontory projects a long way north from northern Scandinavia.[21]
P. Apianus	1530	A large promontory projects a long way north from northern Scandinavia.[22]
L. Finnaeus	1531	A complete blockage extends to the North Pole and beyond.[23]
S. Grynaeus	1532	Shows a passage.[24]
G. Hartmann (globe)	c. 1533	'The Ambassadors' Globe', shown in Holbein's picture 'The Ambassadors'. A land bridge connects Greenland to northern Scandinavia.[25]
J. Vadianus	1534	A complete blockage extends to the North Pole and beyond.[26]
J. Zeigler	1536	A land bridge connects Greenland to northern Scandinavia.[27]
O. Magnus	1539	The 'Carta Marina' shows a clear sea route round Scandinavia.[28]
J. Maillard	1543	Solid land between Norway and Greenland.[29]
S. Cabot	1544	The 'Carta Marina' shows a clear sea route round Scandinavia.[30]
J. Honterus	1546	A picture of a globe shows a passage.[31]
G. Gastaldi	1546	A clear sea passage round Scándinavia and across the top of Asia.[32]
P. Descaliers	1546	A broad promontory extends north, almost to the North Pole.[33]
A. Salamanca	1550	A narrow sea passage round the north of Scandinavia which peters out further east.[34]
G. Gastaldi	1550	A clear sea passage round Scandinavia and across the top of Asia.[35]

As shown above, some of the charts showed an enormous promontory extending northwards from Scandinavia. Others showed solid land connecting the north of

Scandinavia to Greenland, making the sea to the west of Norway a large enclosed bay, and yet others showed a large bay of the Atlantic (the *Hafs-botn*) extending eastwards over the north of Scandinavia, but ending in the White Sea. Very few showed a clear water route for the North-East Passage.

Notes and References

FOREWORD

1 I do not doubt that John Cabot (with an English crew) was the first European (after Leif Eiriksson in AD 1000) to set foot on mainland America, in 1497. He, however, was of Genoese origin, like several other famous explorers, and the route that he followed was basically that of the Bristolian entrepreneurs of the 1480s, who in turn had followed the Basque fishermen to the cod banks of Newfoundland.

2 All of the references to R. Hakluyt's book, *Principal Navigations* [1589], are to the Everyman edition published by J.M. Dent (London, 1907) in eight volumes, unless stated otherwise, as this is the one most widely available. However the photolithographic facsimile edition, edited by D.B. Quinn and R.A. Skelton (2 vols, Cambridge, Hakluyt Society, 1965), is also referred to on occasion, as it contains valuable background material.

3 S.H. Baron, 'Russia and Central Asia', in L.E. Pennington (ed.), *A Purchas Chronology* (2 vols, London, Hakluyt Society, 1997), vol. I, p. 279

4 Hakluyt, *Principal Navigations* (1589), D.B. Quinn and R.A. Skelton, eds (1965), p. xxxv

5 Ibid., Sig. 4

6 L.B. Wright, *Religion and Empire: the Alliance between Piety and Commerce in English Expansion* (North Carolina, University of North Carolina, 1943), pp. 3–7, 41–3

7 Hakluyt, *Principal Navigations*, Everyman, vol. I, p. 6

8 G.B. Parkes, *Richard Hakluyt and the English Voyages* (New York, American Geographical Society, 1928), pp. 125 and 127

9 British Library, Cotton MSS, Otho E VIII, folios 11–16 ; Hakluyt, *Principal Navigations*, Everyman, vol. I, pp. 247–54

10 The various authors (in chronological order) who have told something of the story of the early Tudor explorations in their works include:

Samuel Purchas, *Hakluytus Posthumus or Purchas his Pilgrims* [1625] (20 vols, Glasgow, Maclehose edn, 1906), vol. V, p. 249

J. Moxon, *A Collection of Some Attempts Made to the North East and North West for the Finding of a Passage to Japan, China, etc.* (London, Joseph Moxon, 1676)

H. Willoughby, 'The Voyages of Sir Hugh Willoughby, Richard Chancellor and others to the Northern Parts of Russia and Siberia', in J. Pinkerton (ed.), *A General Collection of the Best and Most Interesting Voyages and Travels in All Parts of the World* (London, Longman, Hurst, Rees and Orme, 1808), vol. I, pp. 1–15 and 23–9

J. Barrow, *A Chronological History of the Voyages into the Arctic Region* [1818] (repr. Newton Abbot, David and Charles, 1971), pp. 64–75

Captain J. Burney, *A Chronological History of North Eastern Voyages of Discovery* (London, Payne and Foss, 1819), pp. 28–32

A. Hyde, A.C. Baldwin and W.L. Gage, *The Frozen Zone and its Explorers: a Comprehensive History of the Voyages, Travels, Adventures, Disasters and Discoveries in the Arctic Region, etc.* (Hartford, Connecticut, R.W. Bliss, 1880)

R.W. Cotton, 'Stephen Borough, the Navigator', *Transactions of the Devonshire Association*, 12 (1880–1), pp. 332–60

N.A.E. Nordenskiold, *The Voyage of the Vega Round Asia and Europe* (2 vols, London, Macmillan, 1881), vol. I

J.A. Williamson, *Maritime Enterprise, 1486–1558* (Oxford, Clarendon Press, 1913), pp. 307–37 (a particularly good account)

J.D. Rogers, 'Voyages and Exploration: Geography: Maps', in C.T. Onions (ed.), *Shakespeare's England* (2 vols, Oxford, Clarendon Press, 1916), vol. I, pp. 179–81

F.R. Dulles, *Eastward Ho! The First English Adventurers to the Orient – Richard Chancellor and Others* (London, John Lane, 1931), pp. 1–36

Sir J. Marshall-Cornwall, 'An English Arctic Expedition, 1553', *History Today*, 27 (1977), pp. 741–6

K.R. Andrews, *Trade, Plunder and Settlement: Maritime Enterprise and the Genesis of the British Empire* (Cambridge, Cambridge University Press, 1984), pp. 64–71

D. Loades, *England's Maritime Empire: Seapower, Commerce and Policy, 1490–1690* (Harlow, Pearson Education, 2000), pp. 56–7 and 66–8

INTRODUCTION

1 Richard Hakluyt, 'Preface to the Second Edition, 1598', in Hakluyt, *Principal Navigations*, Everyman, vol. I, p. 21

2 Ibid., p. 354

3 'Good luck befriend thee, Son; for at thy birth/The faery ladies danced upon the hearth.' John Milton (1608–74), 'At a Vacation Exercise in the College', D. Bush (ed.), *Milton: Poetical Works* (London, OUP, 1974), p. 55

4 T.O. Lloyd, *The British Empire, 1558–1995* (2nd edn, Oxford, OUP, 1996), p. 258. Lloyd points out that between 1870 and 1914, when the empire was at its zenith, Britain invested £1,700 million in countries within the empire but that, in the same period, Britain invested as much, if not more, in countries that were not in the empire, such as the USA, Argentina, and other South American and European countries. In other words, the commercial empire was, in financial terms, something like twice the size of the political empire at that time.

5 H.G.C. Mathew, 'The Liberal Age, 1851–1914', in K.O. Morgan (ed.), *The Oxford Popular History of Britain* (Paragon Book Service, Oxford, 1998), p. 559

CHAPTER 1

1 E.B. Knoebel, 'Astronomy and Astrology', in C.T. Onions (ed.), *Shakespeare's England* (2 vols, Oxford, Clarendon Press, 1916), vol. I, pp. 444–5

2 E.M.W. Tillyard, *The Elizabethan World Picture* [1943] (London, republished Pimlico, 1998), pp. 49–60

3 J. Gardiner and N. Wenborn (eds), *The History Today Companion to British History* (London, Collins and Brown, 1995), p. 479

4 In 2004, the population of Keighley was 49,800; of Macclesfield 50,300; of Stourbridge 55,900; and of Weymouth 53,900; see www.world-gazetteer.com/index.htm

5 Gardiner and Wenborn, *Companion to British History*, p. 610. For comparison, in the 2001 Census the population of England was 49,138,831, and that of Greater London was 7,172,036; see www.statistics.gov.uk/census 2001

6 J.B. Black, *The Reign of Elizabeth, 1558–1603* (2nd edn, Oxford, OUP, 1959), p. 237; P.J. Bowden, *The Wool Trade in Tudor and Stuart England* (London, Macmillan, 1962), p. xvi; C.M. Cipolla, *Before the Industrial Revolution: European Society and Economy, 1000–1700* (3rd edn, London, Routledge, 1993), p. 262; D.C. Coleman, *The Economy of England, 1450–1750* (London, OUP, 1977), p. 61. The other 15 per cent of the export trade was divided (in order of value) between raw wool, woolfells, lead, tin, corn, beer, coal and fish. Coal exports were just beginning to be significant, at about 12,000 tons a year at the start of Queen Elizabeth's reign. Black, *Reign of Elizabeth*, pp. 236–7

7 Bowden, *Wool Trade*, pp. 13 and 43

8 Ibid., p. 38

9 Fulling, also known as tucking, refers to the cleansing and thickening of cloth.

10 Bowden, *Wool Trade*, p. 107

11 C. Carpenter, *The Changing World of Weather* (Middlesex, Guinness Publishing, 1991), pp. 58–60

12 W.G. Hoskins, *The Age of Plunder: the England of Henry VIII, 1500–1547* (London, Longman, 1976), p. 87

13 J.D. Mackie, *The Oxford History of England: The Earlier Tudors* (London, OUP, 1952), p. 602

14 N. Heard, *Tudor Economy and Society* (London, Hodder and Stoughton, 1992), p. 18

15 J. Guy, *Tudor England* (Oxford, OUP, 1988), p. 184; Coleman, *Economy of England*, p. 47

16 N. Heard, *Edward VI and Mary: a Mid-Tudor Crisis?* (London, Hodder and Stoughton, 2000), p. 41

17 E. Kerridge, 'The Movement of Rent, 1540–1640', *Economic History Review*, 2nd series, 6 (1953–4), pp. 16–34, at 25; H.A.R. Fischer, *The Great Wave: Price Revolutions and the Rhythm of History* (London, OUP, 1996), p. 79

18 Fischer, *The Great Wave*, pp. 6, 74 and 78

19 A. Fletcher, *Tudor Rebellions* (3rd edn, Harlow, Longmans, 1983); Heard, *Tudor Economy and Society*, p. 13; Rosemary O'Day, *The Tudor Age* (London, Longman, 1995)

20 Bowden, *Wool Trade*, pp. 6, 89 and 112; D.C. Coleman, *Economy of England*, p. 56; R.B. Wernham, *Before the Armada: The Growth of English Foreign Policy, 1485–1588* (London, J. Cape, 1966), pp. 190 and 202. According to Bowden (p. 112), 'The shortcloth was a fictional cloth of 24 yards into which different types of woollens were translated according to a standard table for the purposes of customs assessment.'

21 W. Shakespeare, *Henry VIII* I, ii, 31–7

22 As early as 1392, some 300 English ships were said to have visited Danzig (modern Gdansk); G.D. Ramsay, *English Overseas Trade during the Centuries of Emergence* (London, Macmillan, 1957), p. 98.

23 'Ships from Blacknie [Blakeney] in the Countie of Norfolk' had made regular voyages north-west to Iceland – see Hakluyt, *Principal Navigations*, Hakluyt Society, p. 520 – as did ships from Dunwich – E.R. Cooper, 'The Dunwich Iceland Ships', *Mariner's Mirror* 25 (1939), pp. 170–7 – and ships from Bristol – see E.M. Carus Wilson, *Medieval Merchant Venturers* (London, Methuen, 1954), pp. 108–24. A total of 149 English ships sailed to Iceland in the year 1528; M. Oppenheim, *A History of the Administration of the Royal Navy and of Merchant Shipping in relation to the Navy 1509–1660* (London, Bodley Head, 1896), p. 89

24 G.V. Scammell, 'Shipowning in the Economy and Politics of Early Modern England', *Historical Journal*, 15 (1972), pp. 385–407

25 Two ships had sailed to Morocco in 1551 and 1552; Hakluyt, *Principal Navigations*, Hakluyt Society, pp. 85–8; T.S. Willan, *Studies in Elizabethan Foreign Trade* (Manchester, Manchester University Press, 1959), pp. 94–7 and 184–7

26 There is a suggestion that the English may have reached Guinea during the reign of Edward IV (1461–83) in D.B. Quinn, 'Edward IV and Exploration', *Mariner's Mirror*, 21 (1935), p. 275 *et seq.*

27 Bristolian entrepreneurs had followed the Basque fishermen across the Atlantic to the fishing grounds of Newfoundland. D.B. Quinn, *England and the Discovery of America, 1481–1620* (London, George Allen, 1974), p. 5; J.A. Williamson, *The Ocean in English History* (Oxford, Clarendon Press, 1941), pp. 13–22; A.A. Ruddock, 'John Day of Bristol and the English Voyages across the Atlantic before 1497', *Geographical Journal*, 132 (1966), pp. 225–33. John Cabot (of Genoa) had sailed from Bristol to the mainland of America in 1497; see D.B. Quinn, *England and the Discovery of America*, p. 93 *et seq.*; I. Wilson, *John Cabot and the Mathew* (Tiverton, Redcliffe Press, 1996), pp. 32–8. John Rut had made an ineffectual attempt to find a north-west passage at 53° N in 1527 and then sailed down to Puerto Rico. See J.A. Williamson, *Maritime Enterprise, 1485–1558* (Oxford, Clarendon Press, 1913), pp. 252–7; and Hakluyt has a brief note about 'two faire ships', one of which was called the *Dominus Vobiscum*, which apparently sailed to the Strait of Belle Isle between Newfoundland and the Labrador coast in 1527, where one ship was wrecked. The other returned safely but made no report of her findings. See Hakluyt, *Principal Navigations*, Everyman, vol. V, pp. 336–7

28 R. Marsden, 'The Voyage of the *Barbara* to Brazil, Anno 1540', *The Naval Miscellany* (London, Naval Records Society, 1912), vol. II, pp. 3–66

29 Hakluyt, *Principal Navigations*, Everyman, vol. VIII, pp. 13–15

30 M. Lewis, *The Hawkins Dynasty: Three Generations of a Tudor Family* (London, George Allen and Unwin, 1969), p. 43; J.A. Williamson, *Hawkins of Plymouth* (2nd edn, London, A & C Black, 1969), p. 27

31 Hakluyt, *Principal Navigations*, Everyman, vol. VIII, p. 15

32 Lewis, *Hawkins Dynasty*, p. 43

33 Roger Barlow, *A Brief Somme of Geographie* [1541], republished E.G.R. Taylor (ed.) (London, Hakluyt Society, 1932), series 2, no. 69, p. 180

CHAPTER 2

1 Memorial plaque to Stephen Borough in St Mary's Church, Chatham (now the Medway Heritage Centre Trust): '. . . Stephen Borough . . . was borne at Northam in Devonshire ye xxvth of Septemb. 1525.' The only reason to query his date of birth is that Chanter says it was in 1526 rather than 1525, though he gives no reason for this statement. J.F. Chanter, 'The History of Borough', in *Transactions of the Devonshire Association*, 58 (1926), pp. 193–208, at 195

2 The two commonest spellings of the family name were Borough and Aborough, but there were many other variations, sometimes even in the same document, including Abrough, Aburgh, Atborough, at Borowe, Borrows, Burrough, Burrow and Burowghe. For consistency, I use Borough for Stephen's surname throughout this book.

3 P.L. Dickinson, Richmond Herald, College of Arms, personal communication (6/3/1998) (re grant of Arms to William Borough, Stephen's younger brother, confirming that Walter was William's father, and therefore also Stephen's).

4 *Will of John Borough (Aborough)* Abstract of (Exeter, West Country Studies Library, OM

Collection 8/36). An uncle of Stephen Borough, he died in 1570 or 1571. John Borough's will mentions brothers Walter and Thomas; wife Christian; sons David and Peter; daughter Agnes; son-in-law John Hernaman; and daughter's son, another John Hernaman.

5 The presence of the nurse and the numbers of the other servants in the household are estimates derived from the numbers of servants in other small yeoman farms, in J. Youings, *Sixteenth-century England* (Harmondsworth, Penguin, 1984), p. 375

6 Stephen's younger brother William was also born at Borough, confirming that the family was still there in 1536, and that Borough was where Stephen spent his boyhood years. *Will of Stephen Borowghe* [1 July 1584], Courtesy of Helen Orme, Centre for Kentish Studies, County Hall, Maidstone, Kent ME14 1XQ (also reprinted in *New England Historical and Genealogical Register* 51 (1897), pp. 274–5). The will mentions Stephen's wife Joane; son Christopher; daughters Judith, Susan, Mary, Anne and Elizabeth; brother William; and his houses at Barking, Gravesend and Chatham.

7 M. St C. Byrne, *Elizabethan Life in Town and Country* (London, Methuen, 1954), p. 177; J. Shuter, *Tudor Children* (Oxford, Heinemann, 1996), p. 6

8 According to the contours of the 1:25,000 map, *Bideford and Atherington* (Southampton, Ordnance Survey, 1969) SS 42/52. (This was long before almost all of the present-day houses of Northam were built.)

9 'The tower serveth for a mark (as men say) for sailors that bear with the bar': T. Risdon, *A Chorographical Description & Survey of the County of Devon* [1605–30], (Plymouth, Rees and Curtis, 1811, reprinted Barnstaple, Porcupines, 1970), p. 288. The whitewashing of Northam church tower is in D.W. Gale, *Northam Parish Church* (2nd edn, 1989), p. 9

10 John Aborough died in 1570 at the age of 76. *Will of John Borowghe of Northam* (Abstract) (Exeter, West Country Studies Library, OM Collection 8/36). The many different spellings of his surname included all the variations of Stephen's (see n. 2), and many others as well (sometimes different spellings in the same document) including a borough, Aborough, Aborrowe, Aborroughe, Aburges, Borrow(e), Bruges, Deborough, debowrove, De Burghe, Teboro, Teborough(e), Teborow(e) and Toborow. Aborough was the most commonly used form of his surname, and in this book he is called John Aborough throughout, for the sake of consistency. John Borowghe (Aborough) mentions his brothers Walter and Thomas Borough by name in his will.

11 T.L. Stoate (ed.), *Devon Lay Subsidy Rolls 1524–7* (Bristol, T.L. Stoate 1979), p. 116; T.L. Stoate (ed.), *Devon Lay Subsidy Rolls 1543–5* (Bristol, T.L. Stoate 1986), p. 103

12 The family tree on p. 7 has been researched and compiled from Stoate, *Devon Lay Subsidy Rolls 1543–5*, p. 103, which lists John Borough @ £20, David Borowe @ £4, William Borow @ £10 and Walter Borowe @ £1. There were ninety-two names in the parish, the highest assessments being Richard Chapell @ £50, followed by John Borough and David Bocombe @ £20 each. See also:

Administration of Estate, Eleanora Aborough [Stephen Borough's first wife] (Probate Records of February 1562) at Family Records Centre, 1 Myddleton Street, London. vol. I, p. 36, folio 182(1), p. 58, in which she is described as 'daughter of John Smithe of parish of Clive (pecul. jurisd.)'. The parish of Clive is in Shropshire (E.C. Peele and R.S. Clease, *Shropshire Parish Documents* (Shrewsbury, Shropshire County Council, 1894), pp. 134–6), and the description of 'pecul. jurisd' is due to the fact that it came under the Royal Peculiar Court of St Mary's, Shrewsbury, for the purposes of probate. Her husband is described as Stephen Aborough of Ratcliffe.

J.L. Chester and G.J. Armytage, *Allegations for Marriage Licences Issued by the Bishop of London, 1520–1610* (2 vols, London, Harleian Society, no. XXV, 1887), vol. I, pp. 26 and 50

F.T. Colby, *The Visitation of the County of Devon in the Year 1620* (London, Harleian Society, vol. VI, 1872), p. 168

National Archives, Kew, Exchequer King's Remembrancer, Ancient Deeds, E 211/600. A grant of 6 Eliz [1564] to Agnes Aborough and William Aborough, of Middx., mariner: a *Grant of land in Stoke, Hartland, Devon*.

A.J. Howard and T.L. Stoate (eds), *Devon Muster Roll for 1569* (Bristol, 1977), pp. 117–18, which lists John Boroughe @ G7 + 1 corselet, Peter Boroughe @ G7 + 1 harquebuse, Walter Boroughe (jun.) as archer and Peter Boroughe as harquebusier. ('G' indicates that the assessment was on goods rather than lands, and 'G7' was a modest assessment, which required the provision of one bow, one sheaf of arrows, one steel cap and one bill.)

Will of John Borowghe of Northam (John Aborough, Abstract of will).

A Grant of Arms to William Borough (letter from Richmond Herald, College of Arms, 1998). William was the brother of Stephen. The letter confirms that William's father, and thus also Stephen's father, was named Walter.

Administration of Estate of John Rabelo [19 May 1572]. Probate Records, vol. II, p. 36, folio 216. At the Family Records Centre, 1 Myddleton Street, London. ('John Rabelo of the Precinct of St Katherine by the Tower of London, sailor, left the lease of a house to Stephen Borough of Ratcliffe, Co. Mssx, sailor.') This house, later described as Stephen Aborrowe's house at Barking, appears in the 1582 Subsidy Roll for London, Tower Ward, St Mary, Barking assessed for £20: R.G. Lang (ed.), *Two Tudor Subsidy Assessment Rolls for the City of London, 1541 and 1582* (London, London Record Society, 1993), p. 284

Hakluyt, *Principal Navigations*, Everyman, vol. II, p. 172: 'Sundrie letters written [from Persia] by Christopher Burrough [Stephen Borough's son], sent to his uncle Master William Burrough' from Persia, in 1581.

Will of Stephen Borough, 1584.

Burial Record of Stephen Borough, at St Mary's Church, Chatham [1584], Courtesy of City Archivist, City of Rochester upon Medway: 'Stephen Aboroughe, Esquire, was buried 14th July 1584.'

J.L. Vivian, *The Visitations of the County of Devon, Comprising the Heralds' Visitations of 1531, 1564 and 1620* (Exeter, Eland, 1895), pp. 340 and 528

Memorial Plaque to Stephen Borough in St Mary's Church, Chatham.

Will of David Borowe, of Northam (Abstract) (Exeter, West Country Studies Library, OM Collection). Will proved 12 July 1576. Mentions wife Anne (his executrix); brother Peter Borough; cousin John Hernaman; son John Borough and his children. Also mentions Blackmores, Thornes, Zelye, Badgelholles. (He owned half a boat with Thomas Zelye.)

Will of Peter Borowghe, gent. of Northam (Abstract) (Exeter, West Country Studies Library, OM Collection). Will proved 23 June 1587. The will mentions wife (unnamed), cousins, and Mathew and John Hernaman.

Will of Ann Boroughe, of Northam, Widow (Abstract) (Exeter, West Country Studies Library, OM Collection). Will proved 21 August 1589. Mentions Thomasin Borough, Ann Thorne, Agnes Borough, various Bagelholles, several Blackmores, several Sellyes, some Hernamans and John Borough, son of William Borough, who is her executor, but does not give any relationships.

T.L. Stoate (ed.), *Devon Taxes 1581–1660* (Almondsbury, T.L. Stoate, 1988), p. 129 (lists Ann Burrough, widow @ G4; Peter Burrough @ G6; and Christina Burrough @ G10).

Will of William Burrowghe (of Limehouse) (transcript in *New England Historical and Genealogical Register* [1897], pp. 274–5). Will proved 28 November 1598. Mentions his first wife Judith, buried at Stebunheth (Stepney); second wife Lady Jane Wentworth; sisters Agnes, Margery and Jane; cousin Thomas Leigh; children Walter and Mary (?by Judith); brother Stephen (deceased); Stephen's widow (unnamed); Stephen's children Elizabeth, Ann, Mary, Judith = John Vassall (William Borough's nephew) and Susan = King (also some connection to Sir Henry Palmer, and to Lady Elizabeth, Countess Dowager of Rutland – Sir Henry Palmer was an admiral who succeeded William Borough as Controller of the Navy in 1598).

Will of Joanne Burrough (of Chatham, widow) (Abstract) (Exeter, West Country Studies Library, OM Collection). Will proved 3 May 1604. Mentions daughters Mary, Elizabeth, Anne = Wright, (Susan) = King and Judith = Versall.

Will of Thomas Leigh (Abstract) (Exeter, West Country Studies Library, OM Collection). Will proved 29 August 1609. It mentions his wife, Agnes, who kept Burrough dwelling; son William; and daughter Agnes = Arthur Giffard. His various properties included Borough, and others at Northam, Abbotsham, Frithelstock, Barnstaple, Witheridge and Delbridge, and a windmill, ships and boats.

Carole Pavitt (of Chelmsford, Essex), *Letter about the Borough Family* and the Vassall connection (1999).

13 International Genealogical Index of the Church of Jesus Christ of Latter-Day Saints (the 'Mormon Index'), http://www.familysearch.org. This may not be absolutely accurate, as it relies, I believe, on the diligence of a large number of Mormon volunteers for its compilation.

14 J.F. Chanter, 'Borough, or Burrough, in Northam and its Inhabitants', *Transactions of the Devonshire Association*, 58 (1926), pp. 193–208, at 196

15 J. Youings, 'Three Devon-born Tudor Navigators', in M. Duffy et al. (eds), *The New Maritime History of Devon* (London, University of Exeter and Conway Maritime Press, 1992), pp. 32–4, at 32

16 Christian was not uncommon as a name for girls. For instance, Richard Grenville (1490–1550), grandfather of Sir Richard Grenville of the *Revenge*, had nine children, one of whom was a daughter called Christian.

17 *Will of John Borough* (Abstract), OM Collection (see n. 13)

18 Youings, *Sixteenth-century England*, pp. 196, 231 and 371

19 Cloam ovens are peculiar to Devon and adjacent areas. They are earthenware ovens, usually built at the side of the kitchen fireplace and used principally for making clotted cream.

20 R. Bovett, *Historical Notes on Devon Schools* (Exeter, Devon County Council, 1989), pp. 228–9

21 When the property came up for sale in 2003, it was learned that the same long upstairs room had survived until only recently, when the present owners had had the room subdivided to make it into several bedrooms. *Sale Brochure* (Bideford, Bond, Oxborough and Phillips [Estate Agents], 2003)

22 N. Orme, 'The Dissolution of the Chantries in Devon, 1546–8', *Transactions of the Devonshire Association*, 111 (1979), pp. 75–123, at 101, 110 and 122. The religious guild was a fraternity founded in the fifteenth century in honour of John the Baptist and George the Martyr, and it had a chapel of St John in the church. It raised money by quarterly contributions from its members, and it also owned quite a lot of land that had been donated, and these assets were used for the benefit of the parish.

The Crown, in the form of Edward VI, attempted to dissolve all the religious guilds, claiming that their funds were being put to superstitious uses. To evade this, the various properties that the fraternity owned were transferred into the custody of two individuals (they were 'granted and confirmed to Thomas Vallett and Philipp Braunton, wardens of the store and light of the fraternytie of St. John'). This was to lead to some skulduggery in Northam, as a certain Thomas Collemore informed the Crown that the fraternity were attempting to 'conceal lands' from the Commissioners for the Dissolution of Religious Guilds. The case was contested in the Court of Star Chamber in London between 1558 and 1566 (National Archives, Kew, PRO STAC 5, B4/34). One of the people involved in defending the assets of the fraternity was Stephen's uncle, John Aborough, but the case went against them and the lands were confiscated, some of them passing to Collemore as a reward for his informing. However, these lands, worth 116s 3d a year, reverted to the Crown soon afterwards. It seems that the villagers of Northam had made it impossible for Collemore to administer his ill-acquired property, and he was forced to exchange it for some other reward. The story does have a happy ending, as a certain Thomas Leigh, a wealthy man who later married into the Borough family, bought back the confiscated properties and granted the rents from them to the feoffees to be used for the good of the parish. D.W. Gale, *Northam Parish Church* (2nd edn, 1989), pp. 6 and 7

23 National Archives, Kew, *Land Revenue Accounts*, PRO LR 6/104/4; National Archives, Kew, *Abstract of the Chantry Certificate for Devon, 1548*, PRO E 301/80, quoted in Orme, 'The Dissolution of the Chantries', pp. 101, 110 and 122.

24 Appledore remained in the parish of Northam until 1844, when it became a separate parish. D. Carter, *Illustrated History of Appledore* (Swindon, D. Carter, 2000), p. 52

25 Captain W.J. Slade, *Out of Appledore* (London, Percival Marshall, 1959), plates 4 and 7. The original photos, by Mr Fox of Cardiff, are in the Photographic Collection of the Print Room at the National Maritime Museum, Greenwich.

26 Slade, *Out of Appledore*, p. 7

27 T.S. Willan, *River Navigation in England, 1600–1750* (London, Cass, 1964), p. vi; T.S. Willan, *The English Coasting Trade, 1600–1750* (New York, Kelly, 1976)

28 B. Greenhill, 'Editorial Preface', in Slade, *Out of Appledore*, p. xvii

29 E. Carus Wilson, *Medieval Merchant Venturers* (London, Methuen, 1954), p. xxxii; D.W. Waters, *The Rutters of the Sea: the Sailing Directions of Pierre Garcie* (New Haven and London, Yale University Press, 1967), pp. 3–43; J. Vanes, *The Port of Bristol in the Sixteenth Century* (Bristol, Bristol Branch of the Historical Association, 1995), p. 9

30 P. Cumberlidge, *Bristol Channel and Severn Pilot* (London, Stanford Maritime, 1988), pp. 125–8

31 A.J. Slavin, *Politics and Profit: a Study of Sir Ralph Sadler, 1507–1547* (Cambridge, Cambridge University Press, 1966), p. 14

32 Lois Lamplugh, *Barnstaple: Town on the Taw* (Chichester, Phillimore, 1983), p. 35. There could have been a grammar school in Bideford in Stephen's time, but there is no evidence for it until the 1580s. M. Goaman, *Old Bideford and District* (Bristol, Cox and Cox, 1968), pp. 27–8

33 N. Orme, *Education in the West of England, 1066–1548* (Exeter, University of Exeter, 1976), pp. 12, 30, 112–13.

34 Youings, *Sixteenth-century England*, p. 40

35 G.V. Scammell, 'Manning the English Merchant Service in the Sixteenth Century', *Mariner's Mirror*, 56 (1970), pp. 131–54, at 136

36 'Gromet' or 'grummett' (apparently from Low Latin *gromettus*), a youth or servant, who ranked above the ship's boy but below ordinary seamen. P. Kemp (ed.) *The Oxford Companion to Ships and the Sea* (Oxford, OUP, 1976), p. 357. Also called 'gromal' – see J.A. Williamson, *Maritime Enterprise, 1485–1558* (Oxford, Clarendon Press, 1913), p. 364

37 G.M. Thomson, *Sir Francis Drake* (London, Futura, 1972), p. 14

38 Chanter, 'Borough, or Burrough, in Northam and its Inhabitants', p. 196; 'Mormon Index', http://www.familysearch.org

39 *Will of John Borough* [1556] (Abstract) (Exeter, West Country Studies Library, OM Collection 8/36), d. 1570 or 1571 (see n. 13)

40 M. St C. Byrne (ed.), *The Lisle Letters* (Chicago, University of Chicago, 1981). vol. I, pp. 248–9, 397–9, and vol. II, pp. 58–60

41 Public Record Office, High Court of Admiralty 24, folio 5, *John a Borough contra John Andrewes.*

42 *Letters and Papers, Foreign and Domestic* (1539, 3 March), no. 432, p. 173

43 *Administration of Estate, Eleanora Aborough.* Family Records Centre (see n. 13)

44 E.D. Harris, 'Genealogical Gleanings in England', *New England Historical and Genealogical Register*, 51 (1897), p. 289; Chester and Armitage, *Allegations*, vol. I, p. 26 (26 March 1563)

45 *Will of Stephen Borowghe* [1 July 1584]: *Will of Joanne Burrough* (Abstract) [1604]

46 *Administration of Estate of John Rabelo* [1572]. This is Stephen Aborrowe's house, at Barking, which appears in the 1582 Subsidy Roll for London, Tower Ward, St Mary, Barking, assessed for £20. National Archives, Kew, Exchequer King's Remembrancer, Subsidy Rolls E 179/251/16, quoted in R.G. Lang (ed.), *Two Tudor Subsidy Assessment Rolls for the City of London, 1541 and 1582* (London, London Record Society, 1993). (An assessment for a sum as large as £20 indicates that the house must have been substantial.)

47 *State Papers Domestic, Addenda* (1547–1625), National Archives, PRO 15/22/folio 10 (microfilm). 'Register of merchant ships of England in 1572', compiled by Thomas Colshill.

48 *Will of Stephen Borowghe* [1 July 1584].

49 Information from *A Gazetteer of the Inns, Taverns and Public Houses of Gravesend and Milton* (quoted in a letter from Roger Ivens, Research Archivist, Centre for Kentish Studies, Maidstone, 14/12/2001).

50 It had been suggested that his 'house in Chatham called Goodsight' may have been close to the house of Sir John Hawkins, which later became the site of Hawkins Hospital, on the corner of Rochester High Street and Boundary Lane. (The site is now a disused department store.) S.M. Dixon, Borough Archivist, Civic Centre, Strood, Rochester (personal communication, October 2001).

51 A.A. Ruddock, 'The Earliest Records of the High Court of Admiralty (1515–1558)', *Bulletin of the Institute of Historical Research, London*, 22, part 66 (1949/November), pp. 139–51, at 145

CHAPTER 3

1 Richard Chancellor, 'Account of the 1553 voyage', in Hakluyt, *Principal Navigations*, Everyman, vol. I, p. 267

2 U. Lamb, 'Casa de la Contratación', in S.A. Bedini (ed.), *Christopher Columbus and the Age of Exploration: an Encyclopedia* (New York, Da Capo Press, 1998), pp. 111–12

3 The English merchants had established a small community at San Lucar, the port of Seville. In 1517, they had obtained extensive privileges from the Duke of Medina Sidonia, including limitations on the amount of customs duties they paid and a plot of land on which to build a church of St George. San Lucar became the English headquarters in Spain. Robert Thorne, one of the English merchants there, made a fortune, being worth £17,000 when he died. J.A. Williamson, *Maritime Enterprise*,

1485–1558 (Oxford, Clarendon Press, 1913), p. 216

4 Robert Thorne, 'A Declaration of the Indies and Lands Discovered, etc.', in Hakluyt, *Principal Navigations*, Everyman, vol. I, pp. 212–16

5 This is the account of the 1553 expedition that Clement Adams took down 'as he received it at the mouth of the said Richard Chanceler' on Chancellor's return in 1554. Hakluyt, *Principal Navigations*, Everyman, vol. I, p. 267

6 Ibid.

7 S. Purchas, *Hakluytus Posthumus or Purchas His Pilgrimes 1625* (20 vols, Glasgow, Maclehose, 1905–7), vol. XIII, p. 5

8 *State Papers Foreign*, Russia I, folio 133, quoted in T.S. Willan, *The Early History of the Russia Company 1553–1603* (Manchester, Manchester University Press, 1956), pp. 2–3

9 L.B. Wright, *Religion and Empire: the Alliance between Piety and Commerce in English Expansion, 1558–1625* (Chapel Hill, University of North Carolina Press, 1943), pp. 41–4

10 Hakluyt, *Principal Navigations*, Everyman, vol. I, p. 244–6

11 Calendar of the Patent Rolls (1554–5), pp. 55–9

12 F.J. Fisher, 'Commercial Trends and Policy in Sixteenth-Century England', *Economic History Review*, 10 (1940), pp. 95–117 (esp. 96–9, 103); J.D. Gould, *The Great Debasement: Currency and the Economy in Mid-Tudor England* (Oxford, OUP, 1970), p. 89

13 D.C. Coleman, *The Economy of England, 1450–1750* (Oxford, OUP, 1977), p. 56; R. Davis, *English Overseas Trade, 1500–1700* (London, Macmillan, 1973), pp. 11–16; Gould, *Great Debasement*, p. 89; D. Loades, *England's Maritime Empire: Seapower, Commerce and Policy, 1490–1690* (Harlow, Pearson Education, 2000), pp. 63–5; N. Heard, *Tudor Economy and Society* (London, Hodder and Stoughton, 1992), p. 55; G.D. Ramsay, *England's Overseas Trade in the Centuries of Emergence* (London, Macmillan, 1957), pp. 21–3; R.B. Wernham, *Before the Armada: the Growth of English Foreign Policy, 1485–1588* (London, J. Cape, 1966), pp. 190, 202–5. R. Brenner takes a different view. He holds that the English overseas mercantile expansion was import-led from the start, and that the effects of the 1551 exchange rate crisis have been much exaggerated. R. Brenner, *Merchants and Revolution: Commercial Change, Political Conflict and London's Overseas Traders 1550–1663* (Cambridge, Cambridge University Press, 1993), pp. 5–12. Most of the other European voyages of expansion may well have been 'import-led', but the early English voyages to Russia do seem to have been in search of outlets.

14 Hakluyt, 'Epistle Dedicatorie to Sir Robert Cecil', in Hakluyt, *Principal Navigations*, Everyman, vol. I, p. 44

15 A. Konstam, *Elizabethan Sea Dogs* (Oxford, Osprey Publishing, 2000), pp. 5–6

16 Richard Chancellor, 'The newe Navigation and discoverie of the kingdome of Moscovia, etc.', in Hakluyt, *Principal Navigations*, Everyman, vol. I, p. 267

17 It was Stow who described them as the two 'principall doers', J. Stow, *Annales* [1631], p. 609, quoted in T.S. Willan, *The Muscovy Merchants of 1555* (Manchester, Manchester University Press, 1953), pp. 78, 98

18 Willan, *The Muscovy Merchants*, pp. 78, 92–3, 102–3, 122

19 Oviedo, 'Historia General de Indias' [Seville, 1535], quoted in L. Stephens and S. Lee (eds), *The Dictionary of National Biography* (London, OUP, 1917, repr. 1973), pp. 619–22

20 This was John Dudley, a later Lord Lisle than John Aborough's erstwhile employer. He subsequently became the Duke of Northumberland.

21 J. Wheeler, *A Treaty of Commerce* [1601], repr. Facsimile Text Society, G.B. Hotchkiss (ed.) (New York, New York University Press, 1931), p. 269

22 L. Picard, *Elizabeth's London: Everyday Life in Elizabethan London* (London, Phoenix, 2004), p. 264

23 Hakluyt, *Principal Navigations*, Everyman, vol. I, pp. 318–29

24 W.R. Scott, *The Constitution and Finance of English, Scottish and Irish Joint-Stock Companies to 1720* (3 vols, Cambridge, Cambridge University Press, 1910–12, repr. 1993), vol. I, p. 17

25 Hakluyt, *Principal Navigations*, Everyman, vol. I, p. 267

26 The curious title of consul, given to the four deputy heads of the Muscovy Company in 1555, may reflect the Italian source of the original joint stock concept. However, having said that, I note that E.M. Carus Wilson in *Medieval Merchant Venturers* (1954, Methuen, London), p. 99, describes the term 'Consul' as it was used in 1296, when the English wool merchants at Antwerp obtained a charter from the Duke of Brabant which allowed them to set up a 'fellowship' or 'hanse' in that city, with the right to hold courts of their 'compagnie' and to elect their own 'Captain or Consul'. Thus the use of the word 'consul' may have other origins and other connotations.

27 *Calendar of State Papers, Foreign and Domestic*, Edward and Mary 1555, 26 February, pp. 55–9. Anthony Hussey was a judge and a shipowner as well as being a great merchant adventurer, and John Southcote seems to have been a judge. Willan, *The Muscovy Merchants*, pp. 104–5, 122

28 CSP, F & D 1555, 26 February, pp. 55–9; Willan, *The Muscovy Merchants*, pp. 4–11

29 S. Cabot, 'Ordinances, Instructions and Advertisements of and for the intended voyage for Cathay' [1553], in Hakluyt, *Principal Navigations*, Everyman, vol. I, p. 239

30 Hakluyt, *Principal Navigations*, Everyman, vol. I, p. 241

31 CSP, F & D [1554–5], pp. 55–7

CHAPTER 4

1 Hakluyt, *Principal Navigations*, Everyman, vol. I, pp. 244–5

2 Ibid., pp. 244–6. There must have been some significance in the ships having Spanish names, but there is no evidence as to what it was. It might have been some devious ploy by the wily Cabot, but it does seem odd that they were given Spanish names during the Protestant regime of Edward VI (January 1547 to July 1553).

3 It was not unusual to find Dutchmen working on English ships at this time. For instance, Scammel mentions a London ship, working to Spain early in the sixteenth century, which had two Flemings (alias 'olde Duchemen') as quartermasters, an Italian master's mate, a Dutch bosun's mate and a Dutch master cook. National Archives, Kew, High Court of Admiralty 13/3, folios 136, 152v., quoted in G.V. Scammell, 'Manning the English Merchant Service in the Sixteenth Century', *Mariner's Mirror*, 56 (1970), pp. 131–54, at 134

4 Hakluyt, *Principal Navigations*, Everyman, vol. I, pp. 267–8

5 John Stow remarked of Ratcliffe in 1598 that 'The first building at Ratcliffe in my youth (not to be forgotten) was a fayre free schoole, and Almshouses, founded by Anice Gibson, wife of Ni Gibson, grocer. But of late years shipwrights and (for the most part) other marine men, have builded many large and strong houses for themselves and smaller for saylers.' John Stow, *A Survey of London* [1603], in C.L. Kingsford (ed.) (2 vols, Oxford, Clarendon Press, 1908), vol. II, p. 71

6 The term 'spritsail' is also used for a four-sided fore-and-aft sail supported by a sprit, a long diagonal spar from the foot of the mast to the peak of the sail, typical of Thames barges.

7 F. Howard, *Sailing Ships of War, 1400–1860* (London, Conway Maritime Press, 1979), pp. 43–87

8 Ibid., p. 43. D.W. Waters, 'The English Pilot: English Sailing Directions and Charts and the Rise of English Shipping, 16th to 18th Centuries', *Journal of Navigation*, 42/3 (1989), p. 318

9 C.S. Knighton and D.M. Loades (eds), *The Anthony Roll of Henry VIII's Navy: Pepys Library 2991 and British Library additional MS 22047 with related documents* (London, Navy Record Society, 2000), p. 78

10 Tumblehome exists when a ship or boat is broader near the waterline than it is at the level of the deck, i.e. the hull becomes narrower higher up.

11 Unknown, 'Elsinore Castle and the Entrance to the Baltic' (engraving, mid-sixteenth century), reproduced in N. Williams, *The Sea Dogs* (London, Weidenfeld and Nicolson, 1975), pp. 240–1

12 British Library, Cotton MS Augustus 1, I, 22; 23, in John Thompson, *Dover Harbour and Ships* (drawing, 1538)

13 A wale is an extra thickness of timber fastened to the outside of the hull, running in a fore and aft direction, to strengthen the hull and to protect it from damage when lying alongside a stone quay or another ship.

14 National Archives, Kew, PRO MPF 75 (SP 64/1), 'The Smerwick Map' (drawing, 1580)

15 N.A.M. Rodger, *The Safeguard of the Sea* (2 vols, London, HarperCollins, 1997), vol. I, p. 479

16 T. Glasgow, 'Elizabethan Ships Pictured on the Smerwick Map: Background, Authentication and Evaluation', *Mariner's Mirror*, 52 (1966), pp. 157–62. Artist unknown. The action that is illustrated took place on 9 November 1579, and the map was sent by Admiral William Winter to Secretary Walsingham on 24 December 1580. Winter's fleet is shown attacking a contingent of some 800 Spanish troops who had landed at Smerwick on the Dingle Peninsula in south-west Ireland and had occupied Fort Gold there.

17 National Archives, Kew, State Papers, PRO 12: 243: 283, W. Borough, *Proportion in building of Shyppinge* [c. 1586–90]

18 Dr O. Roberts, Dept of History with Nautical Studies, University of Wales, Bangor, personal communication (June 1998)

19 Tonnage is a measure of the cubic capacity of a ship. The original tun was a barrel (appropriately enough in view of the large quantities of wine imported from Gascony to England) holding 252 gallons of wine each (these are old gallons, similar to US gallons today). Such a barrel measured about 4 feet 6 inches long and about 3 feet 2 inches in maximum diameter. (It should be said that the stated tonnage of a particular ship seems to have varied from time to time, probably depending on who it was that was making the estimate).

20 W.O. Salisbury, 'Early Tonnage Measurement in England', *Mariner's Mirror*, 52 (1966), pp. 41–51, at 45, 173–80, 329–40

21 R. Barker, 'A Manuscript on Shipbuilding, circa 1600, copied by Newton', *Mariner's Mirror*, 80/1 (1994), pp. 16–29, at 26 and 20

22 M. Rule, *The Mary Rose* (London, Conway Maritime Press, 1982); J.P. Delgado, *Encyclopedia of Underwater and Marine Archaeology* (London, British Museum Press, 1997), pp. 264–6

23 Delgado, *Encyclopedia*, p. 25

24 O.T.P. Roberts, 'An Exercise in Hull Reconstruction Arising from the Alderney Elizabethan Wreck', *International Journal of Nautical Archaeology*, 27/1 (1998), pp. 32–42

25 M. Redknap, 'Reconstructing Sixteenth-Century Ship Culture from a Partially Excavated Site: the Cattewater Wreck', in M. Redknap (ed.), *Artefacts from Wrecks* (Oxford, Oxbow Books, 1997), pp. 73–86

26 http://www.maryrose.org/ship/ship1.htm

27 A.J. Holland, *Ships of British Oak: The Rise and Decline of Wooden Shipbuilding in Hampshire* (Newton Abbot, David and Charles, 1971), pp. 27–8

28 http://www.maryrose.org/ship/ship1.htm; Redknap, *Artefacts*, pp. 73–86

29 M. Morris, 'Naval Cordage Procurement in Early Modern England', *International Journal of Maritime History*, 11/1 (1999, June), pp. 81–99, at 86

30 Hakluyt, *Principal Navigations*, Everyman, vol. I, pp. 267–8

31 Fernando Duro, *Armada Espanola*, p. 121, quoted in M. Oppenheim, *A History of the Administration of the Royal Navy and of Merchant Shipping in Relation to the Navy from 1509–1660* (London, Bodley Head, 1896, reprinted Shoestring Press USA, 1961), p. 103

32 Hakluyt, *Principal Navigations*, Everyman, vol. I, p. 268

33 F.L. Colville, *The Worthies of Warwickshire who Lived between 1500 and 1800* (London, H.T. Cooke, 1870), pp. 813–18; J. Hamel, *England and Russia* [1854], trans. J.S. Leigh (London, Frank Cass, 1968), pp. 11, 18

34 D.B. Quinn, 'Sailors and the Sea', in N.A. Allardyce (ed.), *Shakespeare in His Own Age: Shakespeare Survey 17* (Cambridge, Cambridge University Press, 1964), pp. 21–36, at 29

35 Hamel, *England and Russia*, pp. 21, 15

36 C. Falkus, *Life in the Age of Exploration* (London, New York, Readers' Digest Association Ltd, 1994), pp. 32–3

37 Hakluyt, *Principal Navigations*, Everyman, vol. I, p. 269

38 'Richard Chanceler, Grand Pilot, borne in Bristowe' occurs as a note in the margin, in Hakluyt, *Principal Navigations*, Hakluyt Society, vol. I, p. 281. (It is not in the Maclehose or Everyman editions.)

39 When Chancellor described the Tsar's preparations for war he said, 'I have seene the Kings Majesties of England and the French Kings pavilions, which are fayre, yet not like unto his.' Hakluyt, *Principal Navigations*, Everyman, vol. I, p. 258

40 Roger Bodenham, 'The voyage of M. Roger Bodenham with the great Barke Aucher to Candia and Chios in the yeere 1550', in Hakluyt, *Principal Navigations*, Everyman, vol. III, pp. 8–12

41 Ephemerides are astronomical almanacs, predictions of the future positions of the main celestial bodies, for the benefit of navigators.

42 G.V. Scammell, *Ships, Oceans and Empire: Studies in European Maritime and Colonial History, 1400–1750* (Aldershot, Variorum, 1995), vol. II, p. 133

43 C.A. Fury, *Tides in the Affairs of Men: the Social History of Elizabethan Seamen, 1580–1603* (Westport, Connecticut, Greenwood Press, 1996), p. 18

44 Hakluyt vii (Maclehose edn), p. 286, acc. to Scammell, 'Manning the Merchant Service', p. 133

45 Scammell, 'Manning the Merchant Service', p. 133

46 A.A. Ruddock, 'The Earliest Records of the High Court of Admiralty (1515–1558)', *Bulletin of the Institute of Historical Research, London* (1949, November), vol. 22, part 66, pp. 139–51, at 144

47 Hakluyt, *Principal Navigations*, Everyman, vol. I, p. 268

48 Ibid., pp. 244–6

49 National Archives, PRO, High Court of Admiralty 1/34, folio 331, quoted in Scammell, 'Manning the Merchant Service', p. 142

50 Knighton and Loades, *Anthony Roll*, pp. 38–9

51   Hakluyt, *Principal Navigations*, Everyman, vol. I, pp. 244–6

52   J. Vanes (ed.), *The Ledger of John Smythe [1538–1550]* (London, HMSO for Bristol Record Society Publications, 1974), ledger entry (1539), folio 61

53   J.T. Tinniswood, 'Anchors and Accessories, 1340–1640', *Mariner's Mirror*, 31 (1945), pp. 84–105

54   Hakluyt, *Principal Navigations*, Everyman, vol. I, p. 340

55   Ibid., pp. 244–6

56   J.E.G. Bennell, 'English Oared Vessels of the Sixteenth Century', *Mariner's Mirror* 60 (1974), pp. 178–9. Morris stated that 'The term pinnace had come to describe a range of vessels from over a hundred tons down to the larger ship's boats', R. Morris, *Atlantic Sail* (London, Aurum Press, 1992), p. 70, and Baker wrote, in a very similar vein, that 'Pinnaces ranged from small open pulling boats . . . to relatively large seagoing vessels that carried the normal [three-masted] ship rig of the period', W.A. Baker, *The Mayflower and Other Colonial Vessels* (London, Conway Maritime Press, 1983), p. 75. See also G. Blackburn, *The Illustrated Encyclopedia of Ships, Boats, Vessels and other Water-borne Craft* (London, John Murray, 1978), p. 259, and Mariner's Museum, *A Dictionary of the World's Watercraft* (London, Chatham Publishing, 2000), pp. 456–7

57   Hakluyt, *Principal Navigations*, Everyman, vol. I, pp. 244–6

58   T. Glasgow, 'Dimensions of mid-Elizabethan Shipboats', *Mariner's Mirror*, 51 (1965), p. 183

59   Hakluyt, *Principal Navigations*, Everyman, vol. I, p. 268

60   British Library, Cotton MS Faustina C II, folio 110v and 111 (*A Licence from King Edward VI authorising the provisioning of the ships*); National Archives, Kew, High Court of Admiralty Exemplifications 5, folio 157, quoted by T.S. Willan, *The Early History of the Russia Company, 1553–1603* (Manchester, Manchester University Press, 1956), p. 3

61   J. Vanes, *The Port of Bristol in the Sixteenth Century* (Bristol, University of Bristol, 1995), p. 93. Biscuit or 'biskay' was the Tudor equivalent of our long-life bread.

62   E.A. Bond (ed.), *The Travels of Sir Jerome Horsey: Russia at the Close of the Sixteenth Century* [1856], pp. 185–6, quoted in Quinn, 'Sailors and the Sea', p. 22. Sir Jerome Horsey was describing the victualling of navy ships to the Tsar in 1576.

63   E. Windeatt, 'The Fitting out of Two Vessels against the Spanish Armada at Dartmouth in 1588', *Transactions of the Devonshire Association* 12 (1880), pp. 312–21

64   Vanes, *Port of Bristol*, p. 101

65   Hakluyt, *Principal Navigations*, Everyman, vol. I, p. 272

66   R. Hope, *A New History of English Shipping* (London, John Murray, 1990), p. 63

67   Rule, *The Mary Rose*, pp. 107–9

68   I. Friel, 'Frobisher's Ships: the Ships of the North-Western Atlantic Voyages, 1576–1578', in T.H.B. Symons (ed.), *Meta Incognita: A Discourse of Discovery: Martin Frobisher's Arctic Expeditions, 1576–1578* (2 vols, Quebec, Canadian Museum of Civilisation, 1999), vol. II, pp. 299–352, at 309

69   Redknap, 'Reconstructing Ship Culture', p. 83

70   Falkus, *Life*, p. 38; C. Mudie, 'Mathew and Naval Architecture', *International Conference on Historic Ships* (London, Royal Institute of Naval Architects Conference, 1996, 24 May), p. 6

71   There is the inventory of the *Great Bark* of 1531 (L.G. Carr Laughton, 'Documents: the Inventory of the Great Bark, 1531', *Mariner's Mirror*, 5/1 (1919), pp. 21–2, and extensive inventories of the *Gabriel, Judith, Michael* and *Aid*, four ships of Frobisher's fleets of 1576–8, in Friel, 'Frobisher's Ships', pp. 299–352, and other inventories in many of the High Court of Admiralty Examinations of the time.

72 National Archives, Kew, High Court of Admiralty 1/34, folio 331. Two men who had been working on the rigging of the *Edward Bonaventura* ran away to visit one of their wives, at ?Rokkesall in Essex. One of the two was apprehended a week or so later in King's Lynn. He claimed only to have tarried one night at Rokkesall, and then gone on to Ipswich and (Great) Yarmouth in the hope of catching up with his ship, but did not. The reason he was apprehended was because he was still wearing the 'Jerkyn and a pair of sloppis blew with a red gard', the uniform that he had been issued with.

73 C.W. and P. Cunnington, *Handbook of English Costume in the Sixteenth Century* (London, Faber and Faber, 1962), p. 194

74 Rule, *Mary Rose*, pp. 199–201

75 Vanes, *The Ledger of John Smythe*, folio 61 (1539)

76 G.V. Scammell, 'Shipowning in England c. 1450–1550', *Transactions of the Royal Historical Society*, 5th series, 12 (1962), pp. 105–122, at 112

77 Hakluyt, *Principal Navigations*, Everyman, vol. I, pp. 232–41

CHAPTER 5

Helgeland is in northern Norway and extends up the coast from about 65° to 67° N.

1 *Calendar of Letters, Despatches and State Papers, Spanish*, vol. XI, Edward and Mary, in R. Tyler (ed.) (London, 1916, reprinted Liechtenstein, Kraus-Thomson, 1969), p. 39, *Letter from Jehan Scheyfee, Imperial Ambassador in England, to the Bishop of Arras, Secretary to the Emperor on 11 May 1553* (on the same day as the expedition ships were 'valed' down the Thames past Greenwich).

2 D. Crystal (ed.), *Cambridge Encyclopedia*, 2nd edn (London, Cambridge University Press, 1994), p. 392. The stadium was a unit of length used by the Greeks and later by the Romans. It was equal to 600 Greek feet, but the length used for a foot varied, and the length of a stadium could be 150, 185, 192 or 225 metres.

3 M.W. Richey, 'Astronomy and Astrology', in S.A. Bedini (ed.), *Christopher Columbus and the Age of Exploration* (New York, Da Capo, 1998), p. 50

4 E.G.R. Taylor, *Tudor Geography, 1485–1583* (London, Methuen, 1930), pp. 2–3

5 Richey, 'Astronomy and Astrology', p. 50

6 B. Wooley, *The Queen's Conjuror: the Life and Work of Dr. Dee* (London, HarperCollins, 2002), p. 167

7 Nearly all of his work was in manuscript form, and a great deal of it was destroyed when his house was ransacked in 1583, so that much of it can now only be deduced from excerpts and quotations in the works of his students and other contemporaries. *The Oxford Dictionary of National Biography*, H.G.C. Mathew and B.H. Harrison (eds), (Oxford, OUP, 2004); E.G.R. Taylor, 'John Dee and the Nautical Triangle, 1575', *Journal of the Institute of Navigation, London*, 8 (1955), pp. 312–25, at 319; E.G.R. Taylor, *The Mathematical Practitioners of Tudor and Stuart England* (Cambridge, Cambridge University Press, 1970), p. 21

8 J. Crossley (ed.), *Autobiographical Tracts of Dr John Dee* (Manchester, 1851), p. 5, quoted in H. Wallis, 'England's Search for the Northern Passages in the Sixteenth and Early Seventeenth Centuries', *Arctic* 37/4, pp. 453–72, at 455; Taylor, *Tudor Geography*, p. 78

9 J. Dee, *The Compendious Rehearsal* [1592], quoted in Taylor, *Tudor Geography*, p. 256

10 Taylor, *Tudor Geography*, p. 78

11   J. Dee, *The Compendious Rehearsal* [1592], quoted in F.R. Johnson, *Astronomical Thought in Renaissance England: a Study of the English Scientific Writings from 1500 to 1645* (New York, Octagon Books, 1968), p. 139

12   Taylor, *Tudor Geography*, p. 76

13   J. Dee, *The Astronomicall and Logisticall rules and canons to calculate the Ephemerides* [1592], quoted in Taylor, *Tudor Geography*, pp. 253–4

14   J. Dee, *General and Rare Memorials pertaining to the Perfecte Arte of Navigation* [1577], quoted in Taylor, *Tudor Geography*, p. 263

15   Taylor, *Tudor Geography*, p. 191 (Appendix 1A, List of John Dee's Geographical and Related Works)

16   Robert Thorne, in Hakluyt, *Principal Navigations*, Everyman, vol. I, pp. 216–31 and 212–16

17   R. Thorne, map of the world [1527], in R. Hakluyt, 'Divers Voyages touching the Discoverie of America' [1582], in Hakluyt, *Principal Navigations*, Hakluyt Society, vol. II, p. 176.

18   Robert Copeland, *The Rutter of the Sea* [1528], in D.W. Waters, *The Rutters of the Sea: the Sailing Directions of Pierre Garcie* (New Haven and London, Yale University Press, 1967), p. 67

19   Anon., *Rutter of the English Coasts* [1408], J. Gairdner (ed.) (London, Hakluyt Society, 1889), series 1, vol. LXXIX

20   Alexander Lindsay, *A Rutter of the Scottish Seas* [c. 1540], I.H. Adams and G. Fortune (eds) (Maritime Monographs and Reports, no. 44, Greenwich, National Maritime Museum, 1980)

21   Waters, *The Rutters of the Sea*, p. 67

22   J. Bateley (ed.), *The Old English Orosius* (London, OUP for the Early English Text Society, 1980), pp. xxiii, lv and lxxxvii–viii

23   British Library, Lauderdale (or Tollemache) MS, Additional 47967, quoted in Bateley, *Old English Orosius*, p. xxiii

24   Hakluyt, *Principal Navigations*, Everyman, vol. I, pp. 56–9

25   G. Jones, *A History of the Vikings* (London, OUP, 1968), p. 124

26   Snorri Sturluson, *Heimskringla, The Olaf Sagas* [1220–30], trans. S. Laing, Everyman edn (London, J.M. Dent, 1915), p. 271

27   G.A. Blom, 'The Participation of the Kings in the Early Norwegian Sailing to Bjarmeland (Kola Peninsula and Russian waters), and the Development of a Royal Policy Concerning the Northern Waters in the Middle Ages', *Arctic*, 37/4 (1984), pp. 385–8

28   G. Jones, *History of the Vikings*, pp. 60–3

29   S. von Herberstein, *Rerum Moscoviticarum Commentarii* [1549], trans. R.H. Major as *Notes upon Russia*, 2 vols, 1851 and 1852, B. Picard (ed.) (London, Hakluyt Society, 1969), series 1, nos 10 and 12

30   S.H. Baron, 'Herberstein and the English 'Discovery' of Muscovy', *Terra Incognita*, 18 (1986), pp. 43–54, at 47 (footnote 17)

31   Ibid., pp. 43–54

32   The Scot called David employed as a 'herald' by King John of Denmark made sea voyages round the north of Norway from Russia to Denmark with Jury Manilovitch Trachaniot in 1501, and with Istoma in 1496 and in 1507. He is mentioned by von Herberstein (von Herberstein, *Rerum* (1557), ed. R.H. Major, in *Notes upon Russia* (2 vols, London, Hakluyt Society, 1851–2), vol. I, pp. 105–9. Hamel found a letter from the Tsar, Vassily Ivanovich, to King John of Denmark in which the herald is called David Kochen (from which Hamel deduced that his real name was Cocker). J. Hamel, *England and Russia* [1854], trans. J.S. Leigh (London, F. Cass, 1968), pp. 54,

59, 60, 79–81. David Cocker, or Cock or Corran, was a Scot in Danish service from 1496, as Danish King of Arms. He was the Danish Envoy to Moscow in 1506, 1507, 1513, 1514, 1519 and 1527. T. Riis, *Should Auld Acquaintance be Forgot: Scottish–Danish relations c. 1450–1707* (Odense, University Press, 1988), p. 24; D. Fedosov, *The Caledonian Connection: Scotland–Russia Ties. Middle Ages to Early Twentieth Century: a Concise Biographical List* (Aberdeen, University of Aberdeen, 1996), p. 24

33 Baron, 'Herberstein', pp. 48–51

34 R. Eden, 'Epistle to the reader', in his *A treatyse of the new India* [1553], quoted in S.H. Baron, 'Herberstein', p. 48

35 Taylor, *Tudor Geography*, p. 79

36 F. Nansen, *In Northern Mists: Arctic Exploration in Early Times* (2 vols, London, Heinemann, 1911), vol. II, p. 237

37 A.E. Nordenskiold, *The Voyage of the Vega round Asia and Europe*, trans. A. Leslie (2 vols, London, Macmillan, 1881), p. 56

38 Taylor, *Tudor Geography*, pp. 79–83

39 *Encyclopedia Britannica*, 'Abu al-fida' (2001) (CD)

40 Pliny, *The Natural History of Pliny*, trans. and ed. J. Bostock and H.T. Riley (6 vols, London, G. Bell, 1890), vol. II, p. 36 (Pliny, Book VI, Chapter 20)

41 R. Johnson, 'Certain notes unperfectly written', in Hakluyt, *Principal Navigations*, Everyman, vol. I, pp. 352–6, at 354

42 Taylor, *Tudor Geography*, p. 81

43 Ibid., pp. 131–2

44 Ibid., p. 132

45 R.A. Skelton, *Explorers' Maps: Chapters in Cartographic Discovery* (London, Routledge and Kegan Paul, 1958), p. 103

46 R.W. Cotton, 'Steven Borough, the Navigator', *Transactions of the Devonshire Association*, 12 (1880–1), pp. 332–60, at 335

47 Baron, 'Herberstein', p. 45

48 W.E. Garrett (ed.), *National Geographic Society Map, Soviet Union* (Washington, NGS, 1990)

49 Ibid.

50 Taylor, *Tudor Geography*, p. 80

51 H. Wallis, 'England's Search for the Northern Passages in the Sixteenth and Early Seventeenth Centuries', *Arctic*, 37/4 (1984), pp. 453–72, at 454.

52 R.A. Skelton, T.E. Marston and G.D. Painter, *The Vinland Map and the Tartar Relation* (Yale, Yale University Press, 1965)

53 Roger Barlow, *A Brief Summe of Geographie* [1541], E.G.R. Taylor (ed.) (London, Hakluyt Society, 1932), series 2, vol. LXIX, pp. 43 and 64

54 M.S. Anderson, *Britain's Discovery of Russia, 1553–1815* (London, Macmillan, 1958), p. 18

55 E. Spenser, *The Faerie Queene* [1590–6], in R. Morris (ed.), *The Works of Edmund Spenser* (London, Macmillan, 1899), p. 147 (Book II, Canto XII, verses 22–4)

56 *Webster's Dictionary* (London, G. Bell, 1934), p. 2170

57 Hakluyt, *Principal Navigations*, Everyman, vol. I, p. 345

58 Olaus Magnus, *Historia de Gentibus Septentrionibus* [1555], pub. as *Description of the Northern Peoples*, P. Foote (ed.) (2 vols, London, Hakluyt Society, 1996), series 2, nos 182 and 187, vol. I (no. 182), p. 100

59 Magnus, *Historia*, vol. II (no. 187), Book XXI, Chapter 25; D. Farson and A. Hall, *Great Mysteries: Monsters of the Deep* (London, Bloomsbury, 1991), pp. 170–1

CHAPTER 6

1 *Calendar of Letters, Despatches and State Papers, Spanish*, vol. XI, Edward and Mary 10 April 1553, R. Tyler (ed.) (London, 1916, reprinted Liechtenstein, Kraus-Thomson, 1969), *Despatch from Jehan Scheyfee, the Imperial Ambassador in London to the Bishop of Arras, Secretary to the Emperor, Charles V*. Carsees = kerseys, coarse woollen cloth used particularly for making hose.

2 Sir Hugh's account, in his own hand, survives, though much singed around the edges, in British Library, Cotton MS, Otho E VIII, folios 11–16; Hakluyt, *Principal Navigations*, Everyman, vol. I, pp. 247–54. Sir Hugh Willoughby and Richard Chancellor both wrote accounts of this voyage.

3 Hakluyt, *Principal Navigations*, Everyman, vol. I, p. 271

4 Ibid., pp. 241–3

5 Ibid., p. 271

6 www.greenwichfoundation.org.uk. There had previously been an imposing riverside house at Greenwich called Bella Court, built by Humphrey, Duke of Gloucester and brother to Henry V. However, in 1447 he fell foul of Queen Margaret of Anjou, who took over Bella Court and renamed it the 'Palace of Pleasaunce' or 'Placentia Palace', often referred to as 'Greenwich Palace'. It became a favourite Tudor palace and it was here that Henry VIII, Mary Tudor (Mary I) and Elizabeth I were born, and it was associated with the development of the navy nearby. The Royal Palace of Placentia was demolished in 1694. (M. Lincoln, B. Reid and L. Rivett, *Henry VIII at Greenwich* (Greenwich, National Maritime Museum, 1991).) There are pictures of Greenwich and Placentia Palace by van de Wyngaerde in 1558, printed in F. Barker, *Greenwich and Blackheath Past* (London, Historical Publications, 1993). Henry VIII's tiltyard, armoury and banqueting hall have recently been excavated by the Channel 4 Time Team in the lawns in front of what is now the National Maritime Museum at Greenwich (www.channel4.com/history).

7 Hakluyt, *Principal Navigations*, Everyman, vol. I, p. 271

8 Ibid.

9 Loach argues that Edward VI did not die of tuberculosis, as had generally been thought, but of a 'suppurating pulmonary infection', and that his decline in 1553 was rapid and unexpected. J. Loach, *Edward VI* (Yale, Yale University Press, 2000), pp. 159–69, esp. 162

10 Hakluyt, *Principal Navigations*, Everyman, vol. I, pp. 248–9

11 British Library, Cotton MS, Augustus 1, I, 53, *Caundishe's Chart of the Thames Estuary*. It is inscribed 'Richard Caundish made this Carde'. According to Taylor, the date of Caundish's chart is 1547, E.G.R. Taylor, 'Instructions to a Colonial Surveyor in 1582', *Mariner's Mirror*, 37/1 (1951), pp. 48–62, at 52. However, one of the charts in a list of charts that were in the possession of Henry VIII in or about 1533 sounds very much like *Caundishe's Chart of the Thames Estuary* from its description in *Letters and Papers, Foreign and Domestic*, Henry VIII, vol. XXI, Gairdner and Brodie (eds), part 2, p. 458, no. 19. The fact that this chart does not show any fortifications at the entrance to the Orwell also supports its date as being about 1533, and not 1547. A.H.W. Robinson, *Marine Cartography in Britain* (Leicester, Leicester University Press, 1962), p. 22 and Plate 5.

    Caundish had worked with John Aborough on 'the King's waterworks at Dover' and was the uncle of Thomas Cavendish, who circumnavigated the globe in 1586–8.

12 E.D. Morgan, 'Glossary', in J. Gairdner (ed.), *Sailing Directions for the Circumnavigation of England and for the Voyage to the Straits of Gibraltar, 1408* (London, Hakluyt Society, series 1, no. 79, 1889), p. 32

13 Richard Proude, 'The New Rutter for the Sea' [1541], British Museum, Lansdowne MS 285, printed in Gairdner, *Sailing Directions*, p. 12

14 Robinson, *Marine Cartography*, p. 23

15 I have not been able to positively identify Walsursye. The most plausible candidate is Walberswick, about halfway between Orwell Wands and Holmhead, but the village of Walton, north of Felixstowe and near the mouth of the Orwell, is another possibility.

16 E.D. Morgan, 'Glossary', in Gairdner, *Sailing Directions*, p. 32

17 A league is 3 miles (or 3 nautical miles when at sea, where a nautical mile is 1.15 of a statute mile): C.C. Chapman, *How Heavy, How Much and How Long?* (Dursley, Lochin Publishing, 1985), pp. 20–1.

18 Hakluyt, *Principal Navigations*, Everyman, vol. I, pp. 248–9

19 F.T. Tinniswood, 'Anchors and Accessories, 1340–1640', *Mariner's Mirror*, 31 (1945), pp. 84–143; Hakluyt, *Principal Navigations*, Everyman, vol. I, p. 340, in which Stephen Borough describes how he borrowed an anchor with 140 fathoms of cable from the Russian, Gabriel.

20 Hakluyt, *Principal Navigations*, Everyman, vol. I, p. 249

21 'Pickerie' was petty theft; and being ducked at the yard arm involved being lowered into the sea on the end of a rope with your hands tied together until you nearly drowned (some did) and then being hauled up again.

22 Hakluyt, *Principal Navigations*, Everyman, vol. I, pp. 249, 271–2

23 Ibid.

24 This is an anchor-weighing shanty from R. Wedderburn, *The Complaynt of Scotlande* [*c.* 1550], A.M. Stewart (ed.) (Edinburgh, Scottish Text Society 1979), p. 32, folio 32v. *Virer* (French to turn), e.g. *virer au cabestan*; *pourbossa* may relate to the *bosses de boussoir*, the anchor stoppers at the cathead, A. Moore, 'The Complaynt of Scotland Sea Scene', in *Navy Records Society* XL, Naval Miscellany II (1912), pp. 67–84, at 76, notes 3 and 4

25 Hakluyt, *Principal Navigations*, Everyman, vol. I, p. 249

26 B.M. Willett (ed.), *Philip's Universal Atlas* (London, George Philip, 1983), map 74

27 H. Swain, *Return to Murmansk* (London, Seafarer Books, 1996), p. 54

28 Their first landfall was also described as being at 66° N. This would have put it some 60 miles further south than 12 leagues south-east of Rost. However, their latitude measurements may not have been entirely reliable at that time. (They found the latitude of the Islands of Rost to be 66° 30' N, when actually they are at 67° 30' N.)

29 Denmark, Norway and Sweden had been united until 1523, when Sweden, under Gustavus Vasa (1523–60), broke away. G. Barraclough (ed.), *Times Atlas of World History* (London, Times Books, 1978), p. 188

30 Hakluyt, *Principal Navigations*, Everyman, vol. I, p. 250

31 J. Brown and M. Sinclair, *Scandinavia: The Rough Guide* (4th edn, London, Rough Guides, 1997), p. 317; D. Taylor-Wilkie, *Insight Guides: Norway* (Singapore, APA Publications, 1994), p. 327

32 Brown and Sinclair, *Scandinavia*, p. 317; E. Welle-Strand, *2,500 Miles on the Coastal Steamer* (Bergen, Nortrabooks, 1993), p. 39

33 His epic story is recounted by Purchas, in S. Purchas, *Hakluytus Posthumus or Purchas, His Pilgrimes* [1625] (20 vols, Glasgow, Maclehose, 1905–7), vol. XIII, pp. 417–37

34 J. Armitage and M. Brackenbury, *Norwegian Cruising Guide* (2nd edn, London, Adlard Coles, 1996), p. 53

35 Hakluyt, *Principal Navigations*, Everyman, vol. I, pp. 99–100. This story of Nicholas de Lynn and the ship-swallowing whirlpool was apparently included in an account of a

voyage by a certain James Cnoyen of Hartzevan Buske, which came to Mercator, who sent it to Hakluyt in a letter, but it appears that Hakluyt may not have received the letter until the 1570s, too late for the 1553 expedition to have known about it. E.G.R. Taylor, *Tudor Geography, 1485–1583* (London, Methuen, 1930), p. 133

36 Olaus Magnus, *Historia de Gentibus Septentrionalibus* [1555], P. Foote (ed.), *Description of the Northern Peoples* (London, Hakluyt Society, 1996), series 2, no. 182, pp. 100–2. The expedition leaders may well have heard about the maelstrom, even though Olaus Magnus's book describing it was not published until two years later.

37 Hakluyt, *Principal Navigations*, Hakluyt Society, vol. II, p. 268. 'Stanfew' seems to be the same place as 'Sterfier', which appeared in a note on the outside cover of Sir Hugh Willoughby's account of the voyage, where he had written 'Our Shippe being at an anker in the harbour called Sterfier in the Island Lofoote'. 'Stanfew' has alternatively been identified as Stamsund, an old whaling harbour some 16 miles south-west of Svolvær (S. Aronson, Royal Norwegian Embassy, London, personal communication, 27 November 2002) or as Steenfjord, on the west coast of the Lofotens, by A.E. Nordenskiold in *The Voyage of the Vega around Asia and Europe*, trans. A.Leslie (2 vols, London, Macmillan, 1881), vol. I, p. 61

38 Armitage and Brackenbury, *Cruising Guide*, p. 57

39 Hakluyt, *Principal Navigations*, Hakluyt Society, vol. II, p. 268; E.D. Morgan and C.H. Coote, *Early Voyages and Travels to Russia and Persia by Anthony Jenkinson and other Englishmen* (2 vols, London, Hakluyt Society, series 1, no. 72, 1886), vol. I, p. 252; Aronson, personal communication 2002

40 Hakluyt, *Principal Navigations*, Everyman, vol. I, p. 410

41 Armitage and Brackenbury, *Cruising Guide*, pp. 75–6

42 Hakluyt, *Principal Navigations*, Everyman, vol. I, p. 272

43 Hakluyt, *Principal Navigations*, Everyman, vol. I, p. 251

44 Ibid., pp. 272–3

45 P. Kemp, *Convoy: Drama in Arctic Waters* (London, Brockhampton Press, 1999), p. 17

46 A. MacLean, *HMS Ulysses* (London, HarperCollins, 1994), pp. 106–7

47 Hullock = a mere fragment of a sail kept standing to hold the vessel's head to the wind in a storm (obsolete). *Webster's New International Dictionary* (2nd edn, G. Bell, London, 1934), p. 1211.

48 Hakluyt, *Principal Navigations*, Everyman, vol. I, p. 251

49 R.W. Cotton, 'Stephen Borough, The Navigator', *Transactions of the Devonshire Association*, 12 (1880–1), pp. 332–60, at 338; J. Hamel, *England and Russia* [1854], trans. J.S. Leigh (London, F. Cass, 1968), p. 30; W. Klein (ed.), *The New Soviet Union: Insight Guide* (Singapore, Hofer Ben, 1991); E.D. Morgan and C.H. Coote, *Early Voyages and Travels to Persia and Russia* (2 vols, London, Hakluyt Society, series 1, no. 73), vol. 2, p. 153; T. Rundall, *Narratives of Voyages towards the North West in Search of a Passage to Cathay and India, 1496 to 1631* [1849] (republished London and New York, Burt Franklin, 1970), pp. i–xii; E.G.R. Taylor, 'Instructions to a Colonial Surveyor in 1582', *Mariner's Mirror*, 37/1 (1951), pp. 48–62, at 52; J.A. Williamson, 'England and the Opening of the Atlantic', in J.H. Rose, A.P. Newton and E.A. Berians (eds), *The Cambridge History of the British Empire* (8 vols, Cambridge, Cambridge University Press, 1929), vol. I, pp. 22–52, at 40

50 Purchas, *Hakluytus Posthumus*, vol. xiii, p. 6

51 Nordenskiold, *The Voyage of the Vega*, vol. I, p. 61, footnote

52 J. Barrow, *A Chronological History of Voyages into the Arctic Regions, etc.* (London, Murray, 1818), p. 159

53 Admiralty Chart 2962, *The North Cape to Uyedinyeniya Island*. Nordenskiold, *Voyage of the Vega*, vol I, p. 72; Morgan and Coote, *Early Voyages*, vol. II, p. 253

54 Hakluyt, *Principal Navigations*, Everyman, vol. I, pp. 253–4
55 James Alday, who knew the conditions in Lapland, in 'High Court of Admiralty Examinations 20 (27 April 1576)', quoted in T.S. Willan, *The Early History of the Russia Company, 1553–1603* (Manchester, Manchester University Press, 1956), p. 4
56 Henry Lane, in Hakluyt, *Principal Navigations*, Everyman, vol. II, p. 265
57 Nordenskjold, *Voyage of the Vega*, vol. I, p. 62
58 *Calendar of State Papers and Manuscripts relating to English Affairs Existing in the Archives and Collection of Venice, 1555–1556*, R. Brown (ed.) (London, 1877, reprinted Kraus-Thomson, 1970), vol. VI, part 1, no. 269, G. Michiel, *Despatch to the Doge, Venice*.
59 E.C. Gordon, 'The Fate of Sir Hugh Willoughby and his Companions: a New Conjecture', *The Geographical Journal*, 152/2 (1986, July), pp. 243–7
60 R. Unwin, *A Winter away from Home* (London, Seafarer Books, 1995), pp. 113–14
61 R.E. Byrd, *Little America* (New York, Putnam, 1930), p. 203
62 They were found in a bay called Nokujeff Bay, which is in Lapland, about 300 kilometres east of where Murmansk is now. Two rivers flow into this bay, the Drosdovka at the south end, and a smaller river, the Arsina or Varsina, to the west of the Drosdovka, and it was here, in the mouth of the Arsina river, that they were anchored. Hakluyt, *Principal Navigations*, Hakluyt Society, vol. II, p. 500; N. Casimir, Baron de Bogoushevsky, 'The English in Moscow during the Sixteenth Century', *Transactions of the Royal Historical Society*, 7 (1878), pp. 58–129, at 59; Hamel, *England and Russia*, pp. 82 and 85
63 Ibid., p. 87
64 Nordenskiold, *Voyage of the Vega*, vol. I, p. 67
65 British Library, Cotton MS, Otto E VIII, folio 10

CHAPTER 7

1 Hakluyt, *Principal Navigations*, Everyman, vol. I, p. 14
2 Ibid., p. 273
3 Ibid., p. 336
4 Memorial plaque to Stephen Borough, St Mary's Church, Chatham (now the Medway Heritage Trust Centre)
5 J. Brown and M. Sinclair, *Scandinavia: the Rough Guide* (4th edn, London, Rough Guides, 1997), p. 337
6 Richard Johnson,'Certaine notes unperfectly written', in Hakluyt, *Principal Navigations*, Everyman, vol. I, pp. 352–6, at 353
7 Hakluyt, *Principal Navigations*, Everyman, vol. I, p. 411
8 J. Armitage and M. Brackenbury, *Norwegian Cruising Guide* (2nd edn, London, Adlard Coles, 1996), p. 86
9 D. Taylor-Wilkie (ed.), *Norway: Insight Guides* (Singapore, APA Publications, 1994), p. 337; *Nelles Guide: Norway* (2nd edn, Munich, Nelles Verlag, 2001), pp. 27, 209–10; E. Wellestrand, *2,500 Miles on the Coastal Steamer* (Norway, Nortra Books, 1993), pp. 70–1; H. Swain, *Return to Murmansk* (London, Seafarer Books, 1996), p. 151
10 Hakluyt, *Principal Navigations*, Everyman, vol. I, pp. 273–4
11 Scotland and Denmark had had friendly relations ever since Alexander III of Scotland won the Battle of Largs in 1263, which put an end to the disputes over the sovereignty of the islands to the west and north of Scotland. It was then agreed that the Western Isles (or Sudereys) and the Isle of Man would pass to Scotland for a lump sum of 4,000 marks (a mark was two-thirds of a pound sterling) and an annuity of

100 marks paid annually to Norway, while the Norsemen continued to rule the Northern Isles (Orkney and Shetland). Then, in 1470, James III of Scotland married Margaret, the daughter of King Christian I of Denmark, at which time the rest of the islands came under the Scottish Crown, and there were no more payments of tribute for the Western Isles. M. Lynch, *Scotland: a New History* (London, Pimlico, 1992), pp. 90 and 155. The Hanseatic League also had a trading post at Edinburgh, with connections to Scandinavia and the Baltic. G. Barraclough (ed.), *The Times Atlas of World History* (London, Times Books, 1978), p. 144. A Scot called David (?Cocker) was employed as a 'herald' by King John of Denmark. (See note 32, Chapter 5.)

12 H.R. Fox Bourne, *English Seamen under the Tudors* (London, R. Bentley, 1868), p. 100

13 Hakluyt, *Principal Navigations*, Everyman, vol. I, p. 274

14 G.V. Scammell, 'Manning the English Merchant Service in the Sixteenth Century', *Mariner's Mirror*, 56 (1970), pp. 131–54, at 144

15 Hakluyt, *Principal Navigations*, Everyman, vol. I, 274

16 It was already too late in the year for the sun to have been shining all night. It was 2 August when the fleet was scattered by the storm off Seynam, and it must have taken the *Edward* at least two days to sail over 100 nautical miles to Vardø, where she waited in vain for seven days for the other ships to arrive. The *Edward* could not, therefore, have set off again from Vardø until at least 11 August. The dates above were those of the Julian calendar, which was in use at the time and which was ten days behind the Gregorian calendar we use today. When the date was 2 August in 1553, today we would call it 12 August. The midnight sun shines from 20 May to 20 July at Vardø according to our modern calendar, as previously mentioned. Even as far north as the North Cape, the midnight sun only shines from 14 May until 29 July. Anon., *Cruising with a Difference* (Norway, Scandinavian Travel Service, 1998). The *Edward* could therefore well have experienced twenty-four-hour sunshine earlier on in the voyage, from about 20 May until about 29 July (modern dates, i.e. 10 May– 19 July in Julian dates), but not any later than that, though she would still have had the benefit of a very prolonged twilight.

17 Hakluyt, *Principal Navigations*, Everyman, vol. I, p. 274

18 J. Hamel, *England and Russia* [1854], trans. J.S. Leigh (London, F. Cass, 1968), p. 95

19 Hakluyt, *Principal Navigations*, Everyman, vol. I, pp. 274–5

20 It was not until Peter the Great started ship-building at Archangel'sk in about 1693 that the first Russian vessel big enough to carry goods to other countries was built; Hamel, *England and Russia*, p. 242

21 Hakluyt, *Principal Navigations*, Everyman, vol. I, p. 275

22 The men of the *Edward* may have noticed some long pipes on the shore there, which the nuns of the convent used for extracting salt from sea water by distillation. The convent had obtained permission from the Tsar by an edict of 1545 to run a salt distillation plant; Hamel, *England and Russia*, p. 97. Hakluyt also describes a monastery nearby, called Gostinopolye Monastery, and he mentions salmon fishing there. Hakluyt, *Principal Navigations*, Hakluyt Society, vol. I, pp. 392, 400 and 439

23 Ibid., p. 287; Hamel, *England and Russia*, p. 196. Wild roses grew on Rose Island, together with violets and wild rosemary, and pine and beech trees. The English botanist John Tradescant visited Rose Island, among other sites in Russia, in 1618, and he noted finding a rose there, *Rosa Moscovita*, together with Swedish privet and pinks. Tradescant's account of his journey is in the Ashmolean, 'A voiag of ambussad (to Russia)' (Ashmolean 824 xvi). Tradescant kept a museum, called Tradescant's Ark, on the east side of South Lambeth Road, just opposite Spring Lane; Hamel, *England and Russia*, pp. 255 and 282–4. Named after him, Tradescant Road still runs off the South Lambeth Road in London.

24 Hakluyt, *Principal Navigations*, Hakluyt Society, vol. I, pp. 335 and 385

25 *Dvina Chronicle*, quoted in N. Casimir, Baron de Bogoushevsky, 'The English in Moscow during the Sixteenth Century', *Transactions of the Royal Historical Society*, 7 (1878), pp. 58–129, at 60

26 This mouth of the Dvina is referred to as the Murman mouth (*Murman* means Norseman); Hamel, *England and Russia*, p. 195. W. Klein, *USSR: the New Soviet Union* (Singapore, APA Publications, 1991). Archangel'sk was established by a decree of Tsar Ivan IV, the Terrible, in 1574. It developed into a major lumber port. During the Second World War, it was important for the supply of American tanks and Studebaker trucks to the Russian Army. There were many prison camps in the area, before, during and after the Second World War. R. Van Berkmoes et al., *Russia, Ukraine and Belarus* (Hawthorn, Australia, Lonely Planet, 2nd edn, 2000), pp. 433–9.

27 Jim Row, Bridgend, ex-Merchant Navy, Navigation Cadet, personal communication, 2003.

28 J. Hutchings (ed.), *Insight Guides: Russia, Belarus and Ukraine* (Singapore, APA Publications, 2004), p. 215. In 1991, one of the streets in Severodvinsk was named after Richard Chancellor. In 1998, a memorial stone to the 1553 expedition was set up on Yagry Island (previously known to the English as Rose Island) and, in 2003, ceremonies were held there to mark 450 years of cooperation between Russia and England. (Berkmoes, *Russia, Ukraine and Belarus*.) There is now a long bridge connecting the mainland to Yagry Island. http://english.pravda.ru/main/18/87/343/10619_england.html (30 July 2003)

29 R. Milner-Gulland, *Atlas of Russia and the Soviet Union* (Oxford, Phaidon, 1989), pp. 62–3; R. Wallace, *The Rise of Russia* (Nederlands, Time-Life International, 1967), pp. 76–84. In 1553, Tsar Ivan had just returned from conquering the Tartars in Kazan to the east, his greatest military victory.

30 Hakluyt, *Principal Navigations*, Everyman, vol. I, p. 275

31 The Governor of Dvina was Prince Semen Ivanovitch Mikulinsky Punkoff. Hamel, *England and Russia*, p. 87

32 Hakluyt, *Principal Navigations*, Everyman, vol. I, pp. 275–6. Incidentally, there is a wonderful account of the arrival of the *Edward* at St Nicholas and subsequent events in Dorothy Dunnett, *The Ringed Castle* (London, Century Hutchinson, 1983). It is a work of fiction, but it is soundly based on Dunnett's extensive historical research.

33 Hakluyt, *Principal Navigations*, Everyman, vol. I, p. 279. There were said to be 100,000 inhabitants in Moscow by 1600 – in the Kremlin, the Kitaigorod and the immediate surrounding area. Nearly all the buildings were of wood, with a partially sunken ground floor for storerooms and for the servants, and with the first floor for dining- and reception rooms. P. Bushkovitch, *The Merchants of Moscow, 1580–1650* (Cambridge, Cambridge University Press, 1980), pp. 4, 8.

    However, there were other buildings which were more magnificent, such as the Kremlin, with its 50-foot-high brick walls and twenty fortified towers, the Cathedral of St Michael Archangel and the Uspenski Cathedral (Dunnett, *Ringed Castle*, p. 30). However, St Basil's Cathedral, the ultimate symbol of Russia, which is now Moscow's premier tourist attraction, had not yet been built: it was started in 1555 and finished six years later; *Geographical* (December 2000), p. 63

34 M. Wheeler, H.M. Trevor-Roper and A.J.P. Taylor (eds), *History of the English Speaking Peoples* (12 vols, London, BPC Publishing, 1969), p. 1186

35 Hakluyt, *Principal Navigations*, Everyman, vol. I, p. 294

36 J. Hamel, *England and Russia*, p. 99

37 Henry Lane, 'Letter to M. William Sanderson' [1586], in Hakluyt, *Principal Navigations*, Everyman, vol. II, p. 265

38 Ibid. The robbery by the Flemings was not mentioned until some thirty years later.
39 S. Purchas, *Hakluytus Posthumus or Purchas, His Pilgrimes*, quoted in R.W. Cotton, 'Stephen Borough, the Navigator', in *Transactions of the Devonshire Association*, 12 (1880–1), pp. 332–60.

CHAPTER 8

1 Hakluyt, *Principal Navigations*, Everyman, vol. I, p. 333
2 The narrative of this voyage comes directly from an original account by Stephen Borough himself in Hakluyt, *Principal Navigations*, Everyman, vol. I, pp. 333–52
3 Hakluyt, *Principal Navigations*, Everyman, vol. I, pp. 232–93
4 The *Edward Bonaventura* was the same ship in which Richard Chancellor and Stephen Borough had first sailed to Russia in 1553. (She had returned to London in 1554 and sailed to Russia and back again in 1555.) J. Hamel, *England and Russia* [1854], trans. J.S. Leigh (London, F. Cass, 1968), pp. 142–3
5 Hamel, *England and Russia*, pp. 142–3
6 R. Johnson, 'Certaine notes unperfectly written . . .', in Hakluyt, *Principal Navigations*, Everyman, vol. I, pp. 352–6
7 Hakluyt, *Principal Navigations*, Everyman, vol. I, p. 344
8 Ibid., p. 336
9 The *Anthony Roll* (the list and description of all the ships in the navy in 1546) contains the details of ten vessels that were called pinnaces. Four of them were of 80 tons, four were of 40 tons, and there were two smaller ones, the *Trego-Ronnyger* of 20 tons and the *Hare* of 15 tons. Both of these smaller pinnaces were three-masted, and they carried crews of twenty-five and thirty men respectively (the smaller vessel, the *Hare*, had the larger crew). C.S. Knighton and D.M. Loades, *The Anthony Roll of Henry VIII's Navy: Pepys Library 2991 and British Library Additional MS 22047 with Related Documents* (Aldershot, Navy Records Society, 2000). The *Serchthrift* was probably about the same size as the *Hare* or the *Trego-Ronnyger*, i.e. about 15 or 20 tons.
    One clue as to the possible shape of a pinnace comes from Friel, who found that some pinnaces of 1576 were relatively slender for boats of the time, with length-to-beam ratios of between 4.1 to 1 and 4.5 to 1 (I. Friel, 'Frobisher's Ships: the Ships of the North-Western Atlantic Voyages, 1576–1578', in T.H.B. Symons (ed.), *Meta Incognita: a Discourse of Discovery: Martin Frobisher's Arctic Expeditions, 1576–1578* (Quebec, Canadian Museum of Civilisation, 1999), pp. 299–352, at 315.) Such slenderness of form would have made the pinnace faster, though with less load-carrying ability.
    This notion seems to be supported by Richard Hawkins, who wrote that the function of a pinnace 'is to wait upon their fleet in calms with their oars, to follow the chase, in occasions, and to anchor near the shore when the greater ships cannot without peril'. J.A. Williamson, *The Observations of Sir Richard Hawkins* (London, Argonaut Press, 1933), p. 29, quoted in T. Glasgow, 'Oared Vessels in the English Navy', *Mariner's Mirror*, 52 (1966), pp. 375–6. Indeed, a pinnace was used for just such a task on the 1553 expedition, when they were at the Lofoten Islands: 'then went forth our pinnesse to seeke harborow, & found many good harbours'. Hakluyt, *Principal Navigations*, Everyman, vol. I, p. 250. The one thing that all the different sorts and sizes of pinnaces seem to have had in common is that they were employed for scouting, for message-carrying or for similar support roles to bigger ships. There does therefore seem to be evidence, from both their form and their function, that pinnaces were relatively slender.

10 These estimations are based on Baker's Old Rule, as described in Chapter 4, using 4.2:1 as the length-to-beam ratio, where X is the beam of the vessel in feet.

$$\frac{4.2X \times X \times 0.4X}{100} = 20 \text{ (tons)}$$

   If the *Serchthrift* had been of 16 instead of 20 tons, her measurements, always very approximate, would have been: length of keel 40 feet, maximum beam 9½ feet and depth in hold 4 feet. (Appendix 4 has more detail on these calculations.)

11 Hakluyt, *Principal Navigations*, Everyman, vol. I, p. 334

12 Our Lady of Hollands has been identified as Little Holland in Essex, just north of present-day Clacton. Hakluyt, *Principal Navigations*, Hakluyt Society, vol. I, p. 311

13 Hakluyt, *Principal Navigations*, Everyman, vol. I, 334

14 Ibid., p. 336

15 'St Dunstan's Island' has been very plausibly identified as Bømlo Island, between 59° 35' and 59° 50' N. Hakluyt, *Principal Navigations*, Hakluyt Society, vol. I, p. 313. Stephen Borough describes a 'high round mountaine' to the east of 'St Dunstans Island', which is probably the north–south ridge of Mehamarsat (749 metres) on Stord Island. Borough also describes how 'the land lyeth North and halfe a point Westerly' from there, as indeed it does.

16 'Scoutsnesse' has been identified as Skudenes or Skutesnaes, Hakluyt, *Principal Navigations*, Hakluyt Society, vol. I, p. 313, but I think that this must be wrong. Skudenes has a pleasing alliterative correspondence to 'Scoutsnesse', but it is south of Bømlo Island, when it should be north. Also Borough says that at this headland the land 'trended to the Northwards and to the East of the North', which leads me to suppose that the headland in question was Stadlandet, described as 'a notorious headland' by J. Armitage and M. Brackenbury, *Norwegian Cruising Guide* (2nd edn, London, Adlard Coles, 1996), p. 23

17 Kedilwike has been identified as Kjodvik on the Island of Sørø, or Sørøya; E.D. Morgan and C.H. Coote, *Early Voyages and Travels to Russia and Persia* (London, Hakluyt Society, 1886, reprinted in 2 vols, New York, B. Franklin, Hakluyt Society, series 1, nos 72 and 73), no. LXXII, p. 16; Hakluyt, *Principal Navigations*, Hakluyt Society, vol. I, p. 313

18 Corpus Christi Bay has not been identified, though the entrance to Tana Fjord almost fits Stephen Borough's description of its distance from the North Cape. Hakluyt, *Principal Navigations*, Everyman, vol. I, p. 336

19 The Isle of Crosses has not been identified. It is not the same as Crosse Island, which has been identified as Sosnovetz, in the mouth of the White Sea. Morgan and Coote, *Early Voyages*, p. 22. Point Lookout has been identified as Abramovsky Cape, Hakluyt, *Principal Navigations*, Hakluyt Society, vol. I, p. 314. The Cape Good Fortune mentioned here has not been identified. It is not the same as the Cape Good Fortune that has been identified as Voronov Cape (at the southern end of the Gulf of Mezen), Hakluyt, *Principal Navigations*, Hakluyt Society, vol. I, p. 314. Saint Edmond's Point has also not been identified. It is not the same as the St Edmund's Point described as being in the Gulf of Mezen (possibly Cape Nerpinskiy), Hakluyt, *Principal Navigations*, Hakluyt Society, vol. I, p. 314

20 Hakluyt, *Principal Navigations*, Everyman, vol. I, p. 337

21 Ibid., pp. 337–40

22 Ibid., pp. 372–3

23 The Cape Saint Bernard mentioned here, which is somewhere near the entrance to the Kola Inlet, is not the same as the one that has been located in the Gulf of Mezen, Hakluyt, *Principal Navigations*, Hakluyt Society, vol. I, p. 314

24 Cape Saint John has been identified with Kanushin Cape, at the north-east end of the Gulf of Mezen, ibid., p. 314

25 Hakluyt, *Principal Navigations*, Everyman, vol. I, pp. 339–40

26 Ibid., pp. 339–42

27 Morgan and Coote, *Early Voyages*, vol. II, p. 253 (*Nos* means a headland or cape in Russian)

28 *Admiralty Chart 2962: The North Cape to Uyedinyeniya Island including the Barents and Kara Seas* (Taunton, Hydrographer to the Navy, 1997)

29 Hakluyt, *Principal Navigations*, Everyman, vol. I, p. 343

30 Ibid., p. 343; Morgan and Coote, *Early Voyages*, vol. II, p. 253

31 An explorer in 1895 and 1897 described Kolguev Island as 'dreary, fog-environed and wind-tormented, not one redeeming feature', H.W. Fielden, 'Visits to Barents and Kara Seas, with Rambles in Novaya Zemlya, 1895 and 1897', in *Geographical Journal* (1898, April), vol. 11/4, pp. 333–65

32 This is another Svyatoy Nos, meaning 'Holy Headland'. The other one was called Cape Gallant by Stephen Borough. Morgan and Coote, *Early Voyages*, vol. II, pp. 20 and 253; *Admiralty Chart 2962*

33 Hakluyt, *Principal Navigations*, Everyman, vol. I, p. 344

34 Ibid., p. 344

35 Ibid., pp. 344–5. In his steam yacht in 1895 Fielden was also prevented by ice from going any further east than the Pechora river for some days. (In Stephen Borough's case this happened on 21 July, in Fielden's it was on 27 June.) Fielden, 'Visits to Barents and Kara Seas', pp. 333–65

36 Hakluyt, *Principal Navigations*, Everyman, vol. I, p. 345

37 W.H. Dawbin, 'Baleen Whales', in R. Harrison and M.M. Bryden (eds) *Whales, Dolphins and Porpoises* (London, Merehurst Press, 1988), pp. 44–65, at 45

38 Hakluyt, *Principal Navigations*, Everyman, vol. I, p. 270

39 Once, when the author was sailing off the coast of Angola, a whale swam right underneath us. The yacht was a maxi yacht of 36 tons and 78 feet long, a good deal bigger than the *Serchthrift*, and the whale was probably a Southern Right whale, very similar to its relative, the Northern Right. It was a privilege to sense the power of the whale sweeping below our boat.

40 Ibid., p. 346. The highest mountain on Novaya Zemlya is at the north end of the south island: it is 1,342m high. Novaya Zemlya in the 1970s and '80s was notorious for its two nuclear testing sites. W. Klein (ed.), *USSR: the New Soviet Union* (Singapore, Insight Guides, 1991), pp. 247–8; R. Greenall, *An Explorer's Guide to Russia* (Edinburgh, Canongate, 1994), p. 391

41 Hakluyt, *Principal Navigations*, Everyman, vol. I, p. 346

42 Ibid., p. 347

43 Ibid.

44 Klein, *USSR*, p. 248

45 Hakluyt, *Principal Navigations*, Everyman, vol. I, pp. 352–6

46 D. Hershman, 'Last of the Nomads', in *Geographical* 70/9 (September, 1998), pp. 6–15; Klein, *USSR*, p. 248. These are the people with whom the Stroganov family set up a lucrative trade in furs in the 1580s, according to Purchas: S. Purchas, *Hakluytus Posthumus or Purchas, His Pilgrims* [1625] (20 vols, Glasgow, Maclehose, 1905), vol. XIII, pp. 171–9

47 Hakluyt, *Principal Navigations*, Everyman, vol. I, p. 348

48 Ibid., p. 348

49 Ibid., p. 349

50 Admiralty Sailing Directions, *Southern Barents Sea and Beloye More Pilot* (Taunton, Hydrographer of the Navy, 1996). Burgess states that in the Barents Sea there is on average fog for fifteen days of every month in June, July and August: C.R. Burgess, *Meteorology for Seamen* (4th edn, Glasgow, Brown, Son and Ferguson, 1978), p. 136.

Stephen Borough experienced mists off the coast of Norway on 17 and 18 May, thick mist off the Murmansk coast on 7 June, and 'very mistie' conditions near Kanin Noz on 10 July. The worst time was in August, when they had mist and fog from 8–11, and from 13–18, and further mist when off Kanin Nos again on 29 and 30 August.

51 Hakluyt, *Principal Navigations*, Everyman, vol. I, p. 350

52 Ibid., p. 351

53 Ibid., p. 350

54 The predominant wind in the Barents Sea is north-easterly in the summer, owing to the effects of high pressure at the North Pole and a big low that is usually centred about Afghanistan: S.P. Palmer (ed.), 'Polar Navigation', in *Concise Encyclopedia of Science and Technology* (3rd edn, New York, McGraw-Hill, 1994)

55 Hakluyt, *Principal Navigations*, Everyman, vol. I, pp. 350–1

56 Ibid., p. 352

57 It is not apparent why Stephen Borough felt it necessary to sail west in search of the missing ships. The Muscovy Company wrote to him from London at the beginning of May 1557, saying 'Wee doe perceive that Stephen Burrow . . . is minded to set forth in the beginning of June next, to seek the river of Obi. We pray God to speede him well. . . . We will that Stephen Burrowe doo proceed on his voiage to discover.' Letter from Muscovy Company to Stephen Borough, early May 1557, quoted by Hamel, *England and Russia*, p. 149, but no source given.

Borough set off on 23 May 1557, so very probably the letter did not reach him in time. Incidentally, it was Ivan III who inaugurated a system of posts and post horses: D. Obolensky, 'Italy, Mount Athos and Muscovy: the Three Worlds of Maximos, the Greek', *Proceedings of the British Academy*, LVII (1981), repr. in *Six Byzantine Portraits* (Oxford, 1988), pp. 201–19 and quoted by N. Davies, *Europe: A History* (London, Pimlico, 1997, first pub. London, OUP, 1996), p. 467

58 Hakluyt, *Principal Navigations*, Everyman, vol. I, pp. 367–77

59 Ibid., p. 357

60 Ibid., p. 367

61 Ibid., p. 371

62 British Library, Royal MS, 18D, iii, folio 124, *William Borough's Chart of Northern Navigation, Trondheim to Vaygattes* [?1568]. There is another copy at Hatfield House: R.A. Skelton and J. Summerson, *A Description of the Maps and Architectural Drawings in the Collection made by William Cecil, First Baron Burghley, now at Hatfield House* (Oxford, Roxburghe Club, 1971), catalogue no. 121

63 Hakluyt, *Principal Navigations*, Everyman, vol. I, p. 375

64 Ibid.

65 Some parts of the Kola Peninsula have suffered a lot since the *Serchthrift* sailed along the coast. The area has great mineral deposits, but the sulphur dioxide that has been produced as a by-product has killed off much of the forest. The city of Murmansk was largely reduced to rubble in the Second World War, but was subsequently rebuilt. R. Greenall, *An Explorer's Guide to Russia* (Boston, Zephyr Press and Edinburgh, Canongate Press, 1994), p. 391

CHAPTER 9

1 John Dee, in Preface to *The Elements of Geometrie of the most auncient philosopher Euclide of Megara*, trans. H. Billingsley [London, John Daye, 1570], quoted in D.W. Waters, *The Art of Navigation in Elizabethan and Early Stuart Times* (London, Hollis and Carter, 1958), p. 521

2   G. Chaucer, 'Canterbury Tales, Prologue', in W.W. Skeat (ed.), *The Complete Works of Geoffrey Chaucer* (Oxford, Clarendon Press, 1913), p. 424

3   'We bare roomer' means we sought sea room, i.e. we headed out to sea to find deeper water.

4   Hakluyt, *Principal Navigations*, Everyman, vol. I, p. 252

5   'Polar Navigation', in S.P. Palmer (ed.), *Concise Encyclopedia of Science and Technology* (3rd edn, New York, McGraw-Hill, 1994); C.R. Burgess, *Meteorology for Seamen* (4th edn, Glasgow, Brown, Son and Ferguson, 1978), p. 136

6   Hugh Smith, 'The discoverie made by M. Arthur Pet and M. Charles Jackman, of the Northeast parts . . . in the yeere 1580', in Hakluyt, *Principal Navigations*, Everyman, vol. II, pp. 227–44, at 234

7   Hakluyt, *Principal Navigations*, Everyman, vol. I, p. 349

8   Ibid., p. 352. Another example of his soundings is '45 fathoms and mathes, with small white and black sand', found in the North Sea in 1556. ('Mathes' is apparently a form of grub or maggot that looks like herring bones.) Hakluyt, *Principal Navigations*, Hakluyt Society, p. 316. Other examples are '29 fathoms sand and in manner streamy ground', 15 leagues north of the mouth of the Pechora river on 21 August 1556, and off Cape Race in 1557, where he noted that 'I had where we roade two and twenty fadoome, and the tallow which is taken up is full of great broken shels, and some stones withall like unto small sand congealed together'. Hakluyt, *Principal Navigations*, Everyman, vol. I, pp. 350 and 369 respectively

9   G. Hutchinson, *Medieval Ships and Shipping* (London, Leicester University Press, 1994), p. 168

10   A. Ruddock, 'The Earliest Original English Seaman's Rutter and Pilot's Chart', *Journal of the Institute of Navigation, London*, 14 (1961), pp. 409–31, at 420

11   Hakluyt, *Principal Navigations*, Everyman, vol. I, pp. 344 and 337

12   Admiralty, *South Barents Sea and Beloye More Pilot* (Taunton, Hydrographer of the Navy, 1996)

13   William Bourne, *A Regiment for the Sea* [1574], E.G.R. Taylor (ed.) (London, Cambridge University Press for the Hakluyt Society, 1963)

14   D.W. Waters, 'The English Pilot: English Sailing Directions and Charts and the Rise of English Shipping, 16th to 18th Centuries', *Journal of the Institute of Navigation, London*, 42/3 (1989), pp. 317–54, at 321

15   P. Kemp (ed.), *The Oxford Companion to Ships and the Sea* (Oxford, OUP, 1976), p. 492

16   One knot is a speed of 1 nautical mile per hour. A nautical mile is 6,080 feet, that is 1.15 land miles.

17   Hakluyt, *Principal Navigations*, Everyman, vol. I, p. 250

18   Ibid., pp. 334–5

19   D. Sobell, *Longitude* (London, Fourth Estate, 1996)

20   Waters, *Art of Navigation*, p. 36

21   The Nocturnal from Martin Cortes, *The Arte of Navigation*, trans. R. Eden (London, 1561).

22   The Norsemen refined the observation of the sun by the use of a sundial. One of these, or at least part of one, was found in 1948, in a ruin dated to about AD 1200, in the Eastern Settlement near the southern tip of Greenland. It was a form of sun compass. With this simple device, the shadow of the sun cast on the rim of a hand-held dial by a spike at the centre is used to indicate direction. G. Jones, *A History of the Vikings* (Oxford, OUP, 1968), pp. 192–3; C.L. Vebaek and S. Thursland, *The Viking Compass: Guided Norsemen First to America* (Denmark, Humlebaek, 1992), quoted in Hutchinson, *Medieval Ships*, p. 164. A replica of this device was tested by Sir Robin Knox-Johnston in 1998. To use it, he had to guess what time it was every half hour, and to note then where the shadow fell on the edge of the disc. Using the device, he

found that he was only 9 cables out after sailing 60 miles in his famous yacht *Suhali* (R. Knox-Johnston, television programme, 1998).

The Norsemen had a further refinement for use on days when there was mist or fog, a very common problem in the Arctic in the summer: they used a polarising stone (called a *sólarsteinn*) of calcite, or Iceland spar, to search the sky to try to find where the sun was when visibility was poor. Dr A.D. Grassie, Isle of Arran, personal communication; Jones, *History of the Vikings*, pp. 192–3; B.E. Gelsinger, 'Lodestone and Sunstone in Medieval Iceland', *Mariner's Mirror*, 56 (1970), pp. 219–26

The English certainly noted the direction of the sun at different times but did not, as far as I am aware, use either a sun compass or a *sólarsteinn*.

23 The 'Regiment of the Pole Star' was first published in *c.* 1509. Waters, *Art of Navigation*, p. 45

24 D. Burwash, *English Merchant Shipping, 1460–1540* (Toronto, University of Toronto, 1947, repr. Newton Abbot, David and Charles, 1969), p. 4. The compass, complete with its binnacle (box), and illuminated at night, had been in use on English ships, according to old inventories, since 1410 or 1412. Hutchinson, *Medieval Ships*, p. 168

25 Hutchinson, *Medieval Ships*, p. 168

26 E.G.R. Taylor, 'John Dee and the Nautical Triangle, 1575', *Journal of the Institute of Navigation, London*, 8 (1955), pp. 312–25, at 321

27 The present coordinates of the magnetic poles are 78½° N, 69° W and 78½° S, 111° E, which places them between the north end of Greenland and Ellesmere Island in the Arctic, and somewhere near Vostok, the Russian Antarctic Research Station, in the Antarctic. D. Crystal (ed.), *The Cambridge Encyclopedia* (Cambridge, CUP, 1994), p. 686

28 Pedro de Medina, *Arte de Navegar* [1545], quoted in Waters, *Art of Navigation*, p. 70

29 Jean Rotz, 'Traicte des differences du compas aymante, et de certains poinetz notables ducelluy, etc.' [1542, MS Dieppe, presented to Henry VIII], quoted in E.G.R. Taylor, *Tudor Geography 1485–1583* (London, Methuen and Co., 1930), p. 169; E.G.R. Taylor, 'Jean Rotz: His Neglected Treatise on Nautical Science', *Geographical Journal*, 73 (1929), pp. 455–9

30 Hakluyt, *Principal Navigations*, Everyman, vol. I, p. 344. Other examples of his measurements of variation included 'the variation of the compasse was 7 degrees and a halfe from the North to the West', at 'St James, his island', on 27 July 1556; Hakluyt, *Principal Navigations*, Everyman, vol. I, p. 345. On 6 August, on the Islands of Vaigats, 'I went a shoare, and . . . the variation of the compasse was 8 degrees from the North to the West'; Hakluyt, *Principal Navigations*, Everyman, vol. I, p. 348

31 Ibid., pp. 367 and 368

32 Joao de Castro, for instance, had made measurements of variation during the years 1538–41, S.A. Bedini, 'Declination of the Compass', in S.A. Bedini (ed.), *Christopher Columbus and the Age of Exploration: an Encyclopedia* (New York, Da Capo Press, 1998), p. 208

33 National Maritime Museum, W. Burrowes, *A Discourse of the variation of the cumpass or magnetical needle* [1581], bound with R. Norman, *The Newe attractive, showing the nature, properties and manifold vertues of the Loadstone . . .* (London, John Tapper, 1614)

34 W. van Bemmelen, *Die Abweichung der Magnetnadel: Beobachtungen, Säcular- Variation, Wert- und Isogonensysteme bis zur Mitte des XVIIIten Jahrhunderts* (Batavia, 1899), very kindly sent to me by Dr D.R. Barraclough, British Geological Survey, Edinburgh. The chart shows the compass variation as it was at different places in the 1550s. It shows that magnetic variation has changed considerably since those times. For instance, in the 1550s the magnetic variation in London was about 10° E, whereas in 1995 it was 4° W; in Oslo, it was then about 13° E and in 1995 it was 0° W; and in the White Sea, it was then about 2–3° E, whereas in 1995 it was 12° E. Note that

van Bemmelen assigns positive values to west variation and also to west longitude, i.e. when the compass needle points to the west of true north, he gives the variation a positive sign. (Nowadays it is the convention to show easterly deviation and longitudes east of Greenwich as positive.)

35 The tabular log book was first used by John Davis in 1587, and it first appeared in print in his *Seamen's Secrets* in 1595. J. Youings, 'Three Devon-Born Tudor Navigators', in M. Duffy et al. (eds), *The New Maritime History of Devon* (2 vols, London, Conway Maritime Press, 1992), vol. I, pp. 33–4

36 Kemp, *Oxford Companion*, p. 234

37 Waters, *Art of Navigation*, p. 139

38 Ibid., p. 66

39 Burwash, *English Merchant Shipping*, p. 4

40 Eugenio de Salazar, quoted in *National Geographic*, vol. 200, no. 1 (2001, July), supplement.

41 S.E. Morison, *The European Discovery of America* (New York, Oxford University Press, 1971), p. 153. The best recent description of the astrolabe is *The Planispheric Astrolabe* (Greenwich, National Maritime Museum, 1976). Geoffrey Chaucer wrote a very clear and precise *Treatise on the Astrolabe* in 1391, addressed to 'Litel Lowis my sone'. Skeat, *Complete Works of Chaucer*, pp. 396–418

42 W. Bourne, 'A Regiment for the Sea' [1574], quoted in A. Stimson, 'History of Navigation', in M. Duffy et al. (eds), *The New Maritime History of Devon* (2 vols, London, Conway Maritime Press, 1992), vol. I, pp. 25–31, at 26

43 George Best, 'A True Discourse of the Late Voyages of Discoverie for finding of a Passage to Cathaya by the North West, under the Conduct of Martin Frobisher General' [London, 1578, p. 155], quoted in J. McDermott and D.W. Waters, 'Cathay and the Way Thither: the Navigation of the Frobisher Voyages', in T.H.B. Symons (ed.), *Meta Incognita: a Discourse of Discovery: Martin Frobisher's Arctic Expeditions 1576–1578* (2 vols, Quebec, Canadian Museum of Civilisation, 1999), vol. II, p. 394

44 The first accurate sun tables were devised by Abraham Zacuto and his pupil Jose Vizinho, of Portugal. They appeared in manuscript in 1485 and in print in 1509. M.W. Richey, 'Navigation: Art, Practice and Theory', in S.A. Bedini (ed.), *Christopher Columbus and the Age of Exploration: an Encyclopedia* (New York, Da Capo Press, 1998), pp. 505–12, at 509

45 Leonard Digges, a notable mathematician and a pupil of John Dee's, had also written an almanac specifically for the use of the 1553 expedition, and this may have contained some information about the predicted positions of the sun and stars. Waters, *Art of Navigation*, p. 96. This early edition of Digges's almanac has not survived.

46 E.G.R. Taylor, 'Instructions to a Colonial Surveyor in 1582', *Mariner's Mirror*, 37/1 (1951), pp. 48–62, at 53. It was at about this time that Dee wrote his manuscript 'The Astronomicall and Logisticall Rules and Canons to calculate the Ephemerides by . . . written at the request and for the use of that excellent Mechanician, Master Richard Chancellor'. E.G.R. Taylor, *The Mathematical Practitioners of Tudor and Stuart England* (Cambridge, Cambridge University Press, 1970), p. 315

47 E.G.R. Taylor, *Tudor Geography, 1485–1583* (London, Methuen, 1930), p. 91

48 Dee's traverse table was produced as a companion to his 'parodoxall compas' or circumpolar chart. He called it his 'Canon Gubernauticus. An Arithmeticall Resolution of the Paradoxall Compas'. Waters, *Art of Navigation*, p. 525; E.G.R. Taylor, 'John Dee and the Nautical Triangle', *Journal of the Institute of Navigation, London*, 8 (1955), pp. 312–25, at 320–1. It survives in manuscript: Ashmolean Museum, Oxford, 242, no. 43, Bodleian.

49 Taylor, *Mathematical Practitioners*, p. 318.
50 G. Menzies, *1421* (London, Bantam Pan, 2002), pp. 328–9
51 Taylor, 'Instructions to a Colonial Surveyor', p. 54
52 Kemp, *Oxford Companion*, p. 580
53 Waters, *Art of Navigation*, p. 525; E.G.R. Taylor, 'John Dee and the Nautical Triangle', p. 319
54 Hakluyt, *Principal Navigations*, Everyman, vol. I, p. 339
55 Ibid., p. 343
56 Ibid., p. 346
57 A. Savours, 'A Narrative of Frobisher's Arctic Voyages', in Symons, *Meta Incognita*, vol. I, pp. 19–54, at 26–32
58 Dr Robert Recorde is credited with having introduced the equals sign in 1542; the plus and minus signs had been devised by John Widman in 1489, though they were little used until the seventeenth century. Waters, *Art of Navigation*, p. 245 n.
59 Taylor, 'John Dee and the Nautical Triangle', p. 321
60 The few people in England with an interest in mathematics in the 1550s included John Cheke, a Professor of Greek at Cambridge who came to mathematics from reading Euclid; John Dee, who graduated from St John's College, Cambridge, where John Cheke had been a tutor; the Duke of Northumberland, 'Protector Northumberland', who had been Lord High Admiral, and who had been owner of a substantial number of ships; also several members of his family (including Henry Sidney and also Robert Dudley, who later became Elizabeth's favourite and Earl of Leicester), some of whom had been present at Dee's electrifying lectures on Euclid in Paris; Richard Chancellor, Henry Sidney's protégé; Leonard Digges, Dee's friend, a mathematician and author; Lord Clinton, the new Lord High Admiral, who helped support Digges when he was attainted in connection with Wyatt's Rebellion; Dr Robert Recorde, who wrote *The Castle of Knowledge* and other mathematical works; and William Cunningham, another Cambridge man and author of *The Cosmographicall Glasse*. Taylor, *Mathematical Practitioners*, pp. 18–41, 166–73 and 314–23
61 G.V. Scammell, *The World Encompassed: the First European Maritime Enterprises, c. 800–1650* (London, Methuen, 1981), p. 500
62 Ibid.
63 Taylor, *Mathematical Practitioners*, p. 26
64 Ibid., pp. 5 and 8
65 J. Gullberg, *Mathematics from the Birth of Numbers* (New York, W.W. Norton, 1997), esp. pp. 208–14
66 Waters, *Art of Navigation*, pp. 94–5
67 Taylor, *Tudor Geography*, p. 95
68 Hakluyt, *Principal Navigations*, Everyman, vol. I, p. 378
69 R. Hope, *A New History of British Shipping* (London, John Murray, 1990), p. 104
70 Waters, *Art of Navigation*, p. 341
71 R. Hakluyt, *Epistle Dedicatorie in the First Volume of the Second edition, 1598*, Hakluyt, *Principal Navigations*, Everyman, vol. I, pp. 13–18
72 R.T. Gunther, 'The Newly Found Astrolabe of Queen Elizabeth', *Illustrated London News*, 99 (24 October 1936), pp. 738–9. Thomas Gemini's real name was Thomas Lambrit. He printed the books of Leonard Digges, among others, and he made a 'Universal Astrolabe' in 1552, and other fine astrolabes, including the one made for Queen Elizabeth in 1559.
73 British Library, Lansdowne MS, 10/35
74 A.H.W. Robinson, *Marine Cartography in Britain* (Leicester, Leicester University Press, 1962), p. 24, footnote 5

75 William Borough, 'Necessarie notes to be observed, and followed in your discoverie', in Hakluyt, *Principal Navigations*, Everyman, vol. II, pp. 97–8

76 William Burrough, 'Instructions and notes very necessary and needfull to be observed in the purposed voyage for discovery of Cathay eastwards, by Arthur Pet and Charles Jackman' [1580], in Hakluyt, *Principal Navigations*, Everyman, vol. II, pp. 210–14, at 211

77 Taylor, 'Instructions to a Colonial Surveyor', esp. pp. 59 and 61

78 S.H. Baron, 'William Borough and the Jenkinson Map of Russia', *Cartographica*, 26/2 (1989), pp. 72–85

79 British Library (Old Royal Library 18, D iii), William Borough, *Chart of the Northern Navigation* (*c.* 1558, or 1567–8)

80 It is interesting to note that on the three Frobisher expeditions, which took place in somewhat larger vessels twenty years later, in 1576–8, neither Hall nor any of the other shipmasters make any mention of longitude either. J. McDermott and D.W. Waters, 'Cathay and the Way Thither: the Navigation of the Frobisher Voyages', in Symons, *Meta Incognita*, vol. II, pp. 353–400

81 K.R. Andrews, 'The Elizabethan Seaman', *Mariner's Mirror*, 68 (1982), pp. 245–62, at 260.

CHAPTER 10

1   Hakluyt, *Principal Navigations*, Everyman, vol. I, pp. 254–66

2   Ibid., pp. 266–93

3   Ibid., pp. 294–9. John Hasse (or Harshe), a merchant, was listed as a member of the ship's company of the *Edward Bonaventura*. Hakluyt, *Principal Navigations*, Everyman, vol. I, p. 245. T.S. Willan, *The Muscovy Merchants of 1555* (Manchester, Manchester University Press, 1953), p. 101

4   Hakluyt, *Principal Navigations*, Everyman, vol. I, p. 298

5   J. Hamel, *England and Russia* [1854], J.S. Leigh (ed. and trans.) (London, Frank Cass, 1968), pp. 32–85. Hamel's account of the early relations between England and Russia is especially interesting, as he was himself Russian and thus particularly informative about the Russian people.

6   D. Obolensky, 'Italy, Mount Athos and Muscovy: the Three Worlds of Maximos the Greek', *Proceedings of the British Academy*, 57 (1981), repr. in *Six Byzantine Portraits* (Oxford, 1988), pp. 201–19, quoted in N. Davies, *Europe: A History* (London, Pimlico, 1997), p. 467

7   M.S. Anderson, *Britain's Discovery of Russia, 1553–1815* (London, Macmillan, 1958), p. 3; W. Kirschner, 'Entrepreneurial Activity in Russian–Western Trade Relations during the Sixteenth Century', *Explorations in Entrepreneurial History* 8/1 (October 1995), pp. 245–51

8   J.D. Clarkson, *A History of Russia* (London, Longman, 1961), p. 130

9   Anderson, *Britain's Discovery*, p. 3

10 Hakluyt, *Principal Navigations*, Everyman, vol. I, pp. 241 and 245; Willan, *Muscovy Merchants*, p. 84

11 Hakluyt, *Principal Navigations*, Everyman, vol. II, p. 187

12 Ibid., vol. I, p. 245

13 *Calendar of the Patent Rolls, 1554–5*, pp. 55–9. (Hakluyt gives the date as 6 February, Hakluyt, *Principal Navigations*, Everyman, vol. I, p. 329.) The grant of the Charter was delayed by various political upheavals, which included the problems of the succession after the death of Edward VI on 6 July 1553, Jane Grey's brief reign, Mary's accession

to the throne on 3 August 1553, the beheading of Protector Northumberland, Wyatt's Rebellion in 1554 and Mary's marriage to Philip of Spain.

14 Hakluyt, *Principal Navigations*, Everyman, vol. I, pp. 299–307; Hamel, *England and Russia*, p. 137

15 Hakluyt, *Principal Navigations*, Everyman, vol. I, p. 303

16 Hamel, *England and Russia*, p. 115

17 Hakluyt, *Principal Navigations*, Everyman, vol. I, pp. 307–13

18 E.D. Morgan and C.H. Coote, *Early Voyages and Travels to Russia and Persia, by Anthony Jenkinson and other Englishmen* (2 vols, London, Hakluyt Society, 1886), vol. I, p. lxvii

19 Hakluyt, *Principal Navigations*, Everyman, vol. I, p. 307

20 The rouble was valued by the Muscovy Company at about 12 or 13s sterling. Hakluyt, *Principal Navigations*, Everyman, vol. I, p. 391

21 Ibid., pp. 307–8

22 Ibid., vol. II, p. 267

23 Ibid., vol. I, p. 309

24 Ibid., pp. 311–12

25 Ibid., pp. 313–18

26 Admiralty Chart, 2273, *Dvinskiy Zaliv* (Taunton, Hydrographer of the Navy, 1985); Hamel, *England and Russia* p. 97; Arthur Edwards, 'The Way and Distances from St. Nicholas to the Caspian Sea', in Hakluyt, *Principal Navigations*, Everyman, vol. II, pp. 56–7

27 Hamel, *England and Russia*, p. 139

28 Thomas Randolfe, 'The Ambassage of M. Thomas Randolfe to the Emperor at Russia in 1568', in Hakluyt, *Principal Navigations*, Everyman, vol. II, p. 81

29 Hakluyt, *Principal Navigations*, Everyman, vol. I, p. 308. The rouble was considered to be worth about 13s. Hamel, *England and Russia*, p. 118

30 Hakluyt, *Principal Navigations*, Everyman, vol. II, pp. 73–7

31 Randolfe, 'The Ambassage', p. 82

32 Sir T. Smith, *Voyages and Entertainments in Russia* [1605], quoted in M. Wrett-Smith, 'The English in Russia', in *Transactions of the Royal Historical Society*, 4th series, 3 (1920), pp. 72–102, at 78

33 Christopher Borough described the route and modes of travel in Hakluyt, *Principal Navigations*, Everyman, vol. II, pp. 172–3, and Arthur Edwards gives a note of the distances involved, ibid., pp. 53–7

34 Ibid., vol. I, p. 413

35 Ibid., vol. II, p. 76

36 Hamel, *England and Russia*, p. 194

37 Smith, *Voyages and Entertainments*, quoted in Wrett-Smith, p. 80

38 Hakluyt, *Principal Navigations*, Everyman, vol. II, p. 8

39 N. Casimir, Baron de Bogoushevsky, 'The English in Moscow during the Sixteenth Century', *Transactions of the Royal Historical Society*, 7 (1878), pp. 58–129, at 71

40 S. von Herberstein, *Rerum Moscoviticorum Commentarii* (Vienna, 1549), trans. R.H. Major as *Notes upon Russia* (2 vols, London, Hakluyt Society, 1851, 1852), series 1, 1852, no. 12, pp. 4–5. P. Bushkovitch, *The Merchants of Moscow, 1580–1650* (Cambridge, Cambridge University Press, 1979), pp. 4–8

41 R. Greenall, *An Explorer's Guide to Russia* (Edinburgh, Canongate Press, 1994), p. 107; Herberstein, trans. Major as *Notes upon Russia*, vol. 10, p. 113

42 Hakluyt, *Principal Navigations*, Everyman, vol. II, pp. 135–6

43 'The Priviledges graunted by the Emperour of Russia', 1567, in Hakluyt, *Principal Navigations*, Everyman, vol. II, p. 73. 'And wheras heretofore we have given sir William Garrard and his company in this our kingdome of Mosco the new castle by the

church of S. Maxim behinde the market, they shal there still holde their house as heretofore we have given them, paying no custom for the same.'

44 *Guide to 'The Old English Court, the Museum of the History of Moscow'*, information courtesy of Mr J. Power, personal communication. The 'Old English Court' is now open to the public on a regular basis. It is not far from the Kremlin, on the south side of Varvarka Ulitsa, between the Church of St Maxim and the Church of St Barbara (T. Serkov Varvary, which now houses government offices).

45 The parish of St Dunstan in the East was centred on St Dunstan's Church, which is some 220 yards north of Ratcliffe (where the ships of the 1553 expedition were built), and is in what is now Stepney. (C. Webb, *Suburban London before 1837: Map Showing the Parish Boundaries* (Woking, West Surrey Family History Society, Research Aid 2, 1996).) T.S. Willan, *The Early History of the Russia Company, 1553–1603* (Manchester, Manchester University Press, 1956), pp. 28–9

46 Morgan and Coote, *Early Voyages*, vol. I, p. lxviii. Seething Lane is less than a quarter of a mile north-west of the Tower of London. It adjoins Muscovy Street. The Muscovy Company's headquarters were very close to Sir Francis Walsingham's house, which was also in Seething Lane.

47 Hakluyt, *Principal Navigations*, Everyman, vol. I, p. 406 and vol. II, p. 9; Willan, *The Early History*, p. 286

48 Ibid., pp. 28–9, 135; B. Dietz, *The Port and Trade of Early Elizabethan London Documents* (London, London Record Society, 1972), p. 163; H. Clout, *The Times London History Atlas* (London, The Times, 1991), pp. 58–9; P. Marsden, *Ships of the Port of London: Twelfth to Seventeenth Centuries AD* (London, English Heritage, 1996), p. 21

49 Hakluyt, *Principal Navigations*, Everyman, vol. II, p. 267

50 Ibid., vol. I, p. 357. The Boyars were the Russian hereditary aristocracy, until Peter the Great eventually abolished them in 1711.

51 Ibid., pp. 357–8. The shipwreck is dramatically described by Dorothy Dunnett in her historical novel, *The Ringed Castle* (London, Century Hutchinson, 1971).

52 Willan, *Early History*, p. 52 et seq.

53 G. Barraclough (ed.), *The Times Atlas of World History* (London, Times Books, 1978), p. 162; A.F. Chew, *An Atlas of Russian History* (New Haven and London, Yale University Press, 1967), p. 38

54 See, for instance, British Library, Cotton MS Nero xj, folio 332, Message carried by Anthony Jenkinson from the tsar to Queen Elizabeth [November 1567] for a summary of the tsar's wants. The same letter is reprinted in Y. Tolstoy, *The First Forty Years of Intercourse between England and Russia, 1553–1593* (St Petersburg, 1875), letter 12, pp. 38–9

55 Tolstoy, *England and Russia*, letter 26 (18 May 1570), pp. 96–8

56 Hamel, *England and Russia*, p. 179

57 Morgan and Coote, *Early Voyages*, vol. I, p. xi

58 R.P. and N. Romanoff, *Ivan The Terrible* (New York, T.Y. Crowell, 1975), p. 317

59 Queen Elizabeth's letter declining the tsar's offer of marriage was at one time preserved in a casket in one of the rooms of the old palace in Moscow, A. Maskell, *Russian Art and Art Objects in Russia: a Handbook to the Reproductions of Goldsmiths' Work and Other Art Treasures from that Country in the South Kensington Museum* (London, Chapman and Hall, 1884), p. 236

60 The Tsar threw Bomel out, accused him of conspiring with Sweden and Poland, had him tortured, then whipped with iron wires, then bound to a spit and roasted, and then, still just alive, he was thrown into a prison, where he died.

61 Tolstoy, *England and Russia*, letter 33 (23 March 1572), pp. 128–34, an account of an interview between M. Anthony Jenkinson and the Tsar.

62 Tolstoy, *England and Russia*, p. xxxvi

63 F. Carr, *Ivan, the Terrible* (Newton Abbot, David and Charles, 1981), pp. 172–4

64 Hamel, *England and Russia*, p. 23; E.G.R. Taylor, 'Instructions to a Colonial Surveyor in 1582', in *Mariner's Mirror*, 37/1 (1951), pp. 48–62, at 51

65 E.G.R. Taylor, *Tudor Geography 1485–1583* (London, Methuen, 1930), pp. 90–1

66 G.V. Scammell, 'Manning the English Merchant Service in the Sixteenth Century', *Mariner's Mirror*, 56 (1970), pp. 131–54, at 143

67 L. Stone and J.C. Fawtier Stone, *An Open Elite? England, 1540–1880* (Oxford, Clarendon Press 1984), p. 3

68 *Calendar of State Papers, Foreign and Domestic* (1554–5), Part III, pp. 55–7

69 Hakluyt, *Principal Navigations*, Everyman, vol. I, p. 377. The owners of the *Primrose* (240 tons) were Andrewe Judd, William Chester, Anthony Hickman and Edward Casteline; of the *John Evangelist* (170 tons), Andrew Judd and William Chester; of the *Anne* (160 tons), John Dimocke, and of the *Trinitie* (140 tons), R.T. (It is not known who R.T. was.)

70 Hakluyt, *Principal Navigations*, Everyman, vol. I, p. 379

71 Thomas Alcocke, 'A letter of Thomas Alcocke to the worshipful Richard Gray, and Henrie Lane, Agents in Moscovia, from Terwill in Polonia' [26 April 1558], in Hakluyt, *Principal Navigations*, Everyman, vol. I, pp. 395–7

72 British Library, Cotton MS Nero B xj, folio 332

73 Tolstoy, *England and Russia*, letter 9 [6 December 1569], pp. 29–30

74 *Calendar of State Papers, Foreign*, 1564–6, p. 279; British Library, Royal MS, 13, BI, folio 176v

75 *Calendar of State Papers, Foreign*, 1561–2, pp. 59–60

76 Willan, *Early History*, p. 119

77 National Archives, Exchequer King's Remembrancer, Customs Accounts, E 122/90/11, (1564), quoted in T.S. Willan, 'Trade between England and Russia in the Second Half of the Sixteenth Century', in *English Historical Review* 63 (1948), pp. 307–21, at 309–10. Stephen Borough himself is reported to have shipped fourteen cases of brimstone in the *Swallow* in 1569, R. Baldwin, 'Stephen Borough', in H.C.G. Mathew and B. Harrison (eds), *Oxford Dictionary of National Biography* (60 vols, Oxford, OUP, 2004)

78 Ibid., pp. 381–2

79 Ibid., p. 383

80 Willan, *Early History*, p. 53

81 Hakluyt, *Principal Navigations*, Everyman, vol. I, p. 387

82 A. Hart-Davies, *What the Tudors and Stuarts Did for Us* (London, Pan Macmillan, 2002), pp. 67–8

83 J. Vanes, *The Port of Bristol in the Sixteenth Century* (Bristol, Bristol Record Society, 1995)

84 Willan, *Early History*, p. 65

85 The most useful source on Jenkinson's life and travels is Morgan and Coote, *Early Voyages*

86 Hakluyt, *Principal Navigations*, Everyman, vol. I, pp. 397–9, and 438–64

87 Ibid., p. 398

88 Ibid., vol. II, pp. 9–29

89 Ibid., pp. 73–7

90 Ibid., pp. 136–56

91 Ibid., pp. 30–3

92 Ibid., pp. 33–57

93 Ibid., pp. 108–19

94 Ibid., pp. 119–33

95 Ibid., pp. 201–3

96 The 'Directions' given to Morgan Hubblethorne before his departure for Persia included the instruction, 'If before you returne you could procure a singular good workeman in the arte of Turkish carpet making, you should bring the arte into this Realme, and also thereby increase worke to your company.' Hakluyt, *Principal Navigations*, Everyman, vol. II, p. 203

97 Ibid., vol. II, pp. 172–200

98 Ibid., pp. 200–1

99 Ibid., p. 172

100 Willan, *Early History*, p. 41

101 *Calendar of State Papers, Foreign, Elizabeth*, no. 2415, 12 August 1568. Thomas Bannister and Geoffrey Duckett in St Nicholas to Cecil in London.

102 Hakluyt, *Principal Navigations*, Everyman, vol. II, pp. 133–5

103 T.H. Lloyd, *England and the German Hanse, 1157–1611* (Cambridge, Cambridge University Press, 1991); J.D. Mackie, *The Oxford History of England: The Earlier Tudors 1485–1558* (London, OUP, 1952), pp. 220, and 471–8; Willan, *Early History*, p. 48

104 National Archives, Kew, PRO SP 14/115/109, quoted in R.W.K. Hinton, *The Eastland Trade and the Common Weal in the Seventeenth Century* (Cambridge, 1959), pp. 168–70

105 Willan, 'Trade between England and Russia', pp. 307–21, at 310–13, and 317–18

106 M. Wrett-Smith, 'The English in Russia during the Second Half of the Sixteenth Century', *Transactions of the Royal Historical Society*, 4th series, vol. iii, 1920, p. 95

107 *Calendar of State Papers, Domestic, Elizabeth*, vol. ccxvi, no. 72 (September 1588). 'Causes to move Her Majesty to sign her warrant for 13,504*l* 3*s* 6*d* for a supply of cordage bought for Her Majesty's use in 1587.' Note the enormous sum of money involved and the delay of at least a year before the warrant for payment was signed.

108 National Archives, Kew, Exchequer King's Remembrancer, Port Books, 5/1

109 Hamel, *England and Russia*, p. 209

110 Richard Uscombe, in Hakluyt, *Principal Navigations*, Everyman, vol. II, p. 135 and Anthony Jenknson, ibid., p. 146

111 W. Kirchner, 'Le commencement des relations économiques entre la France et la Russie, 1550–1650', *Revue Historique*, 202 (1949), pp. 161–83

112 Hamel, *England and Russia*, p. 300; R. Unwin, *A Winter away from Home: William Barents and the North-East Passage* (London, Seafarer Books, 1995), pp. 13, 15

113 He notes that the Dutchmen were selling coarse cloth, strong beer, silver platters and dishes and other goods, including otter and fox pelts, in exchange for stockfish from the Lapps. (Stockfish is unsalted fish that has been dried hard in the open air. It is usually cod, haddock, hake or ling.) The Dutchmen were unwilling to tell him what the prices were, either of their goods or of the stockfish. He comments that 'They would not let me understand any of their prises, but as I otherwise understood they bartered 2. Load of silver for 100 of stockfish, and 2. Loade is a doller.' Hakluyt, *Principal Navigations*, Everyman, vol. I, p. 375

114 I. Lubimenko, 'The Struggle of the Dutch with the English for the Russian Market in the C17th', *Transactions of the Royal Historical Society*, 4th series, 7 (1924), pp. 27–51; J.I. Israel, *Dutch Primacy in World Trade, 1585–1740* (Oxford, Clarendon Press, 1989), pp. 43–6

115 Sir Jerome Bowes, English ambassador to Muscovy, 'A briefe discourse of the voyage of Sir Jerome Bowes' [1583], in Hakluyt, *Principal Navigations*, Everyman, vol. II, p. 253

116 J. McDermott, 'The Company of Cathay: the Financing and Organisation of the Frobisher Voyages', in T.H.B. Symons (ed.), *Meta Incognita: A Discourse of Discovery: Martin Frobisher's Arctic Expeditions, 1576–1578* (2 vols, Quebec, Canadian Museum of Civilisation, 1999), vol. I, pp. 147–78

117 S.E. Morison, *The European Discovery of America: the Northern Voyages A.D. 500–1600* (New York, OUP, 1971), p. 545

118 Willan, *Early History*, p. 5

119 Ibid., p. 251.

120 Hakluyt, *Principal Navigations*, Everyman, vol. II, pp. 161–3

121 Hamel, *England and Russia*, pp. 305–6

122 Ibid., pp. 307–38; S. Purchas, *Hakluytus Posthumus or Purchas, His Pilgrims* [1625] (20 vols, Glasgow, Maclehose, 1905–7), vol. XIII, pp. 11–26

123 W.R. Scott, *The Constitution and Finance of English, Scottish and Irish Joint-Stock Companies to 1720* (3 vols, Cambridge, Cambridge University Press, 1910–12, repr. 1993, Bristol, Thoemmes Press), vol. I, p. 130

124 *The New Encyclopedia Britannica*, 15th edn (20 vols, Chicago, Encyclopedia Britannica, 2002), vol. VIII

125 Scott, *Joint-Stock Companies*, vol. I, p. 439

CHAPTER 11

1 G.B. Parkes, 'Tudor Travel Literature: a Brief History', in D.B. Quinn (ed.), *The Hakluyt Handbook* (2 vols, London, Hakluyt Society, 1974), vol. I, p. 100

2 Hakluyt, *Principal Navigations*, Everyman, vol. I, p. xi

3 G. Kish, *North-East Passage: Adolf Erik Nordenskiold, his Life and Times* (Amsterdam, N. Israel, 1973), p. 203

4 D. Loades, *England's Maritime Empire: Seapower, Commerce and Policy* (Harlow, Pearson Education, 2000), p. 74

5 C.P. Lucas, *The Beginnings of English Overseas Enterprise* (Oxford, Clarendon Press, 1917), p. 143

6 *Calendar of State Papers, Venetian* (1581–1591), H.F. Brown (ed.) (London, HMSO, 1894), no. 648, Giovanni Mocenigo, Venetian ambassador to France, Letter to the Doge and Senate in Venice (8 April 1588)

7 P. Dukes, 'Britain and Russia: 450 Years of Contact', *History Today*, 53/7 (2003, July), pp. 9–15, a brief summary of the ups and downs of Anglo-Russian relations.

8 I. Lubimenko, 'A Suggestion for the Publication of the Correspondence of Queen Elizabeth with the Russian Czars', *Transactions of the Royal Historical Society*, 3rd series, vol. IX (1915), pp. 111–22, at 113

9 Hakluyt, *Principal Navigations*, Everyman, vol. II, p. 82

10 *Calendar of State Papers, Foreign, Elizabeth* (12 August 1568), no. 2414, Thomas Randolphe, Letter to Cecil

11 Hakluyt, *Principal Navigations*, Everyman, vol. II, p. 99

12 Ibid., vol. I, pp. 254–66

13 J. Milton, *Paradise Lost* [1663], A. Fowler (ed.) (Harlow, Longman, 1971), Book X, line 291 *et seq.*

14 T.S. Willan, *Early History of the Russia Company, 1553–1603* (Manchester, Manchester University Press, 1956), p. 274

15 V.V. Pitulko et al., 'Humans in the Arctic before the last Glacial Maximum', *Science Magazine*, 303 (2004), pp. 52–6; R. Stone, 'A Surprising Survival Story in the Siberian Arctic, *Science Magazine*, 303 (2004), p. 33

16 L. Sverdlov, 'Russian Naval Officers and Geographical Exploration in Northern Russia (18th through 20th Centuries)', *Arctic Voice*, 11 (1996, 26 November), pp. 1–5, at 1

17 Ibid., p. 1. Mangazea was a settlement on the Taz river, which flows into the bay of the Ob river. It was near where Krasnoselkupsk is now.

18 For a fuller account of the history of exploration of the North-East Passage, see A.E. Nordenskiold, *The Voyage of the Vega round Asia and Europe* (2 vols, London, Macmillan, 1881)

19 A. Engels and R. Howgego, *The Arctic Voyages of Olivier Brunel* (Discoverers' Web, 2004), www.win.tue.nl/~engels/discovery/brunel.html

20 William Burrough, 'Instructions and notes very necessary and needfull to be observed in the purposed voyage for discovery of Cathay Eastwards, by Arthur Pet and Charles Jackman' [1580], in Hakluyt, *Principal Navigations*, Everyman, vol. II, pp. 210–12

21 Richard Hakluyt of Eiton in the Countie of Hereford, Esquire, 'Notes in writing, besides more privie by mouth . . . to M. Arthur Pet and to M. Charles Jackman' [1580], in Hakluyt, *Principal Navigations*, Everyman, vol. II, pp. 214–23

22 Master Dee, 'Certain briefe advices . . . to Arthur Pet and Charles Jackman, to be observed in their Northeasterne discoverie' [1580], in Hakluyt, *Principal Navigations*, Everyman, vol. II, pp. 212–14

23 G. Mercator, 'A letter written to M. Richard Hakluyt of Oxford, touching the intended discoverie of the Northeast passage' [1580], in Hakluyt, *Principal Navigations*, Everyman, vol. II, pp. 224–6, at 224

24 Hakluyt, *Principal Navigations*, Everyman, vol. II, p. 206

25 Hugh Smyth, 'The discoverie made by M. Arthur Pet and M. Charles Jackman, of the Northeast parts, beyond the Island of Vaigats', in Hakluyt, *Principal Navigations*, Everyman, vol. II, pp. 227–44

26 British Library, Cotton MS, Otho E viii, folio 38, Hugh Smyth's *Sketch map: Pet and Jackman's ships in the Kara Strait* [1580]

27 Engels and Howgego, *Arctic Voyages*; P. Horensma, 'Olivier Brunel and the Dutch Involvement in the Discovery of the North-East Passage', *Journal of Polar Studies* (1985), p. 2; Jeanette Mirsky, *Northern Conquest: the Story of Arctic Exploration from Earliest Times to the Present* (London, H. Hamilton, 1934), pp. 40–1

28 Anthony Marsh, 'A Letter to him from a Russian informant' [1584], in S. Purchas, *Hakluytus Posthumus or Purchas, His Pilgrimes* (1625) (20 vols, Glasgow, James Maclehose, reprinted 1906), vol. XIV, p. 293

29 G. de Veer, *The Three Voyages of William Barents to the Arctic Regions, 1594, 1595 and 1596*, 2nd edn (London, Hakluyt Society, 1876), series 1/54; R. Unwin, *A Winter away from Home* (London, Seafarer Books, 1995), pp. 25–9

30 Unwin, *A Winter*, pp. 30–40

31 G. de Veer, *Three Voyages*; Unwin, *A Winter*, pp. 42–229; *The Northern Lights Route* (Tromsø, University of Tromsø, 1999); www.ub.uit.no/northernlights/eng/wbarentsz.htm. Captain Carlsen, a Norwegian whaling skipper, rediscovered in 1871 the remains of Barents's winter camp on Novaya Zemlya. The roof had fallen in and the house was filled with ice and gravel, but all the articles there were perfectly preserved. He took away many of the relics and they are now exhibited at The Hague. Nordenskiold, *Voyage of the Vega*, pp. 300–1

32 Rijksmuseum Volkenkunde, Leiden, *Cornelis de Houtman*, www.rmv.nl/publicaties/3enggano/e/teks/houtman.html

33 Purchas, *Hakluytus Posthumus*, vol. XIII, pp. 294–412

34 G.M. Asher (ed.), *Henry Hudson, the Navigator. The Original Documents* (London,

Hakluyt Society, 1860), series 1/27; Purchas, *Hakluytus Posthumus*, vol. XIII, pp. 294–412; I. Chadwick, *Henry Hudson* (2004), www.ianchadwick.com/hudson

35 Purchas, *Hakluytus Posthumus*, vol. XIII, pp. 194, 205–15, 222

36 J. Woods, *Capt. J. Wood's Attempt to Discover a North-East Passage to China* (London, D. Brown, 1711)

37 Horsens Museum, Denmark, www.pmel.noaa.gov/np/pages/vbering.html

38 L. Sverdlov, 'Russian Naval Officers and geographic exploration in Northern Russia (18th through 20th centuries)', *Arctic Voice*, 11 (27 November 1996). http://arcticcircle.uconn.edu/HistoryCulture/russianexplor.html Cape Chelyuskin is at 77° 43' N.

39 C.J. Phipps, *The Journal of a Voyage . . . by Commodore Phipps and Captain Lutwidge in the 'Racehorse' and the 'Carcase'* (London, F. Newbery, 1774)

40 M. Sauer, *An Account of a Geographical and Astronomical Expedition to the Northern parts of Russia . . . performed . . . by Commodore Joseph Billings in the Years 1785 to 1794* (London, T.C.W. Davies, 1802)

41 O. von Kotzebue, *A Voyage of Discovery into the South Sea and Bering Straits for the Purpose of Exploring a North-east Passage in 1815–1818* (3 vols, London, 1821)

42 Sverdlov, 'Russian Naval Officers', pp. 1–5; http://arcticcircle.uconn.edu/HistoryCulture/russianexplor.html

43 Nordenskiold, *Voyage of the Vega*, vol. I, pp. 311–13

44 Nordenskiold, *Voyage of the Vega* (2 vols); G. Kish, *North-East Passage*, esp. pp. 157–94

45 http://www.brainyencyclopedia.com/encyclopedia/g/george_washington_delong.html

46 F. Nansen, *Farthest North: Being the Record of a Voyage of Exploration of the Ship* Fram, *1893–1896* (London, Newnes, 1898)

47 P. Kemp (ed.), *The Oxford Companion to Ships and the Sea* (Oxford, OUP, 1988), pp. 604–6. (The port at the mouth of the Yenasei river is named Dickson after Oscar Dickson, the Swedish industrialist who was Nordenskiold's long-time sponsor.)

48 There are several opinions as to the exact dates of the 'Little Ice Age', and it seems to have affected different areas at somewhat differing times. According to Lamb, it was 1550–1700 (H.H. Lamb, *Climate: Past, Present and Future* (London, Methuen, 1977), p. 463); it was 1600–1840 according to Sugden (D. Sugden, *Arctic and Antarctic* (Oxford, Blackwell, 1982), p. 177); while C. Carpenter, *The Changing World of Weather* (Middlesex, Guinness Publishing, 1991), pp. 58–62, says that the period from 1550 to 1700 was the coldest in Britain, though the 'Little Ice Age' did not finally end until the middle of the nineteenth century. Sugden points out, for instance, that sea ice was unknown off Iceland in AD 1100, but that it was present for two months each year around AD 1300, and that sea ice persisted round Iceland for two or three months each year from AD 1600 to 1840.

49 *Practical Boatowner* 431, 78 (November 2002); www.vagabond.fr; ebrossier@aol.com; North-East Passage Expedition www.northabout.com

50 The information on the extent of Arctic sea ice comes from satellite observations, supplemented by over 6,000 charts constructed by the Norwegian Polar Institute and the Norwegian Meteorological Institute from the log books of long-dead explorers, the very earliest of which were Sir Hugh Willoughby and Richard Chancellor. http://www.iema.net/article.php?id=2443; http://www.wwf.org.mx/news_old_ships.php; *Cicerone* (The Magazine of the Norwegian Climate Research Centre) (24 April 2000); Kenneth Chang, *New York Times* (8 December 2002)

51 Northabout Debrief www.thepoles.com/story/Northaboutdebrief (16 September 2004)

52 *Guardian* (3 November 2004), p. 18

CHAPTER 12

1 Hakluyt, *Principal Navigations*, Everyman, vol. I, p. 245

2 Ibid., p. 273

3 Ibid., pp. 333–52

4 British Library, Royal MS, 18 D iii, folios 123v and 124v, W. Borough, *Chart of Northern Navigation (Trondheim to Novaya Zemlya)* [1568]

5 National Archives, Exchequer King's Remembrancer, Customs Accounts, PRO E 122/90/11; Port Book 5/1 [1565]; Port Book 5/1 [1571]; British Library, Lansdowne MS, 11, folio 37 [1568]

6 R. Hakluyt, 'Epistle Dedicatorie', in R. Hakluyt, *Divers Voyages touching the discovery of America* [1582] (London, Hakluyt Society), series I, no. VII), 1850, pp. 8–18, esp. 14 and 15. Hakluyt describes the process of examining candidates for pilots and masters in the 'Epistle Dedicatorie' in pp. 866–8 in the third and last volume of the second edition of his *Principal Navigations* [1600]

7 Martin Cortes, *The Arte of Navigation, conteyning a compendious description of the Sphere*, trans. R. Eden, London, Richard Lugge [1561]

8 D.W. Waters, *The Art of Navigation in Elizabethan and Early Stuart Times* (London, Hollis and Carter, 1958), pp. 103–4

9 British Library, Lansdowne MS, 116, folios 6–9, S. Borough, *Three especiall causes and consideracions amongst others wherfore the office of Pilott major ys allowed* [?1561]

10 British Library, Lansdowne MS, 116, folio 4

11 M. Oppenheim, *A History of the Administration of the Royal Navy and of Merchant Shipping in Relation to the Navy . . . 1509–1660* (London, 1896), p. 149; C.A. Fury, 'Training and Education in the Elizabethan Maritime Community, 1585–1603', *Mariner's Mirror*, 85/2 (1999), pp. 147–61, at 148

12 Memorial plaque to Stephen Borough, St Mary's Church, Chatham; British Library, Lansdowne MS, 116, folio 5

13 Waters, *Art of Navigation* pp. 106–7; there is a neatly drawn map of 'Chattam' and the surrounding area, showing twenty-one ships of the fleet at moorings in the Medway, date probably about 1565, author unknown (?Stephen Borough). British Library, Cotton MS, Augustus I. i. 52

14 Waters, *Art of Navigation*, p. 185

15 National Archives, Trinity House Charters, Grants etc., folio 121v, quoted in G.G. Harris, *The Trinity House of Deptford, 1514–1660* (1969), p. 273

16 T. Glasgow, 'Vice Admiral Woodhouse and Shipkeeping in the Tudor Navy', *Mariner's Mirror*, 63 (1977), pp. 253–63, at 260

17 *State Papers, Foreign and Domestic, Addenda (1549–1625)*, 15, 22, folio 10, Thomas Colshill, *Register of Merchant Ships of England* [1572]

18 R. Collinson, *The Three Voyages of Martin Frobisher* (London, Hakluyt Society, 1867), series 1, vol. 38, p. 89

19 I. Friel, 'Frobisher's Ships: the Ships of the North-Western Atlantic Voyages, 1576–1578', in T.H.B. Symons (ed.), *Meta Incognita: a Discourse of Discovery: Martin Frobisher's Arctic Expeditions, 1576–1578* (2 vols, Quebec, Canadian Museum of Civilisation, 1999), vol. II, pp. 299–352, at 315

20 R.A. Skelton and J. Summerson, *A Description of Maps and Architectural Drawings in the Collection made by William Cecil, the First Baron Burghley* (Oxford, Roxburghe Club, 1971), catalogue no. 122

21 D. Wilson, *Sweet Robin: a Biography of Robert Dudley, Earl of Leicester, 1533–1588* (London, Allison and Busby, 1997, first pub. by H. Hamilton, 1981), p. 278; J. Bruce,

Correspondence of Robert Dudley, Earl of Leicester, during his Government in the Low Countries in the Years 1585 and 1586 (London, Campden Society, 1st series, 27, 1844), pp. 461–2, and ibid. in Appendix 1, headed 'A journal of my Lord of Leicesters Proceeding in the Lowe Countries', by M. Stephen Burrough, Admirall of the Fleet', Harl. MS, 6845, folio 26

22 E. Jenkins, *Elizabeth and Leicester* (London, Gollancz, 1961), pp. 306–7

23 *State Papers, Foreign, Elizabeth 1568*: no. 2,414; quoted in E.D. Morgan and C.H. Coote (eds), *Early Voyages and Travels to Russia and Persia* (London, Hakluyt Society, after 1886), vol. I, p. 256

24 R.I. Ruggles, 'The Cartographic Lure of the Northwest Passage: Its Real and Imaginary Geography', in Symons, *Meta Incognita*, vol. I, pp. xix–xxiv

25 G. Kish, *North-East Passage: Adolf Eric Nordenskiold, his Life and Times* (Amsterdam, N. Israel, 1973), p. 135

APPENDIX 2

1 'The Voyage of William Burrough, Captaine of 13 English ships to the Narve, Anno 1570', Christopher Hodsdon and William Burrough, in Hakluyt, *Principal Navigations*, Everyman, vol. II, pp. 133–5

2 L. Stephens and S. Lee (eds), *Dictionary of National Biography* (London, OUP, 1917, repr. 1973), pp. 866–8

3 *Will of William Burroughe* (Abstract) [1598] (Exeter, West Country Studies Library). See also Chapter 2, note 13.

4 Hakluyt, *Principal Navigations*, Hakluyt Society, vol. III, pp. 214–48

5 *New England Historical and Genealogical Register*, 51 (1897), p. 289

6 Ibid., pp. 152, 289

7 D.R. Ransome, 'A Purchas Chronology', in L.E. Pennington (ed.), *The Purchas Handbook* (1997), vol. I, p. 339

8 Mrs C. Pavitt, Chelmsford, personal communication (6/8/1999)

9 *New England Historical and Genealogical Register*, 51 (1897), pp. 152 and 289; *The Copartnership Herald*, vol. 3, no. 26 (April 1933)

10 *New England Historical and Genealogical Register*, 51 (1897), p. 289

11 Ibid.; *Will of Joanne Burrough* (Abstract) [1604] (Exeter, West Country Studies Library). See also Chapter 2, note 13.

12 *Will of David Borowe* (Abstract) [1576] (Exeter, West Country Studies Library). See also Chapter 2, note 13.

13 *Will of John Borough* (Abstract) (Exeter, West Country Studies Library, OM Collection 8/36), d. 1570 or 1571.

14 *Will of Thomas Leigh* (Abstract) [1609] (Exeter, West Country Studies Library)

15 Ibid.

16 *Will of Peter Borowghe* (Abstract) [1586] (Exeter, West Country Studies Library)

17 *Will of Ann Boroughe* (Abstract) [1589] (Exeter, West Country Studies Library)

18 North Devon Local Studies, Barnstaple, *Northam Parish Register* (microfiche)

19 National Archives, Kew, *High Court of Admiralty Examination*, 92, 18 July 1543

20 National Archives, Kew, PRO 15/22/folio 10 (microfilm), *State Papers Domestic, Addenda* (1547–1625): register of merchant ships of England in 1572, compiled by Thomas Colshill.

21 T.L. Stoate (ed.), *Devon Lay Subsidy Rolls 1524–7* (Bristol, T.L. Stoate, 1979), p. 116

22 T.L. Stoate (ed.), *Devon Lay Subsidy Rolls 1543–5* (Bristol, T.L. Stoate, 1986), p. 103.

23 A.J. Howard and T.L. Stoate (eds), *Devon Muster Roll for 1569* (Bristol, T.L. Stoate, 1977), p. 117

24 North Devon Local Studies Library, Barnstaple, *Northam Parish Records*, Grant [1544] 1843A/PF 49

25 Stoate, *Devon Lay Subsidy Rolls 1524–7*, p. 116

26 Stoate, *Devon Lay Subsidy Rolls 1543–5*, p. 103

APPENDIX 3

1 Hakluyt, *Principal Navigations*, Everyman, vol. I, pp. 232–41

APPENDIX 4

1 National Archives, State Papers, PRO 12: 243: 190: W. Borough, *Proportions in Building of Shyppinge* [*c.* 1586–90]

2 W.O. Salisbury, 'Early Tonnage Measurement in England', *Mariner's Mirror*, 52 (1966), pp. 41–51, at 45

3 National Archives, State Paper, PRO, SP 1/ 230, folio 201 *et seq.*, *The Dimensions of the Mary Gonson*, quoted in R.C. Anderson, 'The Mary Gonson', *Mariner's Mirror*, 46 (1960), pp. 199–204

4 N.A.M. Rodger, *The Safeguard of the Sea: a Naval History of Britain 660–1649* (London, HarperCollins, 1997), vol. I, p. 479. The *Aid* was a queen's ship which was hired out as the flagship for the second and third of Frobisher's three expeditions, in 1577 and 1578.

5 I. Friel, 'Frobisher's Ships: the Ships of the North-Western Atlantic Voyages, 1576–1578', in T.H.B. Symons (ed.), *Meta Incognita: a Discourse of Discovery: Martin Frobisher's Arctic Expeditions 1576–1578* (Quebec, Canadian Museum of Civilisation, 1999), pp. 303–5

6 I was happy to find that the method I had used for calculating the approximate dimensions of the expeditions' ships was confirmed when Mr Ian Friel published his use of the same method in 1999, in *Meta Incognita* (see note 5).

7 Friel, 'Frobisher's Ships', pp. 303–5

APPENDIX 5

1 W. van Bemmelen, *Die Abweichung der Magnetnadel: Beobachtungen, Sacular-Variation, Wert- und Isogonensysteme bis zur Mitte des XVIIIten Jahrhunderts* (Batavia, 1899), most kindly supplied to me by Dr D.R. Barraclough, Geomagnetism Group, British Geological Survey, Edinburgh.

APPENDIX 6

1 T.S. Willan, 'Trade between England and Russia in the Second Half of the Sixteenth Century', in *English Historical Review*, 63 (1948), pp. 307–21, at 310–11

2 G.V. Scammell, 'Manning the English Merchant Service in the Sixteenth Century', in *Mariner's Mirror*, 56 (1970), pp. 131–54, at 139

APPENDIX 11

With a note, in brackets, on the locations of the original maps where possible.

1 A.E. Nordenskiold, *Facsimile Atlas to the Early History of Cartography, with Reproductions of the Most Important Maps Printed in the XV and XVI Centuries*, trans. J.A. Ekelof and C.R. Markham (New York, Dover Publications, 1973), p. 49

2 F. Fernandez-Ernesto (ed.), *Times Atlas of World Exploration* (New York, New York Public Library [De Ricci 97], 1991)

3 R. Lister, *Old Maps and Globes* (London, Bell and Hyman, 1979), p. 17 (British Library, No. C.3.d. 8., according to Campbell)

4 R.W. Shirley, *The Mapping of the World: Early Printed World Maps* (London, Holland Press, 1983), Plate 4 (Yale University Library, or in the British Library, according to Nebenzahl)

5 R.V. Tooley and C. Bricker, *Landmarks of Map Making* (Oxford, Phaidon, 1976), p. 53. (Bibliothèque Nationale, Paris, Res Ge A 276: facsimile copy in the National Maritime Museum, Greenwich)

6 Nordenskiold, *Facsimile Atlas*, p. 73

7 T. Campbell, *The Earliest Printed Maps 1472–1500* (1987), Figure 43 (Biblioteca Nazionale, Florence)

8 R. Lister, *Antique Maps and their Cartographers* (London, G. Bell, 1970), Plate 5 (British Library)

9 Fernandez-Ernesto, *Times Atlas*, inside front cover (Arthur Holzheimer Collection, according to Nebenzahl, see footnote 19)

10 Shirley, *Mapping the World*, Plate 31 (Schloss Wolfegg, Baden-Württemberg)

11 Ibid., Plate 32 (National Maritime Museum, Greenwich)

12 Ibid., Plate 36

13 Ibid., Plate 38

14 Nordenskiold, *Facsimile Atlas*, p. xxxv

15 Ibid., p. xxxvii

16 Ibid., pp. 76–7

17 Ibid., p. 78

18 Ibid., p. xxxviii

19 Ibid., p. xxxix

20 Ibid., p. xli (i)

21 Ibid., p. xxxix

22 Lister, *Antique Maps*, Plate 9 (British Museum)

23 Nordenskiold, *Facsimile Atlas*, p. xxxix

24 Ibid., p. xlii

25 This globe, attributed to G. Hartmann, is the hand-held one drawn in minute detail in Hans Holbein's famous picture, *The Ambassadors*, in 1533: H. Wallis, 'England's Search for the Northern Passages in the Sixteenth and Early Seventeenth Centuries, *Arctic*, 37/4 (1984), pp. 453–72, at 457–8; R. Baldwin, *Globes* (London, National Maritime Museum, 1992), p. 2; National Gallery, London, 'Holbein's *Ambassadors*', *Exhibition Guide* (November 1997–February 1998)

26 Nordenskiold, *Facsimile Atlas*, p. 105

27 L. Bagrow, *A History of the Cartography of Russia up to 1600* (Ontario, Walker, 1975), p. 77

28 Bagrow, *A History*, p. 121 (Munich State Library)

29 E.G.R. Taylor, *Tudor Geography, 1485–1583* (London, Methuen, 1930), p. 71 (British Museum)

30 K. Nebenzahl, *Maps from the Age of Discovery* (London, Times Books, 1990), Plate 34. (This world map originated in 1544 but Cabot is thought to have revised it

considerably, and he may well have redrawn the North-East Passage area in about 1550 in the light of John Dee's information.) (Galerie de Géographie, Bibliothèque Nationale, Paris)

31   Nordenskiold, *Facsimile Atlas*, p. 112

32   Bagrow, *A History*, p. 86

33   E. Wright (ed.), *The McGraw-Hill Illustrated History of the World* (New York, 1964), p. 172 (British Museum)

34   Shirley, *Mapping the World*, Plate 79

35   Shirley, *Mapping the World*, Plate 72. Gastaldi's world map was one of the first to show a water passage between the east of Asia and the west coast of North America. This passage later acquired the name 'Strait of Anian'. K. Hakulinen and A. Peltonen, *Nordenskiold Seminar* (Helsinki, Nordenskiold Samfundet i Finland, 1981), p. 62

Index